THE UNTHOUGHT DEBT

Cultural Memory
in
the
Present

Mieke Bal and Hent de Vries, Editors

THE UNTHOUGHT DEBT

Heidegger and the Hebraic Heritage

Marlène Zarader

Translated by Bettina Bergo

STANFORD UNIVERSITY PRESS

STANFORD, CALIFORNIA

2006

Stanford University Press
Stanford, California

English translation © 2006 by the Board of Trustees of the
Leland Stanford Junior University. All rights reserved.

The Unthought Debt was originally published in French in 1990
under the title *La Dette impensée* © 1990, Éditions du Seuil, Paris.

This book has been published with the assistance of the
French Ministry of Culture—National Center for the Book.

Printed in the United States of America on acid-free, archival-quality paper

Library of Congress Cataloging-in-Publication Data

Zarader, Marlène.
    [Dette impensée. English]
    The unthought debt : Heidegger and the Hebraic heritage / Marlène Zarader ;
translated by Bettina Bergo.
        p.   cm.—(Cultural memory in the present)
    Includes bibliographical references.
    ISBN 0-8047-3685-5 (cloth : alk. paper)
    ISBN 0-8047-3686-3 (pbk. : alk. paper)
    1. Heidegger, Martin, 1889–1976.   I. Title.   II. Series.

B3279.H49Z3613 2006
193—dc22

                                                                    2005025807

Original Printing 2006

Last figure below indicates year of this printing:
15   14   13   12   11   10   09   08   07   06

Contents

Translator's Acknowledgements

This translation would not have been possible without the support and counsel of the following persons and organizations: Barty Begley and Marlène Zarader (Université de Montpellier) for their help with the text.Philippe Farah, Département de Philosophie, Université de Montréal for his work on notes and the text. Gabriel Malenfant, Département de Philosophie, Université de Montréal for help with the text. Iain Macdonald for help on thematic questions. Mélanie Walton and Daniel Rhodes, Duquesne University; Michael Nass, Philosophy Department, DePaul University; François Raffoul, Louisiana State University, for help with the translation. James Buckley, Dean, College of Arts and Sciences, Loyola College. The Loyola Humanities Center and its Director, Claire Matthews-McGinnis for their support. Alfred Tauber, Boston University, Center for Philosophy and History of Science. The Radcliffe Institute for Advanced Study, Drew Gilpin Faust, Dean, and Judith Vichniac, Center for European Studies, Harvard University, for support. Robert Gibbs, Department of Philosophy, University of Toronto. Oona Eisenstadt, Department of Religious Studies, Pomona College. Gregory Kaplan, Department of Religious Studies, Rice University. Lia Brozgal, Harvard University, Department of Romance Languages for research. David L. Teasley, Washington, D.C.

THE UNTHOUGHT DEBT

Introduction

Contemporary thought never ceases "coming to terms" with Heidegger. It may think with him, or against him, but rarely without him. At stake is knowing—if only in a very global way—what it is that allows Heidegger's work to occupy this position, commonly recognized today as indisputable.

This question warrants several responses, which we need to see in their progression. In the first place, inasmuch as it takes metaphysics in charge, the work of Heidegger specifically concerns the philosopher (or what remains of him today). It concerns the philosopher in several respects. First, Heidegger's work allows the philosopher to reread the great texts of the tradition in light of the question that is in play in them, even if it is not properly developed therein. Thus, Heidegger makes possible a decisive renewal of the interpretation of philosophical texts. Second, beyond the diversity of these texts, to be focused on the question that shapes them beneath the surface [*souterrainement*] is to grasp them in their unity, until then unnoticed. This is what permits Heidegger to speak of metaphysics in the singular, of "the" metaphysics, and to grasp it as a coherent whole. Third, to circumscribe metaphysics in its unity is to be in the position to grasp it finally in its truth; that is, in one and the same movement to set forth its foundation and to reach its essence, till now unthought. Fourth, reaching the essence of metaphysics, however (if indeed it is this unthought character that constitutes metaphysics itself, at the same time as creating its unity), amounts to casting upon it a gaze that could not be properly its own. And thereby opens the possibility, albeit a distant one, of a resolute "disengagement," directed toward other possibilities, as yet unsuspected.[1]

In a word, the history of metaphysics is replayed in its diversity, referred back to its unity, and thought in its truth: these many gestures make up a single one, since they all come down to putting us in possession of a heritage that was ours, while remaining closed to us. In restoring to the philosopher his past, Heidegger allows him to recognize himself as a man of modernity (i.e., at the end of metaphysics) and to seek out, if gropingly, his new face as a thinker, which is perhaps his future if he is to have one. Such is *one* of the possible meanings of the Heideggerian enterprise, and it would already suffice to account for his prodigious impact on the landscape of contemporary thought.

But Heidegger goes much farther. What he aims at, beyond just metaphysics, is the truth of *Western history* in its entirety. This is in no way to say that, beside everything just presented here, something else would be implied. Simply, in Heidegger's eyes, *in* that which was just presented, something else is implicit. To understand these relationships of implication we must return to the very term *metaphysics* in its Heideggerian usage. If initially it hardly differentiates itself from its current use, it thereafter becomes the object of a dual expansion: a semantic expansion (metaphysics will encompass domains that in early times remained external to it, until it reaches the point where it covers all the constitutive *dimensions* of the West). And a temporal expansion (metaphysics will spill over into periods that escaped it in its early days, until it reaches the point of covering the entirety of Western *history*). Once these two expansions are accomplished (and, each in their time, they are accomplished over the course of the work), we will have passed from the first project (aiming at the one metaphysics) to the second (aiming at the West), or, more precisely, the first project will henceforth signify the second one, and encompass it.

From the beginning of the next chapter, we shall have to follow step by step each of these expansions. For the moment, it is worth our while simply to highlight the movement by which Heidegger is led almost imperceptibly to transform his ambition. He who at first wanted to be the interpreter of a relatively determinate field (which hitherto one called the "history of philosophy," when one still believed, precisely, in the existence of determinate fields) comes to embrace History in its totality, in its past, its present, and its possible future.

Facing this colossal enterprise, what indeed should be the task of the reader today, or more generally of those who attempt to think—in this age known as the "closure [*achèvement*] of metaphysics"—and to think after Heidegger?

I. From One Book to the Other

The first task is undoubtedly a task of reading. Whether it is a matter of reviewing the major axes of the tradition or of opening new paths for research, one cannot seriously claim to stand in the contemporary space of thought if one deprives oneself any reference to the formidable commotion around Heidegger. The sole means for measuring this is to follow again with Heidegger those distressing paths that were cleared by his work.

This task is largely underway today, some sixty years after the publication of *Being and Time*. I myself contributed to it in an earlier study,[2] whose only ambition was to *read* Heidegger (which of course also means to make him readable), and to do so by taking up his work in its entirety from an angle that appeared privileged to me (since it permitted us, precisely, to embrace this entirety): the question of the origin.

Once this reading is finished (even if it is never truly finished), there remains another task. It consists in entering into debate with Heidegger, a debate that has no sense unless it stands resolutely apart from the polemic. Now, there is but one way to avoid this danger, which is to start *from the text*, understood as a text which we must open, from within, to questioning. To open it from the inside is to locate the points, even minor ones, which call for reflection, and to take them thematically as objects. To open the text from within is also to discern there what may be carried by it as inexplicit assertions, presuppositions, and, all in all, as an unthought [*d'impensée*]. Only through this patient labor can a larger discussion begin about the legitimacy itself of Heidegger's interpretation of our history.

As Heidegger has claimed to grasp the meaning of this history, from its origin to its end, our study proposes "to consider what Heidegger's attempt at thinking contributes to the task of understanding our history,"[3] to repeat here the words that were once those of Pöggeler. That is, our study intends to reopen the question posed by the same Pöggeler (who, for his part, responded positively to it): "Is his [Heidegger's] way of taking the itinerary of Western thought in charge required by this thought or not?"[4]

To take seriously such a question, to attempt to work it out, at least in one of its forms, is the aim here. If I insist upon the necessity of a certain detachment (which would go without saying, in a different context), it is because of the highly specific terrain on which we are about to tread, the question of Heidegger and "Judaism." This is a thorny subject, about which sensibilities are more acute than elsewhere. Let us specify, clearly, once and for all, that the present work wants to serve no *cause*. If I come to adopt a critical position vis-à-vis some of Heidegger's assertions, it is in no way because I judge it salutary that Heidegger be subjected "finally" to critique. It is simply because, while engaged on a determinate path, I encountered questions that I was unable to resolve, and that seemed to me could not be resolved within the framework of Heidegger's interpretation of history, and I consequently decided to subject these questions to other interpretations.

In my earlier work, I had followed Heidegger as he traced the metaphysical tradition to its Presocratic beginning—himself led by his questioning in the direction of the unthought of which he remained a bearer. A drawn-out enterprise, since it was not a matter of a single leap, but of a multiform backward march wherein each of the great metaphysical determinations (concerning Being, language, truth, etc.) was referred back to the "fundamental word" that inaugurated it. It was in proceeding to unfold this multiplicity that Heidegger managed to set forth their secret unity: the Greek opening of Being, the original trace toward which all our history must be led back anew, in order to be elucidated by it. To go back to the fundamental words was thus to be prepared to recognize ourselves as what we have always been, albeit unconsciously: inheritors.

It was the whole problematic of the *Andenken* [memory] that I attempted to restore, making a point of neglecting none of the meanderings of the Heideggerian course, all the way to its conclusion. At the end of the enterprise, it appeared to me that, with the assumption of the Greek heritage, the question of our origin was far from being closed; rather, it seemed that the question was perhaps just opening, that it was opening, presently, in Heidegger's own text and starting from it. It was in the text, in effect, that the unsaid remained [*restait du non-dit*], that a certain question came ultimately to impose itself, became almost central, by dint of not being posed by Heidegger. In a word, it was the text itself that now posed a problem.

Therefore everything had to be taken up again in light of that so singularly absent question. To reread the Heideggerian oeuvre, no longer on the basis of the orientations it furnished, but according to another guiding thread: following the trace of a silence, seeking to understand how it functioned, by what means it perpetuated itself, and what that silence produced. Only then should Heidegger's own elaboration of the problem of the origin have some chance to appear in its true dimensions.

II. The Question

When he poses the question of our provenance, Heidegger responds: we are the inheritors of Greece. By this we should understand that the injunction set down [*injonction déposée*] in the fundamental words of the first Greeks constitutes the inception of our history and, in this respect, still determines our present site.

Now, referring our sojourn in its entirety to just the Greek beginning implies that the biblical component (especially the Old Testament, and therefore the Hebraic one) of Western history may be taken as nonsignifying; that is, that it would not have the status of a beginning. And, in fact, Heidegger almost never refers to it, thereby attesting to the negligible character of what had been held, up until then, to be one of the sources of our identity.

It is important, here, not to invert the order of determinations. One believes often enough that it is because Heidegger was able to gauge, as none had done before him, the prodigious impact that the Greek beginning had on thought, that he was led to hold the Hebraic contribution to be negligible. Yet in reality, however decisive the Greek beginning may be, still it could not by itself lead to the erasure of all other determinations. If the Hebraic contribution is so massively excluded, it is not because no further "room" remained for its inscription, but because it had been from the first *forbidden to thinking* [*interdit de pensée*]. It was so excluded thanks to a double reduction, maintained from one end of the work to the other: the reduction of the Bible to the sole Neo-testamentary text (written in Greek), itself reduced to a pure experience, which is that of *faith*. Faith would be the sole object of Revelation, as well as the Bible's sole point of impact on the West. It is only on the ground of this fundamental postulate that Western thought could be said to be Greek in all its parts, including those of its possibilities that the Greeks had not taken up.

From this springs Heidegger's comprehension of Christianity, which is entirely elucidated by two of its dimensions: faith (whose characteristic is to be foreign to the order of thought) and onto-theology (whose characteristic is to be reducible to Greek thought). That means that Christianity's only original trait (faith in the crucified God) in no way concerns thought, and that the trait by which Christianity participates in thought has nothing original in itself: it is never anything but an avatar of what the Greeks already thought, or at least sketched in advance. Yet that also means (i.e., it is only another translation of the same fundamental postulate) that the Hebraic dimension can be passed over in silence, since it has inaugurated nothing, not even within Christianity. The Hebraic dimension has marked neither thought (which is Greek), nor faith (which is Christic and Neo-testamentary).

Thus we arrive at a triple demarcation. First, one may well speak, if one wants, of a *Christian thought*, but it could not be taken for a significant component of the West, since it remains entirely the province [*ressort*] of Greek thought. Second, on the other hand, there could not exist, in any sense of the term, a *biblical thought* (even were it Neo-testamentary), nor even a biblical determination that could be brought to bear on thought, since the Bible only had its impact on Christianity's dimension of faith. The West would thus bear the double mark of the *biblical faith* and of *Greek thought*. Third, it cannot be a question of working back toward some sort of Hebraic source, regardless of whether it is a matter of faith or of thought. We must therefore correct the preceding assertion and say that the West carries the double mark of the *Christic faith* and of *Greek thought*, Christian theology being, for its part, an amalgamation of the two (one as prejudicial to the purity of the first as it is to the import of the second). However, the thinker who knows how to separate faith from thought has finally to do only with Greek thought—or, more rigorously, with the Greek determinations that influenced thought.

This general sketch—which I retrace in broad strokes here, and to which we shall return later in a more precise way—overturns all our received ideas.[5] What had seemed until then to go without saying was that Christianity, including its dimension as *thought*, had been constituted on the basis of two distinct sources: the Greek and the Hebraic sources. This meant that Christianity pointed back to two founding texts, and that the

Books of Exodus or Genesis were as essential to it as the *Iliad* or the *Posterior Analytics*. More broadly, it seemed to go without saying that the Bible constituted a complex universe, which had marked many facets of our identity and left traces in the entirety of our culture, well beyond just the experience of faith, and even beyond what Christianity had retained of it. Heidegger's position is thus manifestly paradoxical. Yet this paradox offers the double peculiarity not only of having been presented (by its author), but also received (by his readers), as its own contrary: namely, as *obvious*.

That it could indeed be presented this way is what its status as a peremptory postulate shows us. Through the reduction of the entirety of the biblical universe to the sole dimension of faith (Christic faith), the Hebraic source of thought is in no way invalidated by Heidegger, rather he *occults* it, to the point of leaving something like a *blank* space in his text. Now it is remarkable that this blank space had posed no problems for the different generations of readers who have followed each other around Heidegger's work. In truth, the blank space so little troubled these readers that this double paradox (the biblical heritage reduced to faith, and the West that is Greek) passes today for an assertion that should go without saying.

That means that we have been present at the reversal of reigning "certainties"; certainties as little questioned in one case as in the other. One used to speak, with an attractive pairing, of the "Judeo-Christian tradition," without it ever having been the object of a properly philosophical elucidation. One speaks today, with a voice not less unanimous, of the "history of metaphysics" and of the "Greek morning," as though these not only suffered no contestation, but even called for no examination. This disguising of the paradox as a certainty is what appears problematic to me.

In this concert of voices we nevertheless note one major exception: Paul Ricoeur.[6] After openly admitting his astonishment to Heidegger himself,[7] and without obtaining a clear answer, Ricoeur will reiterate his question twenty-five years later, in a short paragraph that I take the liberty of reproducing almost whole here—as it seems so capital to me.

What has often astonished me about Heidegger is that he would have systematically eluded, it seems, the confrontation with the block [*bloc*] of Hebraic thought. He sometimes reflected on the basis of the Gospels and of Christian theology, but always avoided the Hebraic cluster [*massif*], which is the absolute stranger to the Greek discourse. . . . This misprision [*méconnaissance*] seems to me to run parallel to Heidegger's incapacity to take a "step backward" in such a way that might permit us to think adequately all the dimensions of the Western tradition. Does the task of rethinking the Christian tradition by way of a "step backward" not require that one recognize the radically Hebraic dimension of Christianity, which is first rooted in Judaism and only afterward in the Greek tradition? Why reflect only on Hölderlin and not on the Psalms, on Jeremiah? There lies my question.[8]

It is precisely this question that I propose to open to discussion, a discussion whose field we must define from the outset. It is in no way a question of playing the historian against the thinker, and of relying on some arbitrary "factual data" to problematize Heidegger's assertions. Such data may well belong to the register of what Heidegger calls *Historie*, but they could not determine the order of his *Geschichte*.[9] In other words, the fact that Christianity was born "objectively" in the Hebraico-Roman milieu, in no way influences the line of thinking Heidegger proposes [*ligne de sens*]: what difference does it make to the thinker that there might have been a Jewish people and a Book, if these remained without posterity—or, more precisely, if *we* are not their inheritors? What value has their pure historic (*historisch*) existence, if the fundamental position in which we stand today can be interpreted—that is, referred back to its truth—without considering their intervention?

On this point one can only subscribe to Heidegger's assertion. Not only is the historial not the historical, but the former receives no order from the latter. It is rather the *Geschichte*—once it is elucidated in its lines of force, hitherto secret—that can make possible another approach to *Historie*, that is, which can allow the approach to be established, not under the dictatorship of facts (which obligate only those who have already decided that it is from these facts that they will take their orders), but in light of a division of meaning [*partage de sens*]. In a word, the multiplicity of events is powerless to account for the "coming" [*avènement*] of a destiny, and thinking is something other than historiography.

Under these conditions, by what right, and especially, from what place, may we suspect that the Heideggerian text is marked by an omission? To this question I can only respond with another one: by what right and from what place can Heidegger speak of a "forgetting" inherent in metaphysics and, thereupon, of an unthought? The answer leaves no doubts: if it is legitimate to impute to metaphysics a forgetting of Being, then that is because Being gives itself continually *in* metaphysics, without being taken into consideration *by* metaphysics. In other words, it is because Being is indeed *its* question (to the point where metaphysics is ultimately nothing other than the history of Being), without nevertheless being recognized and meditated in itself. In this case alone does the concept of the unthought find its relevance. Far from being the other of thought, its outside, the unthought constitutes its heart: that which thought carries with itself, that to which it untiringly bears witness, be it unconsciously.

Starting from the same perspective, I propose to question the eventuality of a forgetting within Heidegger's text. This forgetting could be confirmed only if it turned out that Heidegger himself was located in a line of descent that alone made his words possible and that nevertheless had not been discerned as such. My question is thus the following: can we find in Heidegger's text traces of a heritage that he did not recognize, a heritage that would thus function as the unthought of his text?

III. Elements of Method

1. On the Hebraic Heritage

To be apt to recognize in Heidegger's text references liable to be concealed there, we must naturally have some idea of the original, to which borrowings must be referred in order to be identified as such. That is to say, we require a foregoing knowledge, even partial, of what Paul Ricoeur called the "Hebraic cluster" [*massif hébraïque*]. This is, in itself, a gigantic and proliferating [*foisonnant*] cluster, in which we find inextricably interwoven a language (Hebrew), a text (Bible), a tradition of thinking and writing (Talmudic, midrashic, kabbalistic, etc., literatures), a religion (Judaism), and finally a people with its history and its myths. From what perspective should this cluster be called upon here?

To respond to such a question implies a triple choice:

1. The Hebraic heritage interests us here as a non-Greek component of our culture. Its legacy being constituted in its origin by a founding text, I could just as well have spoken of the biblical heritage. I preferred the qualifier *Hebraic* in order to give the analysis a support other than the Christian posterity of the Bible, which is a posterity in which the Hebraic component is inextricably mixed up with Greek influences. That means that the Jewish reading of the biblical text will constitute the principal support chosen here.

This choice would seem to indicate that the Judaic tradition succeeded in this wager of keeping the Hebraico-biblical heritage pure of any external influences, notably the Hellenistic ones. Yet to believe that would clearly be chimerical. Far from being simply juxtaposed, these different cultures are tied together by the most numerous interferences, even by entire zones of interpenetration. In the case under our attention, we know the most obvious points of contact: the few centuries surrounding the beginning of the Christian era, notably the first and second centuries C.E., during which the encounter between Hellenism, Judaism, and a nascent Christianity took place; the Middle Ages, still more complex since the Arabic influence is added to the encounter here; the modern age, finally, where Jewish culture opens largely to the outside world. Nothing of all this could be contested.

Despite these exchanges, one cannot deny that there is something like a *specificity* proper to each of the cultures in presence. It is this specificity that interests me. To limit myself to a few, trivial examples: it is clear that the God of the promise and of salvation owes more to Yahweh than to Jupiter or to Zeus, and no less clear that a theological concept such as the *causa sui* owes more to Aristotle than to Jeremiah. In a word, it is clear that beside the notions that obviously come from the Greeks, and whose origin we can discern in precise texts, other notions have their sources just as clearly in the Vetero-testamentary texts.

Given that, how could we ask Christianity to provide the framework for the division [*partage*] of these heritages, when it was constituted precisely, and from the outset, as the site of their synthesis? For the problem that interests us here, there was more to be awaited from the tradition that tried to draw simply from the Hebraic source and to assure its transmission. The "Hebraic cluster" will thus be examined on the basis of the Judaic tradition, inasmuch as it rests jointly on the Hebrew language and on the biblical text, and as it is perpetuated in the Jewish interpretation of this text: an interpretation, with its logic and its rhythm, that could encounter other influences without being thereby dissolved in them.

2. The first presupposition of this work is thus that the Hebraic heritage found itself preserved and transmitted—not in a pure way, to be sure, but perhaps purer than elsewhere—in Jewish memory. The second presupposition is that this heritage (like every heritage) is an indissociable fabric

made of *language* and *thought* (or, more generally, of experiences of the world); this is an indissociability that allows us to pass constantly from one to the other, and to rely notably on linguistic facts to deduce the specific relationship that a people maintains with its universe. That means that I am presupposing, more generally, that a language does not constitute an autonomous register that would refer only to itself and about which one could deduce nothing. I am presupposing that the differences separating two languages, for example, are not *merely* linguistic differences, but that they can function as indexes by which to measure divergences in thought; conversely, it is possible to return to the language, on the basis of the thought in question, to hear it resonating in a different manner. In brief, I am presupposing that a circulation is possible, and legitimate, between the different constitutive registers of a single cluster.

Such a presupposition can be challenged.[10] However, if it is compelling here, that is because it is already at work in the two corpuses on which we are calling: in the Jewish tradition as also in the Heideggerian problematic, language is never perceived as a separate domain, which would refer only to itself. Naturally, this convergence remains to be shown.[11] Yet it is so patent that even James Barr, the most virulent critic of the "circulation" between language and thought—bears witness to it in his own way: criticizing the excesses of biblical theology, he refers these to the "philosophical methods of Martin Heidegger,"[12] which he judges just as pernicious as "midrashic novels."[13]

The dual purpose of this study thus invites us to adopt a determinate procedure: concerned to set forth the specificity of the Hebraic cluster, in order to confront it with Heidegger's texts, I will take as my basis not just the Jewish reading of the Bible (first presupposition), but also the *principles* themselves of this reading (second presupposition). That is to say, to carry out this research I will act on the authority of the relationship the Hebrews maintained with their own language, and in the spirit of which Jews have not ceased, thereafter, questioning their own inaugural texts. These principles are all the more imperative in that they are also—as I will endeavor to show—the very ones adopted by Heidegger.

3. There remains a final point. Considering the Hebraic heritage as a signifying totality, I have not felt it necessary to establish clear-cut separations between its different components. I will therefore refer as much

to the classical rabbinic literature (Talmud and midrash), as to the mystical current (notably the Kabbalah). Not that one can erase everything that separates these, and which has so marked the work of, say, Emmanuel Lévinas;[14] but these components interest me here only as the divergent expressions of a single identity. In this sense, the Kabbalah is less an isolated branch than a magnifying mirror: it bears witness in its at times exacerbated way to elements already present in a diffuse fashion in classical Judaism. This is notably the case for the question of language. Now, if I happen to illustrate this with a narrative inspired by a mystical source, then it is with the presupposition that a certain relationship to language, more clearly legible in the Kabbalah, is nonetheless characteristic of the whole Hebraico-Judaic tradition. This whole, in what unity it has, is what shall be called on here.

It is fitting to specify the stakes of this appeal. The threefold presupposition just presented here should allow us to approach the properly Hebraic heritage, inasmuch as it marked the West by the same rights as did the Greco-Hellenistic contribution. However, it cannot here be a question of presenting this heritage for itself. Beside the fact that such a presentation would surpass the bounds of my competence, it would in no way serve the project of this book. My purpose, in effect, is not to establish a confrontation, under the pretence of an exhaustive study, between two distinct "corpuses," and not even to undertake an historic research into the "sources" of Heidegger's work. It consists, rather, in establishing a list of the most patent proximities, in bringing to light a kind of shared space—if only to ask, then (though this is but one question among others, and perhaps not the most essential one), whether this shared space could not be explained in terms of lines of descent or filiation.

The Hebraic heritage must indeed intervene here (which is the reason why it would have to be comprehensively circumscribed), but exclusively *in its relation to Heidegger's work*. It is a matter of bringing this heritage into play, as our reference text—that is, of taking, here and there, certain samplings from it [*ponctions*]—with the sole goal of making this or that aspect of the Heideggerian problematic appear in a new light. My samplings lay claim to no specific erudition in the field of Jewish studies; rather, they stake a claim to something like a *vigilance* toward that which, having marked our culture and our identity, can be found in Heidegger's text without ever having been recognized as such. Perhaps it was ultimately this concern for vigilance alone that led me to seek, on the side of Jerusalem, what Heidegger invited us to find on the side of Athens.

2. On the Texts of Heidegger

My approach to Heidegger's work will follow two principles. In the first place, I will not attempt to enter into the details of the analyses; naturally, I will not avoid being led there sometimes, but that will not be my goal. Rather, my goal will be to present, in as synthetic a manner as possible, a few central questions, with a view to setting forth their lines of force. In this way certain motifs will be brought to light, which, if they were neither isolated nor enlarged, would remain caught up in the threads of the text and would thereby lose visibility.[15]

In the second place, if one seeks that which permeates a work without being named or recognized there, one will not be content with the author's explicit positions relative to the question at stake. Such positions, in effect, which seem to exhaust the problem, say nothing about what is elsewhere in play (it is not impossible, even, that one of their functions would be precisely to mask that there is an elsewhere in the text). I will thus cite Heidegger's text in a deliberately oblique manner. When I pose a question to the work, I will not only seek where Heidegger responds to it explicitly, but where and how the elements of his response "work" the text, even in those places where they are not noted as such.

In clear language: if we limited ourselves to what Heidegger *says* about the Hebraic heritage in order to follow its traces in his work, then our inquiry would be finished quickly. To be sure, we can enlarge the perspective by searching for bits of information in what Heidegger says about Christian theology. And I will not fail to do so.[16] But this can only be an element within a much vaster inquiry: for Heidegger's explicit elaboration of theological questions (or, of what he considers as *the* theological question) in no way exhausts that which, from theology, plays out in his work; simply, it is played out in other sites, under other aspects. It is these aspects that are worth listing and questioning. If Heidegger, who observed such a striking silence on the subject of the Hebraic cluster, is nevertheless in relation with it, then this relation is necessarily secret, caricatural. And it is up to us to disentangle the double skein of the intrigue: we have to show the imprint of the Old Testament heritage on Heidegger's thought, and correlatively, we must show how Heidegger's thought dissimulates this heritage.[17]

But from whom do we get the possibility of such a reading, if not from Heidegger himself? To measure the impact of the Greek morning upon metaphysics, Heidegger did not question—in any case, not in the first place—what metaphysics has said explicitly about the Presocratics. He sought that which betrayed the secret presence and weight of a forgotten "morning," in what metaphysics said about itself (that is, at the same time, by itself and about itself).

Out of fidelity to such a method, I will not take as my basis for this inquiry those themes that are unfailingly called forth the moment we approach the relation between Heidegger and what touches "religion," proximally or distantly. Examples include the question of onto-theology, the relationship of Being to God, or the alternative faith or thinking. I will on the contrary engage in questions that are apparently foreign to the problem that interests us. It is only after having explored these questions that it will be possible to return to the elements that in Heidegger's work are destined to respond directly to our interrogation, elements that we will have the chance, thereafter, to read otherwise.[18] That is to say that the principle, consisting in questioning the text indirectly, shall lead me to adopt a course wholly made up of meanderings and detours. It is worth presenting that course here briefly.

IV. Outline

I will proceed in several stages. In Part I ("Readings"), I will present the elements of the debate, placing side by side certain positions adopted by Heidegger and those positions one may consider to be Hebraic. To situate the framework better, I will first recall the rule of reading or interpretation [*règle de lecture*] that allows Heidegger to make the separation, within the fundamental options of the West, between an experience said to be "originary" and conceptions called "derived" (Chapter 1). Once this rule is clearly set forth, we should no doubt be able to show that it structures the presentation of all the questions that Heidegger treats. Given the impossibility of engaging myself in an exhaustive examination, I will consider two, particularly central, questions: the question of language (Chapter 2) and that of thinking (Chapter 3). I will then examine how Heidegger justifies attributing to the Greek text alone this experience called original, which will lead me to present his theory of interpretation (Chapter 4).

But over the course of these chapters I will also have shown that language, thinking, and interpretation are themselves the object, if not of conceptions, then at least of determinate experiences in the Hebraico-biblical tradition, and that these experiences present close analogies with those which Heidegger credits to the first Greek texts. The entirety of this first part shall lead us to ask whether that which Heidegger takes in charge in his own thinking, to which he assigns the status of the unthought in the Greek text, might not carry the imprint of another text and perhaps of another thinking, themselves never called forth as such.

In Part II ("Problems"), I will set forth—as the title indicates—the various problems raised by the convergence noted in the preceding chapters. I will do this as I attempt to open paths for their elaboration (certain of which will keep the status of hypotheses). Thus I will consider in Chapter 1 the question of Being—a question that apparently presents the greatest difference with the Hebraic positions, but which shall here be interrogated from the perspective of its renewal by Heidegger—and of the conditions for such a renewal. But if the impact of the Hebraic and Vetero-testamentary cluster can be detected in Heidegger's thought, even in those questions most properly his own (which seem also to be the most Greek), then it is appropriate to ask how this impact works in his texts, that is, through what paths is its transmission brought about? This question will lead me to interrogate the relationship of the young Heidegger to theology, such as it may appear in light of the first courses of Freiburg (Chapter 2). Once these different points of view are illuminated, it will be possible to open a larger debate about the place occupied by the Hebraic heritage in Western thought: a place to be delimited not independently of Heidegger's work, but, on the contrary, in terms of the use to which his work has put it (Chapter 3).

To close, we shall have to return to the Heideggerian reading of history, with which this study began, for a reading that can now appear in its problematic character ("Conclusion").

PART ONE

READINGS

Heidegger's Reading of History:
The Split

Most of this first chapter will be devoted to recalling, in a deliberately formal way, what we may consider as the *rule of interpretation* [*règle de lecture*] that guides Heidegger in deciphering Western history. But this demands that we define in advance the notion of "Western history" itself, in its precise relationship to metaphysics.

I. The Field of History and the Metaphysical Field: Heidegger's Evolution

1. The Double Expansion

I already indicated in the Introduction that the term *metaphysics* was the object of a double extension over the course of Heidegger's evolution: one, by which metaphysics comes to cover all the *dimensions* of Western history; the other, by which it covers the entire *course* of this history. It is appropriate to follow each of these two extensions. If the first, as patent, can be the object of a simple review, the second extension is more complex and requires that we examine it for itself.

a. The Semantic Expansion

This expansion is carried out, if not from the *Kehre* itself, then at least during the years of its "maturation" (1936–46, approximately), years during which Heidegger sets up and elaborates thematically—essentially thanks to his contact with Nietzsche—something like a unitary doctrine of "metaphysics," henceforth considered in its essence.

What takes place over the course of this turn? First, there is a quite clear slippage in Heidegger's vocabulary. Whereas, hitherto, the essential object of Heidegger's preoccupations was *ontology* (ancient ontology, traditional ontology), later, the prevalent term becomes that of *metaphysics*. Yet, was this really a change in object? It was rather a displacement of emphasis. In the beginning, what interests Heidegger is the single ontological question, taken up (albeit simply in being renewed) on its own ground; what interests him thereafter is the fullness of this fundamental question (and the positions to which it gives rise) everywhere but on its own ground.

The modification in vocabulary is thus the sign of an enlargement touching on what one might call the "play space" [*espace de jeu*] of the question of Being: from ontology to metaphysics, it is the same question that is intended, but it is understood to be at work in ever larger parameters. Although Heidegger began by awakening this question within the field devoted to it, and which carried it explicitly (perhaps too explicitly to avoid blunting the thrust of Heidegger's questioning), he will thereafter work toward showing that, far from being circumscribed according to the "ontological" field alone, it is this question again that reigns over all the domains of thought from which ontology was traditionally distinguished. That is, not only, as Aristotle perceived, in the other parts of metaphysics (with theology in first place), but in vaster, less clearly defined circles of philosophy (moral or political, for example), and finally within still larger parameters, which normally escape philosophy (everyday behaviors, technology, art, etc.).

In a word, the question of Being overflows ontology. It shapes the entirety of thought and even behaviors characteristic of the European-Western sphere, and it alone is apt, in return, to illuminate this sphere. This global figure of a "West," referred back to its fundamental and until now hidden unity, is what Heidegger will henceforth call metaphysics, separat-

ing himself considerably from the traditional understanding of this term
(as also from the understanding he himself had initially lent it).[1]

Now, how is such an extension legitimated? It is legitimated through
the new way in which Heidegger thinks about the "question" traditionally
reserved for ontology. Once the question of Being becomes that of Being's
withdrawal, it is hardly surprising that the question should be recognized
as everywhere in force (everywhere that one had failed to discern up to
now). And it is precisely because the question reigns through its absence
that it can be said to be forgotten, even where we nonetheless believed it
had been considered: in ontology. In other words, if Being had a positive
presence in one domain at least, then we should have trouble understanding how Heidegger could "impute" it to domains that, up to then, had se-
renely paid it no heed at all; yet, to the degree that this ignorance (under
the term "forgetting" of Being) belongs to the very unfolding of Being, it
follows that this unfolding can exceed the boundaries primitively assigned
to it.

Under these conditions, calling the entirety of the Western sphere
"metaphysics" becomes not only legitimate, but also explicative. It becomes legitimate because this sphere has been referred, integrally, to something like its foundation [*comme à son fondement*], that is, to the question
initially awakened by ontology (although masked by it), an ontology that
therefore indeed constitutes its "essence."[2] It becomes explicative because,
through such a nomination, we are sketching the global face of the West
by unveiling its hidden wellspring [*ressort caché*]: the question of Being.
Such is the first expansion Heidegger carries out touching on the word
metaphysics: beyond mere metaphysics, in the restricted sense of the term,
it henceforth embraces all the dimensions of the thought, even the behavior, that characterizes the West.

b. The Historical Expansion: Presentation

This is but a first step, however. For, although metaphysics—as soon
as Heidegger thinks it through in its essence—does indeed appear indissociable from its history, that "history of metaphysics" is not yet totally
assimilated to the history of the West. Only much later (in what I am inclined to consider as a second turn) does this first determination get modi-

fied, thereby according a second expansion to metaphysics: that by which it comes to embrace, without any "remainder," all of Western history.

The general picture is thus as follows. Starting around 1935, Heidegger gives to the word *metaphysics* an extension wider than what is currently accorded it (and which he himself had accorded it earlier). The exemplary texts include, for the early position on metaphysics, *Being and Time*, and for the transformation, *Nietzsche*. Starting approximately from the 1950s, Heidegger gives to the history of metaphysics temporal boundaries that differ from those that were currently assigned to it (and to which he himself had earlier assigned that history). The exemplary texts for this include, for the earlier position, the entire mature work, but especially *Plato's Doctrine of Truth*;[3] for the transformation, *Time and Being* and *The End of Philosophy*.[4]

It is this second expansion that we must now consider. But if the "turn," which nevertheless offers the guarantee of having been recognized by Heidegger, already constitutes a fragile point of reference, what are we to say about subsequent evolutions! Fluctuating, subtle, and resistant to any strictly chronological grasp, the subsequent evolutions discourage clear divisions. It remains true, however, that the same question may constitute the object, over the course of the work, of a succession of elaborations, which are worth noting and distinguishing even if they find themselves coexisting with or even interpenetrating each other. I will therefore distinguish not so much a before and after in Heidegger, but rather two *configurations*.

2. First Configuration: Metaphysics and Its Margins

The first configuration makes the history of metaphysics into a moment (albeit the most characteristic) in the history of the West. It does so, in the first place, by way of its temporal limits: it begins with Plato and ends with Nietzsche. In the second place and above all, it does so through its intrinsic limitation: here and there amid the historic markers that circumscribe the moment, certain possibilities unfold; these belong de jure to the history of the West, without being reducible, for all that, to a metaphysical wandering. What is the precise status of these possibilities? It consists in their remaining *unthought* (as far as the initial possibilities are concerned), or in being projected further as *to-be-thought* [*à penser*] (as far as the final possibilities are concerned). In one case like the other, the possibilities can therefore not be said to belong to thinking, as the leitmotif of the seminar *Was heisst Denken?* [*What Is Called Thinking?*] attests: We do not yet think.[5]

It remains the case that this unthought inhabits our history, that it unfolds its presence there. Better still: if its specific mode of unfolding, over the course of metaphysics, is the withdrawal that generates the forgetting of Being, then we must not neglect the fact that, everywhere on the metaphysical field, the unthought has other modes of presence, themselves with strongly positive connotations. Inside the field—that is, within the "inaugural illumination" [*éclair inaugural*] that constitutes the "Greek morning"—the unthought is the object of an experience (*Erfahren*) taking the form of a premonition (*Ahnen*). Beyond this—in Heidegger's meditation—the unthought becomes the object of a "memory" in the form of a "commemoration" (*Andenken*).

In this respect the history of metaphysics (which, to be sure, covers the history of what has been "thought" *stricto sensu*) is not yet assimilable to our history as a whole. Beyond the single register of what is thought we have to take account of registers of experience and premonition, of memory, and perhaps of others still—all of them registers that belong by right to the history of the West, which were even prevalent at its outset (which is the whole sense of the "morning"), and which thereby allow the nonmetaphysical to be inscribed *within* this history, if only in an indirect way.

The first configuration thus makes metaphysics into a historial moment that was preceded by . . . and will (perhaps) be followed by . . . This is a configuration particularly legible in *Plato's Doctrine of Truth*. Before the birth of metaphysics—to which the Platonic *idea* attests—something of Being gave itself in its truth and was received as such, at least in the register of experience. At the decline of metaphysics—announced with Nietzsche—this first experience can and must be "recalled to our memory,"[6] in order that "the originary essence of truth" finally be thought in itself. As wandering is not inaugural (and therefore not unsurpassable either), there is no total equivalence [*adéquation totale*] between metaphysics and history.

Now, this subtle nonequivalence finds itself erased in the late texts. There, we observe the setting up of a second configuration in which metaphysics, "occupying" spaces of experience that eluded it hitherto, progressively covers over the entire field of history.

3. Second Configuration: Metaphysics as History

The occupation of spaces of experience that had escaped metaphysics earlier on is effected by a double displacement, the one touching what precedes the metaphysical field, the other, that which follows it. We must consider each of these closely.

a. The Premetaphysical Margin

We have seen that the first configuration left room within history for a nonmetaphysical possibility. The later texts will expel this possibility *outside* of history, *before* its morning, thereby bringing about a double modification: not only will metaphysics be delimited otherwise, but also the nonmetaphysical possibility (that is, the theme of the "originary") that acquires a new status, at the same time that the "Greek morning" is reconsidered. Naturally, there is only a single gesture here, but this can be described according to two perspectives.

Let us consider it first within the perspective of the extension of the metaphysical field. Toward the end of his work, Heidegger took away from the Presocratics the privilege he had so continuously accorded them. Not only was the truth of Being not thought by them (something we already knew), it was not even the object of an experience. Now, only that experience would permit us to establish a difference between the Presocratic beginning and what follows it. Once this experience is erased, the Greek landscape again finds its unity. The best evidence of this reestablished unity is found in *The End of Philosophy and the Task of Thinking*. Giving himself over to a veritable self-criticism, Heidegger recognizes that *alètheia*— far from having been first experienced as disclosure and only afterward thought as rectitude—was first experienced [*éprouvé*] within the perspective of *homoiōsis*. By virtue of this fact, "the assertion about the essential transformation of truth, that is, from unconcealment to correctness, is also untenable."[7]

A text rich in lessons: the dividing line between the initial "experience," which should have been accorded to the Presocratics, and the later metaphysics in which this experience would have been covered over, is here considerably muddled. This muddle alone lets us understand a posteriori certain prior assertions, like the one where Heidegger speaks of the "history of metaphysics, from Anaximander to Nietzsche."[8] These are disconcerting assertions so long as we want to insert them into the first configuration, but they are immediately cleared up as soon as we attach them to the second one. For, if what comes to pass, in effect, with Heraclitus is only and from the outset (*sogleich und nur*) what will be continued in Plato, then the premetaphysical margin is erased. Metaphysics indeed continues to be thought by Heidegger as a derivative construction, but it is recognized as *derivative from the outset*: the morning has lost its radiant form as a "premonition," all of history is a wandering.

That there no longer be a premetaphysical moment in history does not mean, for all that, that thinking should be dispensed from having to return toward a nonmetaphysical possibility. Simply put, with the historial space, assigned earlier to thinking, now being "given back" [*rendu*] to metaphysics, the possibility in question acquires a different status. Thus the configuration we are following here can likewise be described according to this second perspective: no longer from the point of view of metaphysics, but from the vantage point of what precisely escapes metaphysics. In the first case, a certain field saw itself *circumscribed* otherwise than it had been beforehand. In the second case, it is a certain figure (that of the originary) that sees itself *situated* wholly otherwise.

Let us recall rapidly the sites that had hitherto been assigned it. If, in the Marburg era, Heidegger believed he could still situate the originary within metaphysics (thereby opposing the Platonic-Aristotelian beginnings to the later tradition), he works subsequently to rediscover it, sheltered in its mode of an unthought, in Greek words (by which we should understand: in the Greek *language*, at least when it is left to its initial force of nomination, which takes place in the maxims [*sentences*] of the morning thinkers)—whence the opposition, characteristic of the first configuration, between metaphysics (including its beginning) and the Presocratic morning. It is on this ground that we can measure the major displacement introduced by the second configuration: in his taking back from the first Greeks the privilege he had previously accorded them, he is led to set himself apart from the "morning" itself, for the benefit of a site still closer to daybreak, to which one can only have access "starting from the Greeks," but which is nevertheless situated "above and beyond the Greek" (*über das Griechische hinaus*).⁹

Things come to pass as though Heidegger, over the course of his work, *pushed* the originary ever farther *back*: from a hardened metaphysical tradition back to its Platonic-Aristotelian foundation; from thence back to the premetaphysical morning; from the morning, finally, to a daybreak more secret still, and to this day not yet come [*inadvenue*].¹⁰ But that also means—and it is this consequence that merits attention—that, in the very last step of this passage toward the background [*cheminement vers l'arrière*], Heidegger finishes by stepping in some sense outside of the *Greek* itself. The originary, henceforth recognized as already derivative from the very first opening of our history, it is the Greek language itself that imperceptibly loses its privilege as the exclusive shelter of the origin. Parallel to this (though this movement is never thematized in itself), Heidegger's recourse to the German language becomes increasingly frequent. It is as though the German becomes the sole site where the beyond of the Greek language still lies hidden (and can be heard). That is to say, while not abandoning the Greek language—as it resonates in the matutinal words of the first thinkers—Heidegger is increasingly inclined to turn toward the German language, when it is a matter of letting the original essence unfold. He turns toward the German language as it resonates in the call of the poet (in regard to which we do not know whether it is as matutinal, or still more so, than the Greek).

Thus there is some play, in the sense of a wavering, within the Greco-German relationship such as Heidegger presents it. But as he moves within the relationship without setting forth the law of this movement—perhaps without discerning that law clearly—his texts hesitate between several courses. Once unfolded, the original figure sees itself referred back, at one moment, to what sheltered it already in the mode of an unthought within the Greek language, while at another moment it is posited as something to be thought beyond the Greek language itself. Moreover, once the figure is unfolded, in an ever more frequent (though nonexclusive) fashion, on the basis of the German, recourse to the latter language can in turn be understood either as a *detour* permitting a return to the Greek, or as a *break-*

through, allowing the Greek to be surpassed: surpassing not only what was *thought* in Greek, but what was, more radically, *named* there.

I evoke this movement relative to the originary,[11] because it constitutes one of the major repercussions of the expansion of the metaphysical field. But it behooves us to pursue the analysis further. Considering what came to pass *upstream* from this field [*en amont de ce champ*], we have as yet reached but one aspect of its expansion: the displacement outside of history of the premetaphysical margin. The Greek dawn [*l'aube*] having lost its prior privilege, history begins *as* metaphysics; it begins with its own wandering.

b. The Postmetaphysical Margin

Downstream, another remarkable displacement occurs, one I would be tempted to think about as symmetrical. For it has as consequence, ultimately, that history comes to an end at the same time as its proper wandering. As long as we held to the first configuration, we could still imagine that a surpassing of metaphysics, if it were possible, would open the door to an other moment of history, or to another history, less forgetful of Being. Beyond the long wandering to which the metaphysical tradition had condemned the West, it appeared that a return might be possible. This would be a return of thinking to the Being that sustained it and history's return to its long occulted truth. In a word, we, beings belonging to a forgetful modernity, could be awakened *for* Being and *in* history.

Let us consider now the seminar devoted to the course *Time and Being*, a text that constitutes the most complete thematization of the second configuration. The preceding perspectives here find themselves stricken with impossibility. The surpassing of metaphysics, when no longer presented as a task still to come, but as an event finally come to pass (and it comes with "the entry of thinking into the *Ereignis* or appropriation"),[12] appears under a radically new figure. It no longer consists in turning toward Being (as one might have expected), but in being finally able to turn oneself away from Being—as the first "disconcerting" theme of the seminar attests, that of a "leave" given to the question of Being.[13] This signifies that there is, ultimately, only an unthought of Being, or, if one will, that the question of Being is only posed within metaphysics—posed there precisely in not being posed. Likewise the surpassing of metaphysics no longer consists of engaging in a new historial possibility, which would no longer be wandering, but rather of recognizing that history is closed, as the second disconcerting theme of the seminar attests—that of the "end" of history.[14] This means that there is no other history than that of wandering, or, if one will, that the history of Being unfolds only as metaphysics and in metaphysics. It unfolds precisely in not being recognized there.

This double affirmation, characteristic of the final Heidegger (the question of Being can be abandoned, the history of Being is over), allows us to circumscribe the new status accorded to metaphysics. It sketches in effect two essential traits. (1) As Being poses no questions as long as it is perpetuated, in the mode of withdrawal, within metaphysics, it is impossible to envision, *beyond* metaphysics, a return of some kind to Being, or even a memory of it. It is not that in this "beyond" another thinking could not be possible, but such thinking would no longer be that of Being. (2) Since the history of the West is synonymous with the history of Being, and metaphysics espouses this history entirely, the end of metaphysics thus coincides with the end of Western history (and, in truth, of history *tout court*, but we will return to this later). It is not that there might not be a possible future, beyond this closure, but the future would no longer belong to history.

It thus appears that *Time and Being* accomplishes, in regard to the postmetaphysical possibility, what *The End of Philosophy* accomplished in regard to the premetaphysical possibility. These two texts, on condition we hold them together, offer a remarkably integrated [*unitaire*] teaching: that there was no premetaphysical, historial moment, any more than there will be a postmetaphysical historial moment. And it is indeed this that defines the status of metaphysics in the second configuration: the erasure of the margins or, to be more precise, *their expulsion outside of history,* an expulsion leading metaphysics to find itself purely and simply identified *with* history. In effect, it was these margins that, in the first configuration, allowed metaphysics to be situated *within* the history of the West, allowing in turn the history of the West to overflow metaphysics alone. Once the margins disappear, there is no Western history *other than* metaphysics.

It naturally remains possible to contest this division of configurations, which is a division presented here in deliberately cut-and-dried terms, and which is far from being as clear in Heidegger's text. We might consider, notably, that metaphysics is already identified early on (as soon as it is thought in its essence, that is, immediately after the turn) with the totality of history; this also is true (certain texts could attest to this). Yet it seems to me that this identification grows clearer and clearer, more and more complete over the course of the work, and with this the modifications introduced in the final writings find themselves confirmed—at the same time as they are fulfilled. In any case, such an identification may have been more or less precocious, or more or less late, but its existence can hardly be doubted.

c. A Final Expansion?

We should complete this picture by considering a final expansion, which I will evoke much more rapidly. Above, we observed the passage of the history of metaphysics toward the history of the West. But the history of the West, in its turn, becomes History *tout court*, even, in a way still more explicit, that of the planet, or the "entire earth," and so on.[15] This expansion was justified by the fact that the essential determinations, characteristic of the West, have become, through the medium of technology, "planetary."[16] What Heidegger was still calling, at the time of his *Nietzsche*, "European-Western history" is thus each time to be grasped as *world* history. And it is ultimately this world history that is integrally reduced to the history of Being [*l'histoire de l'être*], since its epochs taken as a whole—and its figures, however diverse they might be—may be thought on the basis of the withdrawal of Being. It is not just the ontologies of Descartes or Kant that must be referred back, for clarification, to the Greek commencement or inception [*Anfang*] (where Being, in withdrawing, took its destiny [*se destina*]), but it is also "all the great facts of world history,"[17] like the invention of the Sputnik,[18] the opposition between the politico-economic systems of the United States and of Soviet Russia,[19] the National Socialist ideology,[20] the extension of cybernetics,[21] and so on. All of these are illumined by a single and enigmatic giving [*d'une unique et énigmatique donation*], they are part of the same destiny, they belong to a single essential constellation.

Let us recapitulate the different phases of this analysis. From the beginning to the end of his path of thinking, Heidegger proposed to shed light on the history of metaphysics. Yet, if he first uses the word *metaphysics* in conformity with its current use, it will later become the object of a triple expansion. On the one hand, the word will surpass the single domain of ontology (even of onto-theology, which is certainly recognized as its essence but which in no way exhausts its field of extension), to ultimately cover all the dimensions proper to the West (dimensions of thought and attitude). On the other hand, the word surpasses the limits that had first been assigned it, to finally cover the entire history of the West, from its inauguration to its completion. Ultimately, the two preceding assertions—whose accents concern the West primordially—can themselves be expanded to History as such.

I have spoken till now of a progressive expansion. Yet this project relative to History was, no doubt, already planted, a seed, but in an unspoken fashion, in the first texts. One cannot say, then, that there might have been a precise moment when Heidegger would have expanded his ambition (even if certain texts can function, for us, as markers when it is a matter of measuring this ambition). There was no precise moment, and there could not have been one, because—as in logical implication—the circles gradually show themselves to be concentric. In other words, in Heidegger's eyes (and in those who follow his thought), there is no significant difference between the registers we have distinguished here. The entirety of the movement, far from having to be understood as a gesture of expansion, might consist simply in unfolding, according to vaster and vaster circles, that which was already given (without yet being named, or perhaps recognized) in the starting project.

It thus appears that in attempting to set forth the essence, unthought in itself, of metaphysics, it is indeed the general field of history that Heidegger claims to think, that is, that he attempts to cast light on and to refer back to its truth, hidden till then.

Having thus circumscribed the "object" of our study, we will now consider the *rule of interpretation* [*règle de lecture*] that will guide Heidegger in his deciphering of Western history. In its turn, this rule is the consequence of two major displacements relative to earlier philosophies: one bearing on the beginning, the other on the history that flowed from it.

II. A Beginning Divided, a Dissociation of History

1. The Inception [Le coup d'envoi]

What does Heidegger's specific contribution consist of, on this point? Before its upsurge on the scene of thinking, history (which did not yet call itself that of Being, but, in a more immediate or more descriptive fashion, that of "philosophy") seemed to be sketchable in one stroke, whatever its course looked like, whatever the meaning assigned to it. To speak summarily, one had, at that time, two models at one's disposition.

For the long-dominant model, the inaugural character of the Socratic-Platonic conceptions left no doubts. To be sure, no one failed to acknowledge the existence of thought systems prior to this beginning, but even their name, "Presocratics," indicated well enough their preliminary status, that is, in the final analysis, their prehistoric status. With Nietzsche a new type of reading is set in place. Recognizing Heraclitus or Parmenides as authentic philosophers (and not only, as Hegel would have it, as brilliant precursors), Nietzsche places the accent of the beginning elsewhere than had previously been the case—and this, to the point of seeing in the Platonic *Idea* the beginning of a decline. This bespeaks at once the breadth of the innovation Nietzsche introduced and its limits: an innovation, because he inverted the terms of the traditional schema; limits because, despite this inversion, Nietzsche preserved the traditional schema's outline. The two models—though distinguished to the point of opposition in regard to what they value along the line of history—nonetheless rejoin in a single metaphor of history *as* a line.

This is the metaphor that becomes inoperative with Heidegger. At first sight, it seems given at least formally to taking up Nietzsche's gesture. Like Nietzsche, Heidegger *displaces* the traditional point of departure. Our history begins well before Plato. It is inaugurated by the first Greeks. And it is from them that it receives its decisive impetus. Whence the erasure of the term *Presocratics* and of the double reference which was implied therein, to the benefit of the expressions "initial thinkers" or "morning": at the same time that Socrates loses his preeminence, the Presocratics see themselves confirmed in their inaugural status. Up to this point there is nothing particularly innovative here; another interpretation of the beginning, to be sure (the "moral" one gives way to the "ontological" one), yet it has the same localization—at least in appearance.

In reality, Heidegger does far more than displace the point of departure: he splits it. The prior alternative (either the Presocratics or Plato) gives way to a conjunction: the Presocratics *and* Plato. Thus *a double inaugural register* is set up. On the one hand, the manifest beginning, which opens with Plato; on the other, an "other beginning," hidden, covered over, unknown—which had taken place among the very first Greeks. What is the exact status of each of these? Two elements are worth underscoring.

In the first place, the one like the other has the function of inauguration. On one side, the Greek dawn is the "inception" [*coup d'envoi*] of a certain question, which, under Plato, will fall into forgetfulness. But, on the other side, the Platonic act is not only in a relation (that misrepresents) with what preceded it; to the degree that what preceded it had never been thought, this act has indeed, itself, an inaugural status. We thus find ourselves in the presence, not of an initial moment or a merely derivative stage (to which the Nietzschean notion of "decline" condemned us), but of two initial moments.

In the second place, and paradoxically, the one moment (Platonic ontology) is nevertheless strictly dependent upon the other moment (the initial commencement or inception), since the former constitutes only the resumption of the preceding moment, this time in the mode of a covering over. In this sense, Platonic ontology occupies a secondary or derivative position in relation to the other moment.

How shall we reconcile these two aspects? In other words, can we assert that one moment derives from another, without falling thereby into the linear illusion, into the metaphor of the line (which would erase the inaugural duality)? There is only one solution, which consists in asserting that there are indeed two departure points, but that they do not belong to the same register: they are distributed according to the cleavage between the thought and the unthought. Because of this cleavage they can be said to be *originary*, on the one hand, and *derivative*, on the other—without losing their inaugurating function. The one inaugurates our destiny, without being able to be defined, nonetheless, as the beginning of thought (since it does not belong to its order); the other inaugurates the history of thought, without being the source, nonetheless, of what was therein intended.

Thus we see taking shape, on the same site of inauguration, a gap [*décalage*] between an unthought origin and a thought beginning. While being in a relationship of determination, the originary and the derivative are no longer on the same line; they do not belong to the same "plane" [*plan*]. It is by this breaking up of the point of departure that a wholly other reading of history becomes possible, one that tears it out of the linear schema on which Nietzsche remained dependent. Such is Heidegger's major act.

2. . . . *and what derives from it*

Once the point of departure is divided in two, history can be dissociated: it is no longer that which, manifest, was unfurled on the basis of the Platonic question, but firstly that of another, hidden, question, which opened with the first Greeks. To argue, as the metaphysical tradition had done, for the inaugural character of the Socratic-Platonic conceptions is thus not simply to misunderstand the originary beginning; it is, far more essentially, no longer to have access to more than a single side [*versant*] of history: that is, to condemn oneself to misunderstanding history's essential duplicity.

Of what does this consist? If, from Heraclitus to Plato, there is no debate around a common question, but the setting in place of two distinct registers of questioning, then we find ourselves before a double historial process. On the one hand, manifest history, that of the *leading question* (*Leitfrage*): it begins with Plato, inaugurates its completion in the work of Nietzsche, calls itself metaphysical, and interprets itself, in its truth, as the history of the being-ness of the being. On the other hand, there is the secret history of the fundamental question (*Grundfrage*), which begins with the first Greeks, escapes thought in the very act of its opening, and finds a memory of itself again only with Heidegger. It calls itself the history of Being and is interpreted, in its truth finally dis-covered [*enfin dé-celée*], as the history of a withdrawal.

Such is the schema, at the very least according to a first presentation, necessarily provisional. For, in reality, the history of metaphysics is itself, over the course of its unfolding, the history of Being. In these conditions, can we argue that there are two registers there? Yes and no. No, in the sense that there is, in truth, only one line; yes, however, in the sense that such a line, in all that is most proper to it, is a Fold, one side of which alone is illuminated, the other remaining latent as it were. History thus conceived does more than authorize two registers of reading [*de déchiffrement*], it demands them: history shall have to be considered from the angle of the thought (history of metaphysics) *and* of the unthought (history of Being). Why can we not spare ourselves this unfolding [*dépliement*]? Because only as folded does the line, in its unity, finally become thinkable: our history cannot be illumined in the order of thought except by being referred to the order of the unthought.

That means that Heidegger will not let himself be fixed in either of the two registers: he situates himself at the heart of their conflictual unity. He is the one who can articulate, because he knows how to distinguish. In Heideggerian terms: it is he who, because he is able to recognize the Difference, can think it in the mode of unity.[22]

Let us recapitulate. We have seen a double step taken up to this point: for one, a division of the beginning into two; for the other, and as a result, a breaking open of the line of history, till then conceived as univocal. For Heidegger, it can therefore no longer be a question of what one used to call, in still unitary terms, "the history of philosophy." It is henceforth a question of the history of metaphysics (blind unto itself) *and* of the history of Being (as foundation of the first). Starting from there, a third step becomes possible, directed toward the different questions elaborated over the course of that history.

III. The Splitting of the Questions

1. From the Derivative to the Originary

The framework of the reading having been thus established, each of the positions adopted over the course of the history of metaphysics (corresponding to so many of the questions traditionally constitutive of "philosophy") shall be questioned in view of its possible "latent contents," of which these questions are only a derivation, in the dual sense of their provenance and their secret deviation. Encountering these questions anew and attempting to renew their development [*élaboration*], Heidegger will be led, each time, to a double treatment: (1) a presentation of the reigning conception, which proceeds from what has always passed as the "beginning," that is, the Platonic inauguration; (2) a *step back* [*Schritt zurück*], never before attempted, from this reigning conception, which will henceforth be disclosed as metaphysical—therefore, as derived—toward an essence said to be "originary." This implies bringing to light the specificity inherent in the Presocratic "unthought."

To be sure, as we saw above, the leap toward the originary reaches different sites according to whether we follow Heidegger's mature works or take the last works into account. But, at the end of the path, when thought is invited to pass *beyond* the Greek, it can only do so *from that basis*; and, when it ventures to seek a figure for the origin, situated within the Greek dawn, it can only do so by passing beyond, and behind, *this dawn itself.* That means that even if we integrate into the general economy of the work the last modifications introduced in the late texts, history still only knows one origin. If there is something "more originary," it is thinkable only beyond history or below history. This therefore also means that history, as such, remains Greek, and remains so throughout—remains so, that is, on both sides of the split that crosses it.

In sum, whether we consider it from the angle of thought (i.e., as the history of metaphysics), or from that of the unthought (i.e., as the history of Being), it appears that the entire history of the West can be illuminated by being set into one or the other filiation, that is, by being referred to the one or the other of the inaugural acts. Thus there are two distinct points of departure in Heidegger's problematic (one with a derived status, the other with an originary status). Both are Greek however, and only Greek. While recognizing the existence of a duality, or even an opposition to the origin of our history, Heidegger interprets it in a specific fashion, since he derives it from a single originary "tonality": the Greek language. Such is, it seems, his great contribution to what was until recently called the "philosophy of history."

2. The Two Constants

Now, it is remarkable that, whatever the question approached, the interpretation Heidegger proposes as originary (meaning: originarily Greek, or of Greek inspiration) offers two characteristics, which we find with regularity.

In the first place, there is the extreme difficulty of any act of apportioning between that which can be referred to the "unthought" of the origin and that which must be recognized as the "'to be thought' in the future" [*"à penser" de l'avenir*]—that is to say, between what is brought to light in the mature works as the experience of the first Greeks, and that which is deliberately proposed as a Heideggerian conception. As the two movements of commemoration (of a past always misunderstood) and preparation (of a future as yet unknown), each escapes the thought known until now, the external referent (i.e., the criterion of ancient/new, or Greeks/Heidegger) can no longer come into play, and the distinction remains impossible to make.

How does Heidegger resolve this difficulty? In other words, how does he arrive at preserving the originary status for positions he set forth (which status alone legitimates them), without erasing all that they owe to his own thought? He does so by way of a new theory of interpretation.[23] According to this theory, texts speak only on condition of being questioned, and of being questioned from a perspective already determined. That is to say, Heidegger recognizes that these conceptions are not "really found" in the Presocratic text left unto itself, even as he asserts that they can nonetheless be found in the text, on condition we look for them there.

In the second place, we should note that—if we are able to read a language other than the Greek—each of these conceptions "is found," in a fashion no longer latent but manifest, where Heidegger never dreamed of seeking them, that is, in a wholly other text, the Bible and its commentaries.

If this dual character were to be confirmed, let us admit that there would be a quite troubling coincidence there: on the one hand, certain determinations are referred by Heidegger to the Presocratic texts, although these determinations were never noted there by anyone other than Heidegger. On the other hand, he fails to recognize these same determinations in the biblical text, although they were not just noted there, but also extensively commented upon—and this, well before Heidegger. It is this second assertion that is worth our justifying here. For that task, I will take, as I said, three examples: language, thought, and interpretation.

2

The Question of Language

I. The Double Essence of Language According to Heidegger

1. The Splitting

An early preoccupation of Heidegger, the question of language was the object of an initial, though still provisional, development in the years 1935–40.[1] However, it will only attain its definitive dimension at the beginning of the 1950s: after having attempted to think the *lógos* in the interval,[2] Heidegger again sets about listening to the poem in order to hear, through it, how it is with "essential language."[3]

Over the course of this last period that which had only been sketched hitherto is clearly fixed and thematized. It appears then that Heidegger distinguishes—in order to oppose them in the clearest fashion—two conceptions of language: (1) the one in which the word is essentially *that which designates (das Bezeichnende)*,[4] and therefore where it is apprehended in the category of the sign, from which all the later approaches to language, notably the linguistic ones, will come—a conception whose emergence Heidegger situates with the later Greeks, notably the Stoics; (2) the other conception, of a quite different inspiration, wherein the word is essentially *that which shows (das Zeigende)*,[5] that is, the conception in which there is not signification but appearing, the appearing of the things themselves in their being. It is such an essence of language, qualified as "the most matu-tinal decision,"[6] that shall constitute the initial Greek experience such as it is unfolded, notably in Heraclitus's texts.

We can see that Heidegger applies to this definite question all the elements recognized as constitutive of his general rule of interpretation: (1) A splitting of the question: on the one side, the derived "conception" (the theory called metaphysical: here, language as expression and signifi-cation); on the other side, the unthought "experience" (thereby constitut-ing "what is to be thought": here, language as come to presence, therefore as having an intimate connection with Being itself). (2) An explication of this splitting by way of the existence, not of a simple difference, but of an *opposition* between the late understanding and the originary understand-ing of the same Greek word (here, the word *lógos*: on the one hand, the *ló-gos* as speech [*lógos-énoncé*], on the other hand the *lógos* as gathering [*lógos-recueil*]. (3) Nonetheless, it will be asserted that the understanding called "originary" was never meditated, nor even noticed by the Greeks, and that it can only be attributed to them in an "after the fact" movement.

We should examine thematically what Heidegger considered an "originary essence." But we can discover the very first clues of this in his own *practice* of language. Whence these preliminary questions: how does Heidegger himself relate to language, in what way does he use it, and what can we deduce from such a usage?

2. From Things to Words

No doubt we can say without exaggeration that Heidegger refers *only* to language: his procedure is essentially one of deciphering texts, of atten-tion focused on the words. And this is so, not only when it is a matter of doing a direct reading of a text, but already for any act of thought. When Heidegger aims at the elucidation of a thing (more broadly, of a question-content), he turns immediately toward the *word*. When he asks, for exam-ple, what is dwelling, he questions words (e.g., *wohnen, bauen*) much more than the building itself, or the history of urbanism.[7] The more so, when he asks what are truth, Being, or language themselves, Heidegger ques-tions the "fundamental words" (*alètheia, phúsis, lógos*). One might multiply these examples and show in a very general way that all of Heidegger's questions are always posed to the text before being asked of things. The text is questioned for itself, less in view of what it speaks about, than for what it says, that is, for its *resonance* (understood here as the manner by which the very wealth of language can resonate in the text).

Once the question about the thing is oriented toward the word, how does Heidegger proceed in regard to the latter? Lending a prevalent importance to polysemia, he poses at the beginning: (1) the multiplicity of meanings is the index of a unity; in other words, the different meanings are not simply juxtaposed in one and the same word, "as under the same roof,"[8] but (2) this unity is determined by one meaning among them: the other meanings, as well as their articulation, are rooted in that one meaning. Such is the "proper" or "originary" meaning, the others appearing then as derivative. Once he accomplishes this delimitation, Heidegger uses it thereafter according to a remarkably constant schema: after having deployed the originary meaning, he returns to the habitual one to interpret it, finally, in its truth, that is, in light of the preceding meaning.[9]

The immediate objection to this—of which Heidegger was by no means ignorant—consists in asserting that this passage from one meaning to another is simply a word game, in the pejorative sense of the German term *Spielerei*—a verbal juggling.[10] In responding to this objection Heidegger provides us with primary indications on how he understands, not only the internal functioning of language, but also its relationship to beings.

Let us take up his question again: "Is such a return arbitrary? Is it a game? Neither the one, nor the other."[11] If the passage from one meaning to the other is not arbitrary, then their conjunction within a word is not arbitrary either; it is the expression of a proximity. We should grasp all the implications of such an assertion. To consider that a conjunction of meanings [*conjonction de sens*], played out within language, hints at a connection of essence [*connexion d'essence*] is possible only if we consider that the structure of language is homologous to the structure of "that which is," and consequently, that the conjunction of meanings can be taken as a guide to orient ourselves in the connection of essences.

Yet we ought to be precise: when Heidegger declares that language shows us the direction, and that it is up to us to listen to what language says, he does not thereby mean that language *imposes* a direction that would be properly its own (an order properly linguistic), but rather that language *reveals* the very direction of the essence which lies sheltered within it. This appears clearly in a few highly revealing pages of *What Is Called Thinking?* where Heidegger justifies his practice. If it is a matter of "being attentive to the play of language, of hearing what language actually says when it speaks,"[12] then this is because in truth "it is not we who play with words, it is the essence of language that plays with us."[13] Should this essence of language be understood as an arbitrary linguistic structure, some pure "parade of the signifier"? Not at all. And Heidegger makes no mistake in emphasizing: "Any etymology becomes pure verbal juggling when . . . the unfolding of Being and truth is not experienced as *that on the basis of which language speaks*."[14] That is what Jean Greisch calls a "phenomenology of salutation": "It is *phúsis* itself that is *signified* [*se signifie*] in the word. . . . The word is already a salutation of essence."[15]

Thus, Heidegger's procedure itself attests to a specific conception of the essence of language; this is a conception that founds—and that alone can render intelligible—not only its general relationship to language, but also the highly idiosyncratic usage he makes of polysemia. It is this conception—referred to an unthought experience, one therefore presented as the grasping of the "originary essence"—that we should consider more closely.

3. Characteristics of the Originary Essence

I will limit myself to underscoring three points that appear to me among the most significant.

1. The first point is the specificity of this originary essence relative to all the conceptions of language that are familiar to us. Everything transpires as though Heidegger regressed, on this point, to before one of the decisive conquests of Western thought: the theory of signification, which thinks at once the separation and the tie between the word as a sign and that which it signifies. This was a truly inaugural theory, insofar as it accomplished for the first time the separation between the order of things and the order of words, thereby breaking with the primitive indifferentiation and the magical world that could flow from it. Now, it is precisely from this separation that Heidegger steps back, proposing a wholly different approach to the name.

To name the thing is to "make it come forth," to "call it to presence."[16] Is that to say that before being named in this way the thing was not present? Properly speaking, it could not be, because it had not entered into presence, was not assembled into what it is. That is, the thing was not disclosed; it was not liberated from its shelter.

To follow Heidegger's approach, there is not a being first, then language that would come to add itself to it in parallel fashion, to name it and render it communicable. There is language, and language alone permits the being to come to Being. That is to say that language is not a sector or a domain of beings: it is the condition of their appearing, the opening by which a being can arise and stand forth in presence. In and by language, the being comes to its Being: *language makes things be.*[17]

2. Yet if language thus makes possible "the founding of Being" [*das Sein . . . gründet in der Sprache*],[18] what makes language itself possible and what allows it to unfold *as* language? This is where the double notion of listening and dialogue comes in. It is a notion that we too readily tend to interpret in a horizontal register, as though it were only a matter of the necessary unfolding of the word within an interhuman exchange. But Heidegger says much more. It is not this or that word, but *language itself*, which can unfold its essence only on condition that it is already a listening: the listening to a *call*—which is not of the order of language and which, nevertheless, alone is able to make language possible—the call of Being. To say, as Heidegger does, that to speak it is necessary first to listen, does not mean that I must listen to another word. It also does not mean that every word, in order to unfold, must keep listening to language [*à l'écoute du langage*]; it means first and most basically, that language itself is devoted to receiving that which asks to be opened in it. It only unfolds according to its essence on condition of being docile toward that which lays claim to it. And what thus lays claim to it is Being—or, still more precisely, "the very voice of Being, resonating across all language."[19]

The notion of dialogue presents the same duality of registers. For there to be a community of language within dialogue, in the ordinary sense of the term (i.e., interhuman, horizontal dialogue), it is necessary "to hear together one and the same voice or word."[20] And it is when the speakers assemble around this voice that dialogue is set up. That is to say that even before there is agreement between words, and as the foundation of this agreement, we should consider the vertical agreement, an agreement of that to which every word refers. Hence Heidegger's insistence on the fact that language in its entirety stands in dialogue and presupposes it as its condition: "Dialogue is not a form of language use. It is language that has its origin in conversation."[21] Or again: "Language comes to pass in dialogue, and it is this coming to be (*Geschehen*) that properly constitutes its Being (*Seyn*)."[22] Why insist on this point? In order to indicate that language, which permitted, as we have seen, the institution or founding of Being, nevertheless does not create Being; to the contrary, language presupposes it.

Is this a circle? It is, rather, a movement of mediation. And it is precisely this movement that constitutes the essence of language. Up until now I have presented separately these two aspects: on the one hand, the fact that language could make possible the opening of Being; on the other hand, the fact that what makes language itself possible is already a certain call of Being, to which language responds in unfolding itself. But these two aspects are indissociable from each other. Language permits the founding of Being [*l'instauration de l'être*], yet Being [*l'être*] is nevertheless not reducible to the sole order of language. It is for that reason that this order is defined—and must necessarily be defined—as listening, welcoming, ingathering [*recueil*], and so forth. In this way, the preceding conclusion is completed and illuminated: to be sure there is no Being without language, but there would not be language if language did not reveal Being. Language makes be [*le langage fait être*],[23] but only in the sense that it permits Being to come. That is, that *language lets be.*[24]

Thus it occupies an eminent mediating function. And it is precisely because language is mediation that it is only properly fulfilled in poetry.

3. Being the site in which language remains consistent with its essence,[25] the poet can be defined as he who lets this essence unfold. Yet, because language is in itself mediation—since it finds its essence in the unity that is indissociably reception and donation, welcome and foundation—the poet will incarnate this mediation; he will fulfill it in itself. This is why he appears, in Heidegger's problematic, as the mediator par excellence, the Messenger.[26]

The third significant point thus concerns the status and mission of the poet. Let us recall rapidly his characteristics.[27] The poet is the one who collects the signs from the gods in order, then, to transmit signs to the people; he invents nothing, only receives and transmits. Having collected, "with his pure hands," the "ray of the father" (which could not shine outside the open space of Being), he shares it with the "sons of the earth"; however, he only delivers it after having pacified it, which means that he himself remains exposed to the violence of the lightning flash [*violence de l'éclair*]. *Porte-parole*, messenger, receiver of signs, mediator between men and gods, subject to the horror of the direct relationship with the god, and pacifier of the terrible for human beings: these are the traits of the poet, supreme guarantor of language, thus guardian and watchman over Being and perhaps even, as Heidegger occasionally asserted, "savior" of Being [*die Rettung und Wahrung des Seins*].[28]

Such are some of the lines of force that allow us to account for the specificity of Heidegger's approach. We must now confront these with the status of language in the Judaic tradition, and show why such a confrontation is necessary.

II. The Hebraic Essence of Language

1. Language and Presence: The Biblical Teaching

The central idea around which the entire Jewish experience of language is organized is that language does not have the status of an instrument. It is the crucible of all that is: it is in language that all beings are first held; language is that from which beings can break forth into presence, and it is to language consequently that we must return untiringly to have access to this presence.

The principal attestation of this is provided by the very term that designates the word [*la parole*] in Hebrew: *davar*. Now, we know how frequent it is, in Hebrew, that the same word may have several significations. This plurality is firstly linguistic. But it could not fail to introduce a certain type of relationship to the world, in which the splits that seem natural to us are not precisely performed. That is, that the plurality gives rise to a mode of thought that grasps in their unity, phenomena that other peoples perceive from the outset as distinct. We cannot therefore limit ourselves to establishing a linguistic "juxtaposition": that would be to use a term that Jewish thought would not accept, insofar as it presupposes that there could be a conjunction, in the linguistic register, of certain realities that would remain separated in other respects. Whereas, taking its own language as its guide, the thinking in question let itself be taught by it (notably, by the polysemia of its words) about the fundamental unity of the world.

It is in this framework that we should hear the polysemia of *davar*, which designates simultaneously a *word* and a *thing*. Recall, now, all that Heidegger deduced from the double meaning of *lógos*—meaning at once to say and to posit—or from *aeon*, which says at once Being and beings. It is because the Greek word carries this unity in itself (in the case of *lógos*) or this fold (in the case of *aeon*), that the whole experience of language, on the one hand, and of Being, on the other, such as it gave itself to the Greeks and then to the entire Western world, carries the mark of this primordial command, given by language. We will start here from an analogous principle: to the degree that the word *davar* states, at the same time, the word and the thing, we may rightly consider that the entire Hebraic experience of language remains necessarily marked by this.

All the more that, on this point, the Hebrew language contrasts from the outset with the other languages that also nourished our history, all of which establish a very clear dichotomy between the register of the real and that of language—where the latter is posed from the outset as a separate domain: the Greek dichotomy of *ho lógos* and *ta onta*; the Latin dichotomy of the *res* and the *verbum*, and so on. It all thus comes to pass as though the Hebrew confronted us here with what André Neher called a monist word: "One of those . . . monist words, so common in Hebrew, which respect the deep, original unity of the creation and which protest, by their very existence and by the simultaneous multiplicity of their meanings, against the dualisms . . . of non-biblical cultures."[29] This leads him to a more general conclusion: "Judaism does not know, and it rejects, the Greco-Latin cleavage, readopted by Christianity, and this rejection . . . [is] symbolized in the history of a word."[30]

By itself the word *davar* teaches us, then, that any dissociation between the universe of language and that of Being is foreign to the Hebrew language, as to the experience that proceeds from it. At the same time as the word, the thing itself is given—in a manner that remains to be specified; in language the real is opened, or augured, in some manner.

What the Hebrew language thus says finds itself confirmed by the biblical text, and underscored especially by the Jewish reading of this text.

When we read, at the beginning of Genesis (1:1), that God created the universe through the word [*parole*], that could be interpreted (as it sometimes has been) as the simple assertion of the creative character of God. But it is in no way immaterial that God should be presented, in the biblical narrative, as accomplishing his creative work precisely by way of the word, and not otherwise. This is why Jewish interpreters have never ceased seeing in these first verses the affirmation of the creative power of the word itself. Ultimately, it is not because language is from God that it is sacred (an idea, common to all the great religions of the Book, of revelation), it is rather because God uses language that he is a creator God.

When John declares (John 1:1) that "in the beginning was the Word [*le Verbe*]," he merely translates—and takes the theme up on a new basis, giving it a new sense—a very old tradition, whose reach Christianity reduces by assimilating the Word to the messianic person of Jesus. The most popular of the Jewish interpreters of the Bible, Rashi,[31] proposes what amounts to a broader interpretation of the midrashic books to which John is most probably referring: if creation could be born from the *Said* [*du Dit*] of God, it is only because the Word [*Verbe*], in its purity, is creative. It is in no way simply because it had, initially, sent the world into being, but because it supports it there at each instant. The unity of the *davar* implies that the word [*parole*] accompanies every coming into presence and constitutes, in André Neher's beautiful expression, its "rhythm."[32]

Such is the first key idea: God, in the moment when he creates the universe, uses the word (which is what the biblical text teaches us); that he can do this is because the word, in its purity, is creative (this is what rabbinical exegesis understands). Thus we find ourselves confronted by a determinate comprehension of language: in it is played out the opening of presence.

2. The Practice of Language: Exegesis and Word Games

At this point a new question arises: how should we understand this unity, proper to the *davar*, of things and words? In what direction does the determining relation [*le rapport de determination*] play out? One might give this question its anticipated answer: in the Hebraic-biblical tradition, the existence of things and beings—as well as their mode of being, their history, and so on—is set down in potential in words: *words that therefore serve in no way to designate things, but that instead command them to be.* In other words, if the universe of language contains in germ, and in a manner yet to be unfolded, the entire universe of beings, it is because the former does not belong to the latter: it is its condition of appearing.

To demonstrate this, consider the double practice of language proper to the Judaic tradition: the practice of exegesis (of perpetual commentary, of interpretations always recommended), and, within this, the practice of wordplay. This is a doubly specific practice. In Jewish exegesis, it is not a matter of simply finding the meaning of the text. It is a matter (since the text is the potential of things) of sketching the face of the world. Likewise, wordplay is not simply a matter of making linguistic relationships play among themselves; it is a matter of deciphering relations of essence through the linguistic relations. That is to say, the Jewish tradition uses language in an eminently unique way: it avails itself of it as it would a guide, to orient itself within a given being—thereby attesting that language functions for the tradition as that which decides what the being is, and the fact that it is [*du fait qu'il soit*].

It would be easy to show this in relation to midrashic and Talmudic exegeses. It seems to me more interesting that one can observe this practice at work in the biblical text itself. The best illustration of this is provided, again, by the biblical myths, not so much by their contents as by the rules that presided over their formation. A remarkable study was devoted, a few years ago, to the structure of mythic narratives.[33] Through an extremely meticulous study of the two first books of the Pentateuch, this study shows that the mythical narrative flows entirely from linguistic injunctions: it seems ultimately to have no other objective than to construct narratives that will justify the polysemia of its base word. We know the most famous example: if man is presented as constituted from the dust of the ground (Gen. 2:7)—whereas none of the Mesopotamian creation stories establish such a tie—this is because man (*adam*) is in a linguistic relation with the earth (*adama*). Likewise, if woman (*isha*), is presented as constituted from man (*ish*), and more specifically again from his rib (*tsela*), this is because the feminine (*isha*) is constituted on the basis of the masculine (*ish*), considered as a "side" or genus of language (*tsela*)—and all this, starting from the same radical, that is, from the same linguistic "trunk." We can hardly be surprised, consequently, that they "become one flesh": they have a common root. The same goes for biblical *names*. The individual history of each figure is constructed progressively as a justification of the name they bear; that is, in the majority of cases, to justify the polysemia of this name.[34]

The same principle proves applicable to rites, understood as the cultural dramatization of the myth. Ritual practice consists frequently in "playing" on the euphonic relation between two words, or on the polysemia of one word.[35] That is to say that ritual practice rests not on the symbolism of gestures, as is the case in other traditions, but on a pure linguistic echo. Rites and myths therefore appear as the two expressions, one verbal and the other behavioral, of an identical relationship to language.[36]

I will not multiply examples, which one can find presented very convincingly in the study already cited. The result is that, in the biblical universe, existence is only the manifestation of a reality contained in potential in the word: it is language that engenders existence and determines history; it is language that, properly speaking, makes be [*fait être*].

If we unite the different elements stated up to this point, we find ourselves in the presence of two teachings, one concerning the *way* in which the biblical authors (as well as their exegetes) relate to language and use it, the other concerning the *essence* of language, which must necessarily be presupposed (even if it is not thematized as such) in order that such a practice of language might be imaginable. Let us recall these in their greatest generality.

1. In what manner does this culture relate to language, and what is it seeking through language? It lets itself be carried by language. The biblical text, like the tradition that corresponds to it, rests upon *relations proposed by the language*, in order to discover these relations in the world (i.e., myth), or even to recommence them through gestures (rites). That means that the culture discloses—or forms—the structure of the world on the basis of the structure of language.

2. Yet, if it is appropriate to discover or recommence these relations in this way, that is precisely because it is *not* a matter, for this tradition, of *relations limited to language*, as though the latter constituted a separate and autonomous domain. What is presupposed here is an entire conception of language in its relation to the real. If the Bible can make the structure of the world derive from the structure of language, this is because language

itself has previously been considered as the shelter of all presence. And this is the reason why playing with words allows words to tell us how it is with things; to bring together terms sharing the same root is to allow a closeness of essence to unfold.

Now it is this double teaching that also came out of the Heideggerian problematic. Should one see there only a general acquiescence [*connivence générale*] in the attention paid to language? That would be to cheapen the *specific* tie between the two approaches: if they are attached to each other, this is because they separate from all the other determinations familiar to us. Only accounting for this tie can permit us to make a clear distinction between Heidegger's thought and that of contemporary thinkers, who likewise accord a primordial importance to language and use wordplay, but without situating themselves in the same filiation. For these contemporary figures, in effect, language, grasped as an autonomous structure, remains apprehended under the category of the sign; for the others (i.e., Heidegger and the biblical universe, and for them *alone*), language is the opening up of that which is.

In this way we see all the distance that separates, for example, Lacan's use of language—and notably, his wordplays—from Heidegger's use of it. What opposes them from the outset is that they derive from two different conceptions of language: on the one hand, the structure revisited, on the other, the forgotten *davar*. That is, on one side there is the pure succession of the signifiers [*le pur défilé du signifiant*]—a purely linguistic play, at least at its origin; on the other side, the opening of presence, the play of Being itself. Now it is this play of Being within language that the biblical tradition teaches us, as much through its comprehension of language as through the practice that derives from it.

This is, nevertheless, but a first lesson: language has been defined only in its relation to the real. It is now appropriate to consider it for itself, examining its own mode of unfolding.

3. Language as Dialogue

We can proceed here in the same way as before, that is, drawing support from a practice, in order to deduce a certain conception from it (though it is not explicit). To say that language is dialogical is, in effect, to say two things at the same time: the one concerns the manner by which the word unfolds, in fact, in the Bible; the other concerns the very essence of language, which must necessarily be presupposed by such an unfolding.

Let us consider the first point. It has often been noted that the word, in the Bible, is never simply a word, nor a word about . . . , but always already a word to . . . [*ni parole sur . . . , mais toujours déjà parole à . . .*]. When God speaks, he uses the imperative and optative modes ("Hear, O Israel!" . . . "That I be . . . "). He speaks in the form of an address to an interlocutor, real or potential. This is what the notion of Revelation attests, even before that of the Covenant. As the basis of the biblical universe, as well as of the religions that flowed from it, Revelation is not the simple *expression* of God, manifesting himself in a saying—it has meaning only as an *encounter*: the encounter of the mouth that proffers and the ear that hears. And it could not be anything else, once it was manifested in speech [*dans un dire*]. If God had simply wanted to show himself intransitively, as was the case in other religions, notably pagan ones, he could have shown himself "in the tempest or the fire." However, if he shows himself in a saying, in words (and this is indeed the meaning of the word *revelation*), it is because this saying is addressed to someone who is supposed to receive it.[37] Revelation is thus indissociably the word of God and the word to humans [*parole de Dieu, parole à l'homme*]; it is the one because it is the other, and, if it is the one and the other, this is simply because revelation is a word [*parole*]. What the Bible teaches us here is that the very essence of every word is to be dialogical.

This brings us to the second point; that is, to the being proper of language. If, in the Bible, the word actually comes to pass only as dialogue, this is because language is from the first experienced—insofar as its essence is concerned—according to the double category of the *call* [*appel*] and the *listening* [*écoute*]. Language, in its highest realm, that is, when it is the word of God, is a call; when it is taken up in the human universe, it presupposes someone is listening to this call—it gets structured by the modalities of reception and response [*en mode d'accueil et de réponse*]. As Rabbi Nahman of Bratislava says, in a striking epigram: "For man to write, he must bow forward," which means that to speak one must first listen.[38] This does not necessarily mean listening to words, but being attentive to the divine call, which lays claim to us [*qui nous revendique*] not in the tempest and the fire, but in the "thin voice of silence" (or, according to another translation, in the "subtle voice of silence"; 1 Kings 19:11–12).[39] One can see this clearly in the human word par excellence, which is the prophetic word. Only on the foundation of this vertical structure of language can the horizontal, interhuman dialogue unfold. The prophet speaks to the people, and can be heard by them, because his word remains governed by a call that preceded it.

If the typical example of this structure is the prophetic word, the counterexample is the biblical figures before Abraham, who never speak to each other; they cannot even manage a horizontal dialogue, because they do not yet know how to listen.[40] Revelation is given, but the Covenant is not settled. From the moment the call is heard (and it is heard by Abraham),[41] the human word can arise in itself, consistent with its essence and its truth, structured as dialogue.[42] And it is only then, in the eleventh chapter of Genesis, that the word *davar* itself appears for the first time in the biblical text: an authentic word, a word consistent with its essence, and bearing with it the opening to things: a dialogical word.

We have thus encountered three things, which I now recapitulate: (1) The word, as word of God, is addressed to humanity. This is what accounts for the specificity of the biblical universe, which begins with revelation. (2) For this reason the human word can only unfold upon the horizon of this first call. That means that it becomes itself only on condition of being first a listening. (3) And only if it is inscribed within the framework of this vertical dialogue, always presupposed, can the horizontal one be established.

This dialogical dimension of the Bible is hardly open to debate. The problem is rather that of its relationship to Heidegger. In effect, the possibility of an analogy between the biblical word and the Heideggerian word has been envisaged, precisely in order to contest it. I am thinking especially of Emmanuel Lévinas who, in *Otherwise Than Being; or, Beyond Essence*,[43] presents the specificity of the prophetic word while, in his text on Paul Celan,[44] he evokes in entirely different terms the Heideggerian word. It becomes clear from the confrontation of these two texts that, to Lévinas's eyes, the word in Heidegger's sense, that word that is listening to Being, could not be compared with the biblical word. What distinguishes it fundamentally is that Heidegger's word has nothing to *answer to*; it holds itself, barring insomnia, "within the bed of Being."[45] It is therefore pure self-containment and perseverance with oneself, whereas the word, in its biblical vocation, is unceasingly outside of itself, listening to an other.

The majority of Heidegger's readers share this position,[46] yet it seems problematic to me. It is quite true that we find ourselves confronted with an ineluctable difference: the listening, understood as a listening to Being, opens onto no determinate content (to the point where it is liable to be subjected to almost opposed "calls," as Habermas noted clearly),[47] whereas the listening that is understood as a listening to God is not a pure attitude but a specific listening, exposed from the first to an ethical imperative. It nonetheless remains that the (formal) *structure*, that constitutes the word is analogous in both cases: the word unfolds as (horizontal) dialogue only because it is guided by a call [*ordonnée à un appel*] that comes to it from elsewhere. That is to say that language, in Heidegger as also in the biblical world, in no sense rests upon itself: structured in the modality of opening, of exposure to . . . , language is characterized by a radical heteronomy.

In this sense, that Heidegger could evacuate the entire ethical dimension of the Bible is a fact hard to contest (to which we will return in more detail elsewhere);[48] but that he could take up an *essence* or *structures*, which were originally those of the Bible, in order to think some question, like that of language—that seems to me every bit as evident and merits being questioned as to its meaning and consequences.

Moreover, it is in no way insignificant that this theme of language, as response to a call, should take place in a meditation on Hölderlin, that is, on the poetic experience. This is a poetic experience that is itself, largely, traced upon the *prophetic* experience.

4. Poetry and Prophetism

Once the word must be received before being transmitted, a mediator is implied. In the biblical tradition, this mediator is the prophet; in the Heideggerian conception, it is the poet. Here we find one of the best illustrations of the unavowed dependence I am attempting to set forth. No one would contest, in effect, that the Heideggerian poet might have a prophetic status; moreover, Heidegger himself states this. Yet it has never been stressed, at least to my knowledge, that this status owes nothing to Greek prophetism (which is of another nature), and that it owes everything, on the other hand, to biblical prophetism. Now, not only is this debt, in its specificity, unrecognized by Heidegger, but he explicitly denies it.

If Heidegger recognizes, in effect, that the word of the poet can be called prophetic, it is only to add immediately afterward that this must be understood in the sense of the Greek prophets, as opposed to the biblical ones—as though the biblical prophets were simple soothsayers, while the Greek prophet alone was a prophet "in an essential sense." Heidegger's text reads:

> Their word [that of the poets] is that of predication, but in the rigorous sense of *prophèteuein*. . . . The poets are not "prophets" in the Judeo-Christian sense of this word. . . . We must not overburden the essence of this poetic universe [that of Hölderlin] by making the prophet a seer in the sense of a diviner. . . . The essence of this poet must not be thought in reference to those "prophets" [the biblical prophets].[49]

On this precise point, it seems that Heidegger overreaches his rights of interpretation. To show this it is not necessary to engage in a meticulous description of the two forms of prophetism. It is enough to confront their two central figures: that of the *mantis*, on the one hand, and of the *nabi*, on the other, in order to make the specificity of the second figure apparent. The analysis that follows makes no claims to exhaustiveness; it simply aims to recall a certain number of features characteristic of biblical prophetism—features we in no way find in Greek prophetism but that constitute, nevertheless, so many determinations of the poet in Heidegger.

1. Grasped in its highest figures, like those of Cassandra or Tiresias, the *mantis* is much more than a magician or a caster of spells. He or she is a seer, an authentically inspired one. Yet it is precisely thereby that he or she is distinguished from the *nabi*: in biblical prophetism, emphasis is not placed on vision or even on inspiration. The word is emphasized; more precisely, it is the meditative function of the word that receives emphasis. In other terms, the biblical prophet is not firstly he who receives in his person [*en lui*] the spirit of God, or his breath; it is he whose function is to lend his mouth, he who formulates a word he did not himself initiate. That is to say that what defines his specific essence is the order of language, and that, inside this order, the biblical prophet has the function of the intermediary: the receiver of a word that demands transmission. On the oth-

er hand, the Greek prophet is someone firstly inspired, and only second-arily the mediator and interpreter of a word (*prophètès*).

2. The prophecy of the *mantis* is always, and by definition, tied to the future. The Greek prophet is he who, inspired by God, foresees the future, he who pre-dicts. The biblical prophet sometimes foresees the future, but this is not his essential or exclusive task. He deciphers the invisible mean-ing of the visible. "The prophet is there to read through the words [*pour lire au travers*]. In this way, more than through the act of foreseeing, he re-veals things. He recognizes what is hidden."[50] That means that his prophe-cy has to do with meaning, not with tomorrow: "While the diviner seeks to announce the unexpected, the prophet sees himself invested with a wholly other task, that of stating the invisible. The *nabi* is a hermeneute."[51]

3. While the biblical prophet does foresee the future, the future is pre-viewed only to be pre-vented [*celui-ci n'est pré-vu que pour être pré-venu*]. My remarks are inspired here by the opposition: Cassandra versus Isaiah, such as it is developed by Ernst Bloch and taken up again by André Neher.[52] Cassandra, whether she speaks or not, will have no influence on the events, whereas events will or will not come to be, according as Isaiah speaks or remains silent. We see this clearly in Ezekiel 3:17–20: the destiny of human beings is in the hands of the *nabi*. For this reason, the biblical prophet does more than belong to history; he is its founder. It is with him that history opens and takes on meaning; it is he who announces the mes-sianic hope.

Such are the three central differences that separate the two forms of prophetism. Now, concerning each one of these points, the Heideggerian determinations of the poet are lifted directly from the biblical prophet, not the Greek prophet. The saying of the poet is not a pre-diction: what he re-ceives to share is "the almost unpronounceable superabundance of mean-ing."[53] The poet himself is above all a *porte-parole* or a messenger, an inter-mediary: the poets "are those who stand between men and the gods, and who endure this between-the-two."[54] Finally, "the poet is the founder of a history of humanity;"[55] it is he who determines "a new time;"[56] he "lays the foundations,"[57] and "sanctifies the ground."[58]

But Heidegger does not simply rest at that—and neither does the Bible. The biblical prophet has numerous other characteristics, which are likewise found in the "Heideggerian" poet. I am not claiming here that these characteristics are the exclusive endowment of the biblical prophet (some of them are likewise found in other forms of prophetism), but it is their combination that seems impressive to me.

4. In prophetic experience, as Abraham Heschel notes, God is the subject: the divine call precedes the human awaiting, in radical opposition to every divinatory technique that consists in turning toward God to interrogate him. "But the poet never has the power to reach the sacred through his own meditation, nor to exhaust its essence, nor again to oblige the sacred to come to him by his questions."[59]

5. Hence the status of the word [*parole*] for the prophet: as the objective transmission of a message from elsewhere, it is a response to a call; it inscribes itself in dialogue. "But the gods cannot come into the word unless they themselves summon us [*uns ansprechen*] and place us under this summons [*Anspruch*]. The word that names the gods is always a response to this summons."[60]

6. Exposed to the call, the prophet is torn out of himself, to be confronted with the Terrible; he then feels seized by a sacred fright.[61] "The poets are exposed to the supreme danger. . . . They must grasp in their own hands the flash of lightning that mediates, and themselves endure the storms of the initial [*les orages de l'initial*]."[62]

7. In the last instance, the prophet submits. But that signifies that he accepts crossing the night. For the divine voice is rarely clear. Let us listen to André Neher: "The prophet is not the organ of a self-revealing God but the instrument of a God Who is on the verge of hiding. Our analysis has led us to the recognition that God's movement toward the world is not an approach but a retreat. God takes the prophet's hand and leads him on that secret road which removes him. Prophesy does emerge from the absolute, but from an absolute which becomes darker and darker the more it comes into the open. It is a march with God, but toward the night of the unexplainable."[63] To this Heidegger seems to respond, as if echoing it: "Night is the time that shelters the hidden divine [*Vergangengöttlichen*]. . . . The length of this night can sometimes exceed human powers, to the point that one wishes to sink away into sleep."[64] Jonah does more than wish; learning that God chose him, he falls asleep!

8. As a decryptor of meaning, the biblical prophet is he who gathers the signs. Isaiah and Ezekiel go still farther: resigned to the fact that their

whole being is reduced to showing, they use the term *sign* to designate *themselves.*[65] "The speech of the poet consists in gathering these signs in order afterward to make a sign to his people."[66] And Heidegger, recalling the words of Hölderlin ("ein Zeichen sind wir . . . "), continues: "It is only thus that the poet can make himself show what appears and, in showing it to the others, be himself a sign."[67]

9. Prophecy belongs less to the order of discourse than to the struggle with words [*parole*], to the sparring with language. Jeremiah is not content just to live this: he knows it and states it, presenting ease of speech as the sign of false prophecy (this is the entire theme of Jeremiah 23). The false prophet is the prater: speaking without having received a mission, he remains given to counterfeit images (verse 21). The true prophet knows the weight of the word (verse 36): he must struggle before being able to speak (verse 29), and wait patiently to receive the response (verses 35–37). "Of what does the poetic existence of good dialogue [*être poétique du bon dialogue*] consist? The poet knows. For, he knows false dialogue, and the duplicity of the languages at his disposition. Anti-dialogue [*das Gegenwesen*] is chatter, which is without poetry."[68]

10. The prophet is a watcher (Ezek. 3:17). Like sentinels on the ramparts, he has the task of keeping watch and giving warning (verses 17–19). "The poets, who always have some premonition, hope and keep watch,"[69] says Heidegger, who specifies in another text: "Because the night, in the nocturnal density [*in solchem bergend-verbergenden Nachten*] where it shelters and thus hides [things], is not nothing, it also possesses the calm befitting the silent preparations of what is to come. To the latter must respond a watchfulness [*ein eigenes Wachen*], not that absence of sleep which is merely sleep's privation, but such that it [the watchfulness] knows how to protect the night under its watch."[70]

11. Another point which would, no doubt, have merited taking its place among the differences between biblical prophetism and the prophetism of antiquity is the dialectic of the prophet and the people, such as it is incarnated, notably, in Moses—of whom no equivalent exists among the Greeks, where the prophet always speaks to sovereigns. We find in the Talmud a long discussion about the experience of Israel during the reception of the Decalogue. What could they hear, and what did they hear? Here is the response of the rabbis, as recalled by Gershom Scholem: "The over-

whelming power of the experience would have been too strong for the people, and they could not have borne the divine voice." Whence the mediation of Moses: "Moses alone was able to withstand the divine voice, and it was he who repeated, in a human voice," those words from elsewhere.[71] Let us now listen to Heidegger: "The poet himself, stands between the former—the gods—and the latter—the people."[72] What does he make possible this way? "Now, the sacred [*das Heilige*] has lost its danger for the sons of the earth. . . . The terror of the immediate . . . has transformed, through the peace of the protected poet, into the mildness of the mediated and mediating word [*in die Milde des mittelbaren und vermittelnden Wortes gewandelt*]."[73]

12. Despite this, the biblical prophet is not an exceptional man, gifted with particular powers, and even the suffering he endures is not an attribute of his being: it is inherent in the destiny of human beings, which is to be claimed by God and to exist only in participation with him [God].[74] That means that all people are virtual prophets. Just as it is "man" as such, who, in Heidegger's perspective, "dwells in the world as a poet."

I am in no sense claiming that all these traits might be exclusive to the biblical prophet. A number of them are also found in Greek prophetism, not to mention other forms of prophetism, which we should also bring in here. I am simply noting two facts. In the first place, the majority of traits that characterize the poet in Heidegger's approach are found in the biblical prophet, and vice versa. What is therefore striking is not one or another particular trait, but rather their accumulation. This accumulation is all the more impressive in that not only was it never recognized by Heidegger, but, as we have seen, he explicitly denied it. In the second place, when we observe at precise points (themselves pregnant with meaning), a clear divergence between the Greek prophet and the biblical one, Heidegger's characterization of the poet is *always* drawn from the biblical one, something I cannot fail to find quite remarkable.

Let us state the case clearly. Whether it is a matter of the specific practice of language (as exegesis, as plays on words), of the essence of language in its relation to Being, of its unfolding as dialogue, or of the mediator in whom this dialogue is rightly fulfilled, this chapter has tried to show that we find ourselves in the midst of troubling analogies, to say the least, between Heidegger's approach to language and the approach to which the biblical text, like the tradition related to it, bears witness. It should be understood, once again, that what is troubling is not the analogies themselves, but the silence surrounding them. We will find these analogies and this silence again, around other major questions; chief among them is the question of thought. But it is only after we have noted the frequency with which these analogies and silence appear that we will be able to attempt to reflect on them.

3

The Question of Thought

I. The Double Essence of Thought According to Heidegger

1. The Splitting

As he had done for language, and perhaps more clearly still, Heidegger distinguishes two "essences" of thought [*la pensée*]:[1] (1) the traditional doctrine, as taught by logic, and which was not only the dominant determination but the exclusive one for what "thinking" meant; (2) the original essence, which remains to be thought (since "we do not yet think"),[2] and where, a thousand leagues from its later determination as logic and representation, thinking [*la pensée*] unfolds as fidelity, memory, and thankfulness. This double site leads us to think of distinct *vicinities* [*voisinages distincts*], vicinities that have nothing arbitrary to them insofar as they flow directly from their initial determination. It is because thinking is essentially memory that the thinker is close to the poet (who, among men, has the status of guardian or watchman, who remembers when the others forget, if not the poet? Mnemosyne, mother of the muses . . .).[3] Likewise, it is because thought is essentially logic, in the [Western] tradition, that Heidegger refers the philosopher to his essential complicity with the scholar (*ratio*: "reason," but also and firstly "accounts to be given," "calculation").[4] This means that, in passing from thinking such as it was practiced and conceived over the course of our history, to the other thinking, never yet thought, and which nonetheless alone deserves the name, we shall not be limiting ourselves to modifying a single determination; we shall be swinging, much more broadly, from one order to another. Between these two orders there is no bridge, only the "leap":[5] on the one side is the order of reason (which discovers and grasps), on the other that of memory (which welcomes and preserves). As long as we keep the determination of thinking in the first of these orders, it allows us (or seems to allow, and above all promises) mastery. As soon as we resituate thinking in the second order, thought invites us to docility, it becomes the very site of listening and thus of belonging and obedience [*de l'appartenance et de l'obéissance*].

Once this duality is established, it calls for two questions.

1. How can we, taken up as we are in the metaphysical determination of thought, have any idea of thought's originary essence? This is a question that applies also, and primarily, to Heidegger himself: how does he proceed to express that truth of thought? What is the point of departure from which he accomplishes the leap?

2. At what does he arrive in this way? This will lead him to unfold, as before with regard to language, the characteristics of the originary essence.

The first question could just as well have been asked in the previous chapter. It concerns, in effect, the outline, and the legitimation, of a certain movement that is at work as much in Heidegger's meditation on language as in that on thought: the movement by which, separating himself from the traditional determination, Heidegger unfolds the originary essence. What is, each time, the support or pillar of this unfolding? If I have deferred this question up until now, it is because we can only respond to it by holding language and thought together: the originary essence in both cases remains sheltered in a single initial word, the *lógos*.

2. The Two Paths

a. On Language

Heidegger's meditation rests, according to his texts, upon two distinct points of departure. These points are distinct yet convergent, since, following the paths opened by each of them, Heidegger arrives each time at the same conclusions.

1. The first point of departure is constituted by a renewed listening to the Greek word [*parole*] that provided the impetus for all our subsequent conceptions: *lógos*. To come back to the *lógos* qua initial word is to attempt to let the word resound in the way in which it spoke at the origin, before being "worn out," that is, before being taken up as a guiding word of metaphysics. And, in order to let it resound, Heidegger returns jointly to its "proper" meaning, whose memory etymology retains, and especially to the texts (of thinking) where the word found itself used, texts that thereby play the role of context, on the basis of which it is possible to discern what is originarily said [*son dire originel*]. For this reason he returns to the fragments of the Presocratics, principally those of Heraclitus.

This first path thus has as its departure point the way in which language was "experienced" [*éprouvé*] at the inception of Western history. Armed with indications provided for him by his listening to the Greek language and by his reading of thought's inaugural texts, Heidegger turns toward language in a new way, and can thus propose a definition of it that is no longer metaphysical, without sinking into caprice since it renews the connection with the original injunction, beyond forgetfulness and concealment.

Nevertheless, even as he adopts such a path, Heidegger always takes care to make it clear that, in the Presocratic texts, he could hear the original meaning of the *lógos* resonate only because he himself was already turned in a new way toward language. It is therefore because he already understands language in a determinate way that he can turn back toward the Presocratic texts and discover there something like a prefiguration of this, his conception. Had he not already had it, the new way would not have been revealed to him by these texts.

We recognize the hermeneutic circle here, whose outline was already established by *Being and Time*. What interests me here, nonetheless, is not so much the circle itself as the status of the Presocratic texts within it. The foregoing considerations show clearly that these texts could not be viewed as an effective point of departure. Their real status consists, rather, in this: though they did not themselves open the path, they can be placed retrospectively as a potential departure point. That is to say, they are taken up, despite being characterized as "originary," in an incontrovertible "after-the-fact" mechanism [*mécanisme d'après-coup*]. This is possible despite the characterization of them, or rather because of it, since the after-the-fact mechanism constitutes the very framework of everything "originary" in Heidegger's problematic.[6]

The first path is thus more complex than it first seemed. It is not enough to say that Heidegger starts from the inaugural texts in order to think language otherwise. In fact, he already thinks language otherwise, and this allows him to "encounter" the inaugural texts, or to come back to them, and to show that in them the invitation to this new thinking already lay sheltered, in the modality of something unthought. This is why Heidegger, whatever the paths he adopts in his meditation on language, is inclined to add that we always could have started from these texts. But in fact, we could not have done so, since the texts can only appear as a possible departure point for this path to someone who already finds himself on it: *unterwegs*... [under way, en route]. Therefore, if we want to understand what allowed him to make the "leap," on the basis of which everything can finally be clarified by a new light, then we must necessarily refer to another departure point.

2. The second path is constituted by his meditation on the essence of language: what language is, what is accomplished by it, and according to what modes it actually functions. How does Heidegger propose to arrive at such statements? It is not a matter, for him, of proposing a new "theory" of language, a new conception or representation of it, but rather of accomplishing as far as possible the reverse act (the act that, in its principle, belongs to the phenomenological horizon): to rid oneself, methodologically and deliberately, of all theories, to erase the slate, then to "let language come" in person, such that it could present itself by itself and teach us what it is.[7] To let it come, that means under the circumstances, to let it speak. And, as language speaks in an essential way only in the poem, this second path leads Heidegger toward the listening and the situating (*Erörterung*) of poetic speech [*dire poétique*].

This decision to "let language speak" is apt to be understood in two ways. In one sense, it is simply the expression of a procedure; but the decision could also serve as justification for the path. To the question "What authorizes your affirming that language *is* such as you say it is?" Heidegger would no longer need the mediation of the Greek texts, nor recourse to an initial experience ("What legitimates my assertions is that the Greeks, at the origin . . . "), he could simply limit himself to responding, "What legitimates my assertions is that, given the method I have adopted—which is the phenomenological method—it is language itself that showed itself, and that dictated the characteristics stated in its regard."

Yet Heidegger does not proceed in this way. Just as, earlier on, he called upon the Greeks as confirmation of his own position, while acknowledging that, left to themselves, the Greek texts could not serve as an effective departure point (but only as a retrospective and potential one), he likewise asserts here that language shows itself by itself, while again acknowledging immediately that this monstration cannot take place until I have already approached it. Without this foregoing "approach," language could not have made its own being shine—it would have remained *veiled*. This is a veiling that in no way results from an inadequate attitude on the part of consciousness, but one that belongs to the essence itself of the "thing" in question.[8] Affirming this, Heidegger gives up taking advantage of phenomenological evidence. To be sure, he insists that what he states about language has been gathered, as it were, directly from language. But he also affirms that this could not have been gathered, that is, understood, unless one had already covered half the length of the path, as regards the very terms of the question.

It thus appears that, in both cases—whether it is a matter of setting about to listen to history (i.e., to the Greek texts) or a matter of what opens, in the thing itself, to the present (i.e., the essence of language, where we stand)—Heidegger defines a determinate path, then assigns it a point of departure—but a point of departure that always lacks something, that which would allow it to function as such, to get itself moving. In clear language: the moment we are apt to hear what Heraclitus says, the latter becomes singularly talkative and hands over secrets to us. But he can in fact only confirm these for us, since it was necessary, to have access to them, already "to be in on the secret." In an exactly parallel way, as soon as we are apt to hear what language says, the latter sets about speaking and hands its essence over to us. But to speak more precisely: language confirms, in superabundance, that which we knew about it. If we had not already known it, even in the mode of a premonition, language could not by itself have taught us this.

Again we encounter the circle. It is in no way a vicious circle, and it was Heidegger's contribution to have shown the heuristic wealth of it. But it remains no less true that the question of Heidegger's *real* point of departure, in accomplishing his leap, remains open: the paths he takes, precisely because they are not "naïf" but conscious of their own limits, and at the same time of their conditions of possibility, do not allow us to answer the question posed at the beginning: whence does he get the characteristics of the essence called "originary"? What is his point of departure for the accomplishment of the leap? Let us leave this question in suspense for now, and consider the case of thought.

b. On Thought

The problem knowing whether, on the one hand, Heidegger's meditation on the essence of thought is also warranted by a plurality of paths, or, on the other hand, whether these paths are identical to those that were just evoked in regard to language.

The second part of the seminar What Is Called Thinking?, which can be considered the source of the reference text here, follows a global movement that is particularly revealing. From the first lesson we are confronted with the "split." In presenting the multiple senses of his inquiry, Heidegger draws from the outset a distinction between the determination of thought that has had, for all time, the force of law ("How does traditional doctrine conceive and define what we have named thinking?"),[9] and the true essence ("What are the prerequisites we need so that we may be able to think with essential rightness [*Wesensgerecht zu denken*]?").[10] Over the rest of the seminar, it appears very quickly that the traditional doctrine unfolds, on the basis of the Greek *lógos*, understood as a statement [*énoncé*]— with thought defining itself then as logic and judgment. As to the other essence, it demands that we abandon, at least provisionally, the preceding derivation (from the *lógos* to the statement; from the statement to the principle of noncontradiction, and other logical rules), for the sake of a wholly other line of meaning, whose source lies not in the Greek language, but in the German (the old German word *Gedanc*)—with thought defining itself now as memory, recollection, and gratitude.[11]

Once this split is unfolded, it remains for us to understand, once again, the "leap" leading from the dominant definition of thought to its essence, obscured until now. On an initial appearance, it might well seem that the two terms of the split are represented here in two distinct languages, and consequently, that it would suffice to pass from one language to the other. This is not the case. For the essence of the unthought, at which Heidegger arrives, in the first lectures of the seminar (lectures 1 to 4), by way of a meditation on the German, finally proves to be the very thing that was sheltered in the original saying of the *lógos* (lectures 5 to 11). Now this is therefore an original *lógos* that, in Heraclitus's and Parmenides' texts, did not in fact have the sense of the *lógos*-statement (as in the "middle" lectures, 4 and 5), but altogether the sense of the German *Gedanc*.

Thus we again find our two paths: to accomplish the leap leading outside the traditional doctrine toward the unthought essence, two ways open to us, appearing foreign to one another, yet nevertheless reuniting at their ends, to the point of coinciding with each other. On the one hand, we have the meditation on the original *lógos*, such as it continues to resonate in the Presocratic fragments, a meditation that teaches us the essence of thought experienced at the dawn of our history—just as it had already taught us the inaugural essence of language. On the other hand, we have a listening to the German language, resting upon the guiding words, *Gedanc, Denken,* or *Gemüt*. However, this listening is oriented to language only because it is, in principle, an attention directed to the "thing itself," such as it presents itself in person. And it presents itself in person, it "comes" properly to "presence" (as the meditation on language has taught us), only in its word.

We see at once the difference between, and the proximity of, the two paths taken in order to think language and the paths outlined by the seminar What Is Called Thinking? There is a difference, because the unthought essence is sought and reached in the second case, by way of the interrogation of just the German language, which in the first case had intervened only in an accessory fashion (as, for example, when Heidegger, stating the essence of nomination, questioned the verb *heissen* ["to be called"]).[12] Yet there is a proximity, because over the course of this meditation what is still in question is the unfolding of the thing itself. However, that the thing itself (of thought) could come to us only in its word [*que dans son mot*] is what the previous meditation on language uniquely could make audible.

Two paths, then: the one that takes its source in the most distant past; the other, which is liable to open [*s'ouvrir*] at any moment, provided we are able to let unfold that in which we are taken up. At their endpoint, the two paths say the same thing—and, fundamentally, they could not say anything else, given Heidegger's premises. For the thing itself is always sheltered in the inaugural words, and the inaugural words never say anything (inasmuch as we let them speak) other than the thing itself. If the two paths always reunite, then, this is not because of their proper outlines [*tracé propre*] so much as by dint of the more general framework in which they are caught up, and which from the outset prescribes their ultimate reunion.

It all takes place as though Heidegger—engaged since the turn in a thinking that strives to break with the categories of presence (and who does, in fact, diverge from these, in asserting that Being, as withdrawal, exempts itself enigmatically)—did not manage to get to the end of this rupture. Being is certainly understood as withdrawing essentially, therefore as forgotten, but *it must be the case* (Heidegger seems to think) that it has not always been forgotten. It must be the case that Being is revealed, at least for an instant, in itself [*révélé en propre*], as the withdrawal that it is, and therefore that the decisive act by which it withdraws might have been given all the same. It must be the case, in a word, that, though only in the time of a "lightning flash," and in the sole register of "experience," the truth of Being *has taken place.*

It is into this landscape—characteristic of what I elsewhere called the "second epoch" of Heidegger's trajectory [*parcours*][13]—that we must reinsert the astonishing convergence of the paths. If the act of listening to the thing itself and that of returning to initial experiences always reunite (and reunite in the same separation from the determination that dominated the course of history), this is because, in Heidegger's eyes, the essential and the initial necessarily go together. And, if they go together, this is because the essential gleams—can only gleam—as long as it has not been covered over. To be sure, Heidegger insists firmly on the fact that our entire history is the history of this covering over. But he cannot dispense with a "remainder" [*un "reste"*], even if this remainder is reduced to an instant without density, a pure flash. In this inaugural flash, essence has gleamed.[14]

Once the instant of inauguration is defined in this way, relative to the history that followed it, it must be the case that the essence of the thing itself has been given at the origin (and can therefore be rediscovered in the initial words); just as it must be the case, conversely, that the initial words, when questioned, state the essence of the thing itself. What is at stake in the coincidence of these two paths is thus not some periodic intersection [*recoupement ponctuel*]—whether it concerns thought, language, or truth—that would make the Greeks and the truth come together miraculously. It is, rather, a prior structure of comprehension of history itself.

But these are largely anticipatory considerations. Let us come back to our two paths, such as they are presented in the case of thinking. To accede to its essence, which up until now went unthought, we may start either from its determination as memory, such as is proposed by the *Gedanc*, and then find the essence again at work in the original *lógos* (which is the path concretely followed by the 1952 seminar); or we may start from the original *lógos* and develop on that basis an approach to thinking in its essence (this is the path presented as possible, and followed, for example, in a fragment of the article "Lógos").[15]

Nevertheless, in a manner exactly identical to what had already been observed about language, in each case a portion of the path, however minute, is lacking: the portion starting from which it becomes possible, precisely, to get *en route* [*la mise-en-chemin*]. As earlier, Heidegger recognizes this explicitly: in order to hear, in the word *lógos*, the echo of memory and return thanks, we must start from a point of view or from a horizon of thought that does not come from this word, but which alone permits us ultimately to hear it. This is a horizon of thought that listening to the German language, over the progress of the seminar, was precisely to have prepared. But, then again, how would this listening have been possible if it had not already, in its turn, been prepared by a previous horizon? As Heidegger puts it, etymology hardly proposes more than signs; and "to notice a sign, it is necessary to have already penetrated into the domain from which it comes."[16]

The double path leading to thinking thus only confirms what the Heideggerian progress toward language already taught us. In both cases, Heidegger travels over the hermeneutic circle with remarkable rigor; in so doing, he teaches us about its outline. But he does not inform us about what might serve as support—or what, in fact, served him as support—in the effective accomplishment of the "passage." It is not a matter of legitimation here. Paradoxically, the original essence has only too much legitimacy: it is warranted at once by language (thus, by the thing itself) and by history (the Greek texts). But, as these legitimations are, by their own essence, retrospective, they do not give us what we are seeking, which, more modestly, is an explanation: how could Heidegger have any idea of the originary essence? This question remains open for the moment. Let us leave it at its opening and turn, as we already did with regard to language, toward that which such a leap gives access to: the original essence of thought.

3. Characteristics of the Originary Essence

In the presence of the dominant conception, of what does the unthought "experience" consist? In the path traced by the seminar of 1952, this experience is marked by two words, which shed some light on the radical *Denken*: memory (*Gedächtnis*) and recognition in the sense of gratitude (*Dank*). But this is obviously only the most general framework. Within this framework I would like to restore the principal determinations of thought according to Heidegger, in order to show their connections [*l'articulation*].

1. Thought is neither a behavior of human beings nor a faculty of the subject that would allow it to turn toward . . . What conditions thought from the origin is the *Other*, which Heidegger calls the thinkable [*le pensable*], and which he defines as that which "gives" food for thought.[17]

2. Because it supposes this Other, thought is structured, like language, in the mode of welcome. Since the Other constitutes the active pole of thought, since it is destined for us—and in this way, calls to us—to accomplish thought shall be to receive this gift, to take care of it. And, if the thinkable remains so difficult to think ("we do not yet think"), this is because it only calls to us in concealing itself. Thinking is thus the welcoming of an Other that withdraws and, by means of this withdrawal, lays claim to thought.[18]

3. If that which calls us to think is not a present or a being, if it only signals to us through the fullness of its absence, then it is constantly threatened by the danger of *forgetting*. And it is precisely because the thinkable withdraws that it is indispensable to recall it. To think would thus be to

keep something in memory. This memory is itself redefined by Heidegger, in light of what it was already in the old word *Gedanc*, in which we hear the echo of *Gemüt* [soul, disposition, nature]: the soul gathered into itself. In memory understood this way, it is not a matter of having some fixed memory, but rather of existing wholly in the mode of fidelity.[19]

4. Fidelity to what? Fidelity to that which calls to us, to that silent voice—the silent voice of Being, which speaks in language. This is the reason why thought, having become faithful thought (*An-denken*), will be, indissociably, the memory of the gift and attention to the words in which this gift remains held. To think is to stand listening to language, in order to remember Being.

5. As this donation is what allows thinking itself in its essence, the welcoming of the gift is the memory of a favor, which is *gratitude* [*reconnaissance*]. A gratitude properly abyssal, which could not stand within the limits of some sort of "proportionality," since it consists in commemorating not an arbitrary gift, but its very possibility. To think is to give thanks [*rendre grâce*] at every moment.[20]

Welcome, memory, and gratitude: only on condition of holding these three dimensions together can we approach, if only in a still approximate way, that which *Denken* means. In such an approach, thinking is not only redefined, it is referred to an entirely other site, at the same time as it is understood according to another structure. Thinking becomes opening through and through, the distant echo of that other movement of excentering and extraction from self that, from the first pages of *Being and Time*, defined with the name *Ek-sistence*, the very essence of *Dasein*.[21] In an analogous way, but by other routes, Heidegger attempts to accomplish, here, through a new listening to language, a re-structuring, in the mode of a bursting open [*en mode d'éclatement*] of the act of thinking. The latter then proves to be something wholly different from a property of human beings, and still less one of the intellect. To think, as also to exist, is to be open to an Other that is never given, which nevertheless crosses through us mysteriously, and which, in crossing through us, constitutes us.

The difference with *Being and Time*, nonetheless, is that the entire thematic of the decision has been erased in the meantime. Earlier, one might have imagined that thinking rushed toward the Other: participating in the structure of the project, it was aimed toward . . . Henceforth, the Other continues to determine thinking, but the movement is reversed: thinking becomes pure welcome, a passive reception, from which not only every trace of will, but even and more radically, of desire, is erased.[22] From this we find the serenity, more passive than any awaiting, more passive too than the mystical awaiting, which, according to Heidegger, gives itself over to the divine will.[23] To define thinking as *Gelassenheit* [serenity], is thus to define it by an essential receptivity: renouncing any concern for action, thinking is limited to welcoming that which cannot be represented,[24] and for which we do not even have to be responsible.[25] This is why it is an experience, but in a radical sense for which the primary notion of "passion" could account. Jean Greisch, who has long reflected on Heidegger's *Gelassenheit*, does not go that far; but he casts light on it, following Henri Birault,[26] with the idea of a trial or an experience, presented as the experience of relinquishment [*déssaisissement*]: "What we must try to think, on the contrary, through this notion of experience, is a sort of 'originary passivity,' [since] the experience is always a trial, an upset [*bouleversement*], the *Widerfahrnis.*"[27]

It is not at all sure that we might not find, in some form, the quest for such a relinquishment over the course of Heidegger's entire philosophy; such a relinquishment would serve the pure coming of the thing that demands to be thought.[28] Did not Hegel himself limit his ambition to being "the faithful secretary of what is"? But Heidegger, in his interpretation of history, has the accent placed on the opposite aspect: the distance that separates his approach to thought from that which philosophy taught us to call by this name. Following his analyses, in effect, thinking in the Greco-Western tradition as a whole is a certain faculty guided by reason, consisting in taking or seizing (*greifen*, from whence the word "concept," *Begriff*, is derived) that which is there, facing us (as the German *Gegen-stand* indicates clearly). Thinking is therefore that which com-prehends the present, understood as the totality of what are beings, and which consequently cannot grasp the essentially absent, since, as the philosopher has repeated since his beginnings, that which "is" not, is not thinkable.

We thus find ourselves in the presence of two determinations that differ to the point of opposition. On the one hand, the Heideggerian approach, according to which *to think* is *to welcome, in memory, that which withdraws.* On the other hand, the traditional definition (that is, Greek and metaphysical), for which *thinking is com-prehending, through reason, that which presents itself.*

How does Heidegger conceive the relationship between these two essences of thinking? Not as the product of two different inspirations, and still less of two sources, but contrariwise, according to a bond of filiation. He certainly never stops insisting on the radical distance that separates the grasp of thinking as logic, and its comprehension in terms of memory and fidelity. And he cannot spare this insistence, since it is a matter of showing that the determinations he proposes no longer belong to metaphysics; they are even as far from it as possible. But at the same time, he cannot pass up the reverse movement either, which insists upon continuity—since it is likewise a matter of showing that these determinations are in no way "other" (thus, eventually arbitrary), that they are only the foundation (unthought up until then) of metaphysical determinations. Thus the opposition of the two essences, which Heidegger so masterfully *described*, is *interpreted* by him as a simple mutation within a fundamental continuity. This is what I called the bond of derivation [*lien de dérivation*], in a presentation of its general interpretive structure.[29] This is a bond that attaches an (originary) "experience" to a (metaphysical) "conception," but does so in an eminently paradoxical fashion, since the latter proceeds from the former (as regards its source). Yet the bond makes this attachment while opposing it (for its content), and as radically as possible.

In clear terms, this signifies that the conception of thought as logic derives from, while it covers over, the experience of thought as memory; the conception of language as statement and meaning [*énoncé et signification*] derives from, while covering over, the experience of language as appearing. We can also add: the conception of truth as exactitude derives from, while covering over, the experience of truth as disclosure [*dévoilement*], and so forth. And *it must indeed* be this way, since conception and experience are referred back to the same support, which is the Greek word.

Thus, we again find here, applied to the question of thinking, the three points we already noted as characteristics of Heidegger's general rule of interpretation: (1) the splitting of the question; (2) an explanation of the split through the existence of an opposition between late meaning [*l'acception tardive*] and originary meaning [*l'acception originelle*] of the same Greek word; (3) the assertion, nonetheless, that the original meaning can only be glimpsed when it is taken up at the heart of a new thought, whose paths Heidegger, with a bold *Vordenken*, will prepare.

But this peculiar regularity of structure is precisely what poses problems. Since the opposition and derivation of the two "essences" represent the sketch against which *all* the questions Heidegger approaches must fit, we are justified in thinking that the derivation's motor resides less in the content itself of these questions, than in a decision external (and prior) to them, a decision about the general outline of Western history.

To be sure, Heidegger is always occupied with showing, through the detour of texts, the *internal* filiation between memory and logic, or between appearance and predication. But, in a certain sense, it scarcely matters what the nature is of the questions examined—language, thought, truth, and so on—since the relation [*filiation*] is what is first. Why, within each question, should the content of the "essences" in question matter? What difference does the way in which one derives from the other make, when the essential is set down from the beginning, as the prior framework, and the essential is that the Greeks derive from the Greeks? Or rather, the essential is that *there is* something Greek [*c'est* qu'il y a *du grec*] at the origin of our history (which explains at once its wanderings and its secret truth), always and only Greek, and from this *it must be the case* that all the paths that open in this history, however divergent, however opposed, are always brought back to this Same. These are multiple paths, whose stupefying diversity Heidegger never stops emphasizing, but which, since *there is* but one source, are necessarily understood as the tributaries of a single river: the adventures and misadventures of Hellenism.

The problem is evidently not about knowing whether the "other essence"—which Heidegger sets forth each time as what is "to be thought"— *can* be attributed to the Greek unthought. Evidently it can, and to doubt this possibility would be to misunderstand the very status of the unthought or the unconscious in Heidegger. Yet it is perhaps appropriate to ask ourselves whether this essence is not in fact thought elsewhere;[30] and, if it is, *ought* we still attribute it to the unthought of the Greeks? To respond to such a question I will proceed in the same manner as before. That is, I will again leave Heidegger behind in order to turn toward the Hebraic essence of thought.

II. The Hebraic Frame for a Determination of Thought

On this point a problem arises. If a question like that of language constitutes a major pole of reflection in the tradition inspired by the Bible, when we approach Jewish studies, on the other hand, with a view to discovering the specifically Hebraic comprehension of thought, we are disconcerted by the scarcity of "material" available. To be sure, the biblical text offers us teachings about the spirit (*ruah*)—which we can fruitfully compare with other approaches, like the Greek *pneuma* or the Latin *spiritus*—on wisdom (*khokhma*), or on knowledge (*da'at*). But what is "thinking" exactly? This is what remains singularly indeterminate, as much in the Bible as in the tradition inspired by it. It is not that the texts offer us no element of a reply, but these must be sought elsewhere, under other aspects than as responses to the "question" of thinking. For thinking manifestly *poses no* question here.

The difficulty encountered at the outset of this development thus consists in the fact that we are not able to *confront*, properly speaking, the determination of thinking Heidegger presents as "originary" with its Hebraico-biblical determination, since the latter is not initially legible.

Nevertheless, to recognize that the faculty of thinking did not preoccupy the men of the Bible in no way means that they can not teach us anything about it. More broadly, to recognize that the biblical universe remains foreign (perhaps refractory or rebellious) to the themes, the modes of presentation, and the procedures proper to "philosophy" does not mean that there is nothing there apt to interest a rigorous thinking. Indeed the wealth of such a universe is not just due to the explicit teachings delivered there, but also to all that is found sedimented within it, whose singular code [*chiffre singulier*] marked the West, even (and perhaps especially) when it did not take the form of an object. Such is the case, it seems to me, for the question of thinking. The tradition that interests us has certainly never made of thinking a theme for reflection or investigation; yet, in speaking of what seems to be something wholly different (of that which is, in a sense, something wholly different), this tradition has set up a framework and laid down marking posts, on the basis of which it is perhaps possible for *us* to understand thinking otherwise. On the basis of these it becomes possible to renew our elaboration, and to respond otherwise than did the tradition, when it explicitly took up the question "What is called thinking?"

Is this a question that only the Greeks formulated, and which, moreover, was never posed? To be sure. But something of the response is nonetheless settled deep, in a shattered mode, within the biblical heritage. It remains for us to extract it and to constitute it as such. That means, more broadly, that a task has been left to us by those who never professed to think: not only to hear the suggestions they propose, but above all to make them *our* goods, to restore these suggestions to the field that is our own, and to use them. In a word, it is up to us to construct a determination of thinking, absent as such from the biblical text, on the basis of suggestions given to us by this text.

Is that not, in some manner, what Heidegger does on his side? We have seen above the highly peculiar determination he proposes for thought, which is a determination that, being unable to justify itself directly from the Greek, lives from the passage of "signs," set down in the German language. But no sign, as we know, can decide an orientation of thought: to notice it is never more than to recognize it.[31] If Heidegger is able to discern these signs, it is because he recognized previously, as worthy of thought (and even, in the case before us, as guiding elements *of thinking itself*), a certain number of key words, at once unusual and familiar. They were unusual because philosophy had largely ignored them, according them only the most marginal attention when it did encounter them. Yet they are familiar in that they name essential dimensions of the biblical universe. And no doubt we might say, without exaggeration: they name *the* essential dimensions of this universe.

Calling and listening, memory and fidelity, gratitude and thanksgiving: it is obviously not Heidegger who establishes such notions, which are cardinal in the Bible. But it is not even he who organizes these notions or articulates them in a signifying interplay and sketches, on that basis, the space of their interaction. Already constituted, this space precedes him. Heidegger encounters it and settles there, nourished by it, in order to think anew about a question not taken up there, or which, if it was, had received no distinct form in that space: *thinking*. It is from a space already sketched by these notions, themselves already set forth as prevalent, that his *Denken* takes its lines of force. It is in this space and through it that a new determination of nonmetaphysical thought is made possible.

Is it really necessary to *demonstrate* here that these different terms—taken each in itself as much as in their articulation as a whole [*articulation d'ensemble*]—are characteristic of the biblical world (and it alone), that they properly *define* that world, and that they were bequeathed to us by it? All this is generally known, and the vocabulary in question is to such a degree charged with history (and with a determinate history), that so much evidence discourages any "refined" presentation. I will therefore limit myself to a few suggestions, in the form of a reminder.

We know that biblical existence begins with the Covenant (*Berit*). The latter presupposes that God has a need of man, addresses him, and solicits him. That is why, as Buber pointed out, all of Jewish life is tied to his rhythm, not around an assertorial dogma—I believe, I know—but around an imperative *call*: "Hear, O Israel" (Deut. 6:4). Because God reveals himself to man only by soliciting him, the latter discovers himself and discovers existence, as being-summoned.

As much as the call is presupposed by the Covenant—and as it demands that man correspond to it in every instant in the Law—it is therefore the fundamental structure of the biblical universe. It is to this structure that Paul Ricoeur referred when, questioning Heidegger about the Hebraic heritage, he was able to limit himself to doing so in these terms: "There is a *call*, whether it be that of Moses' wanderings or that of Abraham's uprooting. Can we exclude such a call, which is not Greek, from philosophy?"[32] This is an essential question, the formulation of which is worth specifying. The call constitutive of the biblical world is not Greek, to be sure; and on these grounds it must indeed be excluded from "philosophy" (which, we cannot deny, is Greek). But can we exclude it from *thinking*? Heidegger so little effects such an exclusion that he even performs the opposite move: he restores the call to thinking, to the point of redefining thought, in its essence, by a call.

A recent text of Jacques Derrida underscores the reach and the stakes of this restitution.[33] Meditating on the status accorded the promise, understood as "originary covenant,"[34] in Heidegger's texts from the 1950s—notably, in the seminar text *What Is Called Thinking?* and in the lecture "The Essence of Language"[35]—Derrida concludes, legitimately, that questioning is no longer posed there as thinking's original gesture. Before any questions, there takes place "a response that is produced *a priori* in the form of acquiescence." This is an acquiescence that Heidegger, in *On the Way to Language*, calls the *Zusage* [promise, agreement, consent], and which is like "an originary abandonment to that which is given in the promise."[36] By this we should understand: an originary abandonment to that which, in the very act of promising, lays claim to us and already engages us. Let us note in passing that such an aspect had already been strongly emphasized by Pöggeler: "Questioning however . . . is rather determined by what is promised to it. . . . It is therefore obvious that not the questioning but rather hearing the promise is the genuine gesture of thinking."[37] Pöggeler remarked elsewhere that the definition of questioning as "piety of thinking" already implied this precedence of donation: "Thus questioning is the piety of thinking, *which means* it is the manner by which thinking *submits* to that which must be thought."[38]

Should we see there only a late turnaround, foreign to the path of thinking taken previously by Heidegger? Derrida shows clearly that, though this prevalence of the originary promise takes place properly in the thematic of the *Zusage* (coming effectively later in Heidegger's thought), one can find "indications and signs" of it over Heidegger's entire trajectory—even as early as in that "meaning of the call," already treated by *Being and Time*. Thus it appears that the call, which inaugurates biblical existence in its own right, discovers with Heidegger the same inaugural status: it is what conditions the very possibility of thinking.

That the call might come first, always already awaiting our awakening to it, means that man, in the Bible, begins with *listening*, is defined by it. The displacement of accents from the visual to the auditory has often been noted as one of the essential differences between the two traditions, Greek and Hebraic. Whether it is a matter of specialists of Jewish thought (Scholem, Banon), or of Christian theologians (Boman and Bultmann),[39] they all agree in emphasizing the opposition between the prevalence of seeing and discerning, proper to *theoría*, and that of listening, therefore of obedience, characteristic of the biblical universe.

This accent placed on the auditory element naturally influences the structure of *knowledge* [*connaissance*]. In a universe where man is given over, from the first, to a call and defines himself by listening (which is also obedience), to know cannot mean to take hold of . . . [*se saisir de* . . .], but rather to receive, to welcome. We can see this in the different registers of knowledge characteristic of the Bible and, in the first place, in the knowledge of God. This knowledge is never presented as a cognitive act that would take God as its object. It resides instead in an "experience," taking the form of receptive sympathy: to know him is to listen to him, to trust him, "to recognize that it is he who makes and who gives . . . , which makes us and gives us to ourselves."[40] Now, we know that the verb *ya'da*, "to know," is used in many other contexts, and serves notably to describe love relationships from their first mention (Gen. 4:1). This usage is frequently highlighted,[41] in which theologians are pleased to recognize a sign of the intimate proximity between love and knowledge. But the verb *ya'da* carries another teaching, which David Banon brings to light: in love as in knowledge, the *structure* is not that of "possession" but of "fidelity."[42]

Fidelity to that which gives itself, to that which from the moment of its Revelation has not ceased to continuously give itself, even when man no longer knows how to receive this gift or how to recognize it (and it is thus that God reveals himself in Isaiah: as "the call toward man who no longer listens").[43] Fidelity, then, to that which does not cease to bestow itself, even without being received, *in history*. For the God of Israel is less the master of nature than the partner in a story. When Moses announces to the Hebrews their deliverance, he does not come in the name of the God of the earth and the skies, but in that of the God of their fathers. "Go, you shall reunite the elders of Israel and you shall tell them: Yahweh, God of your fathers, has appeared to me, he, the God of Abraham, Isaac, and Jacob . . . " (Exod. 3:16). And when God addresses his people, it is again in this way that he most willingly presents himself: "I am Yahweh, your God, I brought you out of the land of Egypt, out of the house of bondage" (Exod. 20:2).[44] Over the centuries, rite bears witness to this: it repeats, to be sure, but it repeats a singular event that took place only once; "it does not celebrate the natural year, but rather the historical memory."[45]

Because God only reveals himself in history, there is no other reception possible for this revelation than the form of *memory*. To exist, for man, is first to remember. *Zakhor*, Remember! is one of the most recurrent imperatives of the Bible (it has even been noted that it appeared 169 times in the biblical text!).[46] But the frequency of this verb is less important here than the specificity of the memory to which it invites. Mnemosyne, to be sure, was the mother of the Muses. But all the Greek determinations of memory make of it a faculty for the past—in precise correspondence with the representation of history as a chronological succession of events. This exclusive focus of Greek memory on the past alone is so patent that Heidegger gives up soliciting the Greeks when he attempts to think memory wholly otherwise.[47] It is from the angle of the Old German *Gedanc* that he pulls memory out of its status as one faculty among others—the faculty of retaining the past—to make of it a manner of existing. As the "gathering of faithful thought,"[48] memory thus appears as a collection and focusing of the entire soul upon all of presence [*recueillement de l'âme tout entière sur le tout de la présence*], a presence that includes the past, but not as something elapsed: on the contrary, the past governs and passes through the present, as that which it is incumbent on us to measure and appraise.

Now, it is indeed in this way that memory appears in the biblical universe. We know that the Jewish people, whose major imperative was to remember, developed no historiography, or did so only very late.[49] But the thing is only paradoxical in appearance. It reveals that history is not for the Jews the chronicle of past events, but the inexhaustible source from which springs an always-actual meaning. If history is so important, therefore, it is so less by virtue of its historicity than by its radical contemporaneousness. In this sense, history is not simply behind me, as the totality of *faits accomplis*: it is that which accompanies me, in the present, at every instant and—since the prophets at least—awaits me still, in the future.

This is why, as Yerushalmi puts it, "the call to remember does not arise from a curiosity about the past."[50] Memory is indeed fidelity, but fidelity to a history gathered, at every instant, into the unity of presence, and which can be so because it is fundamentally oriented toward the future.[51] Memory must therefore be thought—as Heidegger saw clearly—as a gathering around a temporal totality, which is at every instant alive.

Whence comes *wisdom*. One of the most profound of contemporary theologians, Paul Beauchamp, could open his chapter on the Wise [*les Sages*] with this succinct expression: "Wisdom declares that all is received."[52] All of wisdom is there, in effect: it is only on condition of relying upon such a definition that we can undertake to say more about it, that is, "to move, with [the definition], following the course of the question."[53] This is a course over which postbiblical Jews will tread untiringly: from the first call, constituting the Covenant and received in obedience, arises the piety of a thinking in the form of a perpetual questioning, which attempts always to understand this call better, to adapt itself more intimately to it, and which questions—in order better to understand. As a midrash says: "It is not incumbent on you, perhaps, to finish the task, but you are not free to give it up."[54] Herein lies, in effect, the sole act of thanksgiving that reaches the level of the originary gift: to respond first, in an abrupt act of obedience; then, in order to respond still better, to unfold the infinite field of the question.

A call and a listening, knowledge taking the form of experience, fidelity, and memory, acquiescence, the play of the question: in all this, as we said, are the cardinal notions of the biblical universe, but without any direct determination of *thinking*. But is that so certain? If thinking does not constitute a specific question here, perhaps this is because, in reference to such a universe, it does not have—cannot have—independence. The ostensible lack may function here as a positive indication: an indication of a decentering movement, of not resting on oneself, conditioning a structure of receptivity and welcome, wherein thinking properly resides.

At this point in the analysis we therefore have two teachings at our disposition. We know, for one—as the absence of any direct determination attests—that thinking is not perceived as a separate faculty that could be defined for itself. On the other hand, we know that inasmuch as thinking exists, it must necessarily take place in the play-space sketched by the cardinal points of covenant and memory, fidelity and gratitude—and must be defined by them.

Is it possible to go farther than this? Is it possible, that is, to find indications in the biblical universe that would permit us to close in better—within this general framework of comprehension—on thinking itself in its specificity? In order to attempt this, it is advisable to attend, not just to the *themes* that occupy a principal place in this universe, but to the *relations* they maintain, as much among themselves as with the entirety of the other questions to which they are tied. For the interplay of these relations sketches subterraneously [*dessine en creux*], at the very interior of the biblical tradition itself, something like a virtual place for thinking. That is to say, the latter, though never approached frontally, is, at the very least, *situated*.

It is thus a matter, beyond simply bringing to light the Hebraic "frame" for a determination of thinking, of recalling the few essential linkages that permit us to circumscribe the *site* that it occupies.

In the first place, there is the injunction for all thinking (whatever definition one will be able to give it) to submit to language [*se soumettre au langage*]. If language, the tongue [*la langue*], is indeed the shelter of all presence, then thinking cannot be determined otherwise than as a listening to language [*écoute du langage*], an attention directed to that which opens essentially in it. And it is indeed this way that thinking is constantly presented in the rabbinic literature: as an effort to *adapt* to what is always already unfolded in the text, even—in the midrashim of kabbalistic inspiration—in the letter itself. The prevalent place accorded to the order of language thus provides a first indication, in the form of an assignation: thinking, inasmuch as it exists, shall necessarily be a docility to language [*docilité à la langue*].

In the second place, if it is fitting to be attentive in this way to language, this is because only in the text [of the Other] is inscribed his trace, whereas outside the text, that Other might seem to be the Absent one, since he never shows his face. Through this, another decisive linkage appears: that which ties all thinking, inasmuch as it exists, to the inalienable dimension of *withdrawal* of what must be thought. We will come back to this at length in a later chapter,[55] but we should indicate it here in passing. Thinking is indeed the reception of a gift, and in this sense it is structured by the presence of an Other, an Other who withdraws; and it is precisely for this reason that thinking can only be a memory.

In the third place, finally, this Other who is revealed, if only in being eclipsed, can reveal himself nowhere else than in the frame of the Covenant, with which the existence of Israel begins. Therefore, thinking could never overhang, or neglect, history. And it must constantly return to the original event that makes it possible quite simply as thinking.

This is a necessary relation with language, with withdrawal, with history: perhaps all this does not allow us to define a singular act called "thinking," but it functions nevertheless to indicate its site.

Now this site is not without its troubling relations of vicinity to that which Heidegger assigned to the "original essence of thinking." How then shall we understand the relationship between the diverse determinations by which Heidegger circumscribes *Denken* (§ I), and those which are suggested, albeit obliquely, in the Hebraic universe (§ II)? This is the question I demurred at asking at the end of the preceding chapter,[56] but which cannot be deferred any longer. We now hold enough elements to attempt to propose an initial development of it, though it is still only provisional.

III. Heidegger, Memory, and Denial

The work Heidegger does in regard to the different constitutive elements of the Hebraico-biblical heritage seems to me to reside in two concomitant acts. The first is his act of taking in charge, thus of memory and safeguarding. The second is what makes forgetting possible, but this is a peculiar forgetting, since it in no way affects the content of what comes to memory. This second act does not consist, therefore, in excluding or making something indiscernible, but rather in bringing something to light, while not recognizing it. It consists in laying open a memory that is not acknowledged as such—better still, which is explicitly forbidden by other assertions. That is why I am inclined to identify here a structure of denial, in the rigorous sense that Freud called *Verneinung*, and whose paradoxical dynamic Jean Hyppolite once highlighted quite masterfully.[57]

1. Heidegger's Taking in Charge

We have seen that a certain number of elements liable to interest thinking were found settled deep in the Hebraic universe. But it is clear that the latter has a style and rhythm all its own, incommensurable with the style and rhythm that govern Western rationality since the Greeks.[58] The elements in question, whatever their potential interest *for* thinking, could not therefore be directly usable *by* thinking, at the very least not by that which, over the course of our history, was called "thinking."[59]

Let us pause a moment at this point. It is not enough to say that thinking unfolded in Greece, with a power and breadth unknown elsewhere. We must add, moreover, that it is also in Greece that thinking was *defined* as such, that it took itself as its object and set its own criteria of identification. It identified itself, in its essence, as logic. That means that Greece bequeathed us at once a certain definition of the essence of thinking (logic), and a field—of questioning and elaboration—considered as being its privileged domain.

If a non-Greek culture intervenes in this field (albeit in its own way and according to its particular procedures), then that means that it has a property enabling it to be thus inscribed and to bring something to the field in its own fashion. But, if that is possible, then it is because a thinking was in action there, a thinking that did not correspond to the Greek comprehension of the term, and which consequently demanded another definition of its essence.

We thus see the linkage: the very fact of borrowing, from the Hebraic universe, determinations recognized as belonging to thinking attests that a thinking was indeed at work therein, even if the culture in question did not trouble itself to define thinking in itself [*en propre*]. And if this thinking is foreign to logic, that is because logic is not the entirety of thinking.

In this sense, the Hebraic heritage holds teachings that concern the very *essence* of thinking. But, foreign to the decisions by which thinking understood itself, these teachings were condemned to go unrecognized by thought and could not serve in return to define its essence. Thus they can be used by thinking only on the explicit condition of being first *given* to it: that is, mediately, at the end of an endeavor at restoration. This is the restoration of certain determinations, neglected up to now, *to* the essence of thinking, beyond the self-understanding of thought such as it is carried out in logic, the discipline of metaphysics.

This is indeed the way—through this process of marginalization [*procès de mise à l'écart*], then of reintegration—that the West seems to have treated, over the course of its history, the Hebraico-biblical legacy. I said above that a certain number of teachings are found sheltered within it, which were not directly *usable* by thinking. In fact (historically), they were not *used* by it. While they concerned thinking in the highest degree, they remained in reserve or in waiting—awaiting the act that would bring them properly to language, and which would, in return, make use of them to redefine thinking itself.

In a more general manner, this can set us on the trail of the status or significance, singular though it is, of the Hebraic heritage in Western history. It is part of that history, has accompanied it over the entire course of its development, and has not ceased questioning it. But it did this in a "wild" way; wild, because this heritage, though constantly present in the West, was not taken up in the consciousness the West had of itself. And how could this surprise us? *Where* did this consciousness play itself out, if not precisely in metaphysics? What exceeded metaphysics, or was foreign to it, may well have haunted the course of our history, belonged to it, and contributed to constituting it, without the West ever recognizing its specificity [*son propre*]. This is because the West only came to the representation of itself in and through metaphysics.

At least until Heidegger. And it is on this point that we can measure the extent of our debt to him. For, Heidegger gave the West to itself; he allowed it to expand its self-understanding of its essence, to recognize all that it carried secretly without having appropriated it until then. But he did this along the edge of a double restoration, whose moments we should distinguish here.

The first moment concerns *thinking*. To abandon the title of philosopher for that of a thinker is to enrich the latter with all that is situated beyond the domain reserved to the philosopher, and which the philosopher had not known how to possess. But we must be precise here. The thinker does not think *more things* than the philosopher: he re-thinks, in another light, what the philosopher already thought. He therefore only thinks what was already thought, but he thinks it on its other side [*en son revers*], neglected up to now. And the history of Being as a whole is not to be sought *elsewhere* than in the history of metaphysics; it *is* this history itself, grasped along the most secret side of its fold. The "surpassing" of metaphysics must therefore not be misunderstood: to surpass (in the sense of *verwinden*) is not to think something else, it is to think the same thing, but otherwise. There lies a point on which many recent interpretations have insisted,[60] and which I emphasized elsewhere.[61]

Nevertheless, this continually neglected other side did not fail to deposit "traces" in our history, traces that could serve as signs showing the way. The principle ones are inscribed in metaphysics itself,[62] but they are covered over to such an extent that, to be able to discover them, it is necessary to be attentive to other traces still, at once stranger and better preserved: those deposited *elsewhere*, in places the philosopher never haunted. That means that to think, but otherwise, the very thing that metaphysics already thought, Heidegger is led to embrace a vaster horizon; he is led to look, as it were, overboard—and this, in order to better return to the text he has under his eyes and to discern that which forever lay there in waiting. In this sense (and in this sense alone), he thinks *more*.

This amounts to saying that from here on he takes the *unthought* in charge. But I want to try to accentuate the most neglected aspect of this unthought: not the withdrawal (of thinking), but its presence (in history). We too often tend, when we present the unthought, to define it only by its relation to what is thought [*au pensé*], which leads to exclusively negative formulations. So, we would say that the unthought is that which, while supporting thinking, has not been taken in charge by it, and so has not been integrated into the metaphysical field. This is perfectly correct, but insufficient. We must again ask *where* it resides, even as it withdraws from what is thought, and where we should question its traces. In metaphysics to be sure, but is it exclusively in the latter? Such a question orients thinking toward the mode of *presence* of the unthought, and toward sites where such a presence, preserved, awaits its release.

Now, these sites are not other than those we inhabit already; they are not other than those over which we have ceaselessly trod during the course of our history, but which always remained *apart* from thinking [*à l'écart de la pensée*] (which does not also mean that thinking did not nourish itself with them and that they, in their turn, remained deprived of thought). In soliciting them, Heidegger gives back to us that which was already our own but which philosophy did not recognize as its own: all that we could encounter, in the mode of dispersal, in the poet, the painter, the prophet, even the everyday working man [*homme de la quotidienneté laborieuse*]. All that seemed to constitute an "elsewhere," about which we did not imagine that it could interest thinking. But now we find that, turned toward sites such as these, the thinker is setting about learning from them and nourishing his work from them in order to occupy them finally, in his turn, *as* a thinker—that is, to reintegrate them into the general field of thought [*champ général de la pensée*].

Such an act of recovery [*reprise*], as we see, surpasses by a wide margin the biblical legacy alone: it touches the entirety of the Western "dwelling." Yet if this dwelling or sojourn can henceforth be taken in charge by the thinker, in its full extent, that is because Heidegger came back to the essence of *thinking* itself, in order to enlarge it. To respond to the promise, to hear, obey, recall, remain faithful, to be grateful: because thinking has been redefined in this way, overflowing in every direction the framework of logic, it can embrace, in its unfolding, the totality of the Western dwelling and in this way flow out over the limits that had been assigned to "philosophy." In a word: Heidegger puts back into the hands of the thinker what was indeed contained in the West, but had remained external to thought [*hors pensée*]. And he can do so, because he first expanded the act of thinking itself, in giving back to it one of its own essential possibilities, which came to him from the biblical tradition in which he did not find himself.

What then is the relationship between this possibility thus released and that which had claimed exclusive rights, up to then, over the domain of thinking, to the point of becoming identified with the very essence of all thinking? Heidegger does not limit himself to unearthing the first possibility: he shows its connection to the "traditional doctrine," a connection that is not a juxtaposition or amalgamation, but really one of unity. And Heidegger is the very first to do so. Up until his work, the West knew only exclusion or juxtaposition, when it attempted to understand itself. Exclusion meant to limit the entirety of Western thought to logic alone, as the history of philosophy had done. Juxtaposition meant underscoring the double components of Western "culture" or of "tradition," and recognizing the Greek *and* Hebraic contribution, the way the theologian or the historian could do. Juxtaposition meant taking the two currents into consideration without ever seeking to think their unity or managing a fortiori to do so, and therefore without ever asking in what respect this unity might interest thinking.

Heidegger shows that when the thinker takes in charge sites he had previously neglected, he passes beyond what the philosopher had called thinking, *without being in some other place for all that.* For this step beyond is recognized as a leap into a region more original than that of philosophy, the only one that could make philosophy possible. What had been hastily considered as an outside was actually the root. There is, therefore, very much an expansion here, and the thinker thinks *more*, but this expansion is a *return* [*un retour*], and the thinker ultimately only inhabits the sites that come back to him. "Indeed, it is not a matter of going farther. We would like only to try to arrive, for once, there where we have our dwelling [*aufhalten/séjour*]."[63] Yet do we not already have our dwelling in memory and fidelity, in the promise and in gratitude? These sites were very much our own—they sketched the face of the West—without our ever having inhabited them as philosophers; now we find them restored to us, we find them back in our care as thinkers, for they have been reintegrated into the very definition of thinking. Such is the first restitution Heidegger accomplished: a restoration, unto thought, of what had remained foreign to it, even as it had been thought's own wealth; this is a return of thinking to a part of its essence that it had deserted.

However, by virtue of this, Heidegger made possible a second restitution, less noted but more considerable: he gave back *to the West* that which the latter did not clearly know was its own. By virtue of the fact that the thinker overflowed the limits of metaphysics in order to think all that was set down in (and constitutive of) the history of the West, he can apply to this history the rigorous procedures that are his own, and thereby *think* this history in its wealth and its fullness—at the same time as he thinks it in its relation to the determinate field called philosophy. That means that the West, in its unity, ultimately finds itself thought, or—which amounts to the same thing—that the West finally thinks itself.

Heidegger thus does more than enlarge the essence of thinking and thereby the field traditionally reserved to the thinker. In this very act, he has given back to our history all that the latter carried within it without having clearly measured it. He made the rigorous connection between what up until then were separated scenes. Concerning the specific question of thinking, this means that, in underscoring the importance of certain determinations *for* thinking, Heidegger restored and resituated them at the same time *within* Western history.

This is to say that he effectively accomplished what he promised. We have shown this from the outset:[64] beyond the mere interpretation of the *history of philosophy*, Heidegger claimed, at the end of his oeuvre, *to think the history of the West.* Now, therein lies what this work has made possible. It leads, beyond the closure of metaphysics, toward the fullness of Western thinking, henceforth grasped in its double essence: as traditional doctrine, centered upon logic, and as original essence, in the form of memory.

Yet this other essence, recognized as belonging to the province of thinking, though without ever having belonged to metaphysics, gets referred to the same word from which logic already derived: the word *lógos.* This can set us on the path of his second act.

2. Denial

The first act was the gesture of taking in charge: attentive to sources neglected up until then, Heidegger drew material from them to nourish and renew thinking in order to raise, in return, the legacy thus unearthed to the dignity of thinking. The second act consists in not recognizing *from whence* he was thus drawing, in not admitting his debt, or, more rigorously (since Heidegger recognized he was a debtor, but it was relative to a wholly other domain [*relativement à un tout autre règne*]), in silencing its *provenance*.

The source is not already the work. I never asserted that Heidegger's determination of thinking might have already existed, in the form it took, within the biblical universe. The preceding pages aimed, on the contrary, to show the radical originality of Heidegger's work: we are indebted to him for having redefined the very essence of thinking and, thereby, for having allowed our history finally to think *itself*, in its fullness. But Heidegger did this on the basis of elements too clearly marked, too much the carriers of a meaning and a history—in short, too possessed, already, of a significant *identity*—for the complete suppression of indications of their source not to appear as an *erasure*.

This erasure was all the more remarkable because Heidegger did not just omit *referring* the words he uses to the universe from whence they came, and where he himself had found them. More radically, he suppressed any mention of this universe in his work. Though he sometimes called upon the New Testament, we find throughout the entirety of Heidegger's opus only the most exceptional allusions to Old Testament writings and to the Hebraic heritage in general.

To be sure, one will say that Heidegger does not fail to come to terms with "religion," understood essentially on the basis of faith (in contrast to thought) and of God (in contrast to Being). We will come back to this at length elsewhere.[65] But to respond with onto-theology to what is said here about the promise or about faithfulness is clearly to refuse to hear. *For, I am not discussing "religion."* I am discussing, and this, since the beginning of this study, a founding text, the tradition derived from it, the coherent universe that it composes, and the place that a certain number of questions like language, thought, or history, occupy in this universe. In short, I am discussing *the very thing* that Heidegger discusses when he rethinks anew language, history, or thought.[66]

And, if I am discussing these things, it is with the sole ambition of recalling, on the one hand, that these questions are fully present in the Hebraic universe, which is in no way reducible to a few doxic statements about faith, and that, on the other hand, Heidegger's specific interpretation of these questions owes a lot to the way in which they were experienced within this same universe. Now Heidegger—who more than anyone else takes up biblical words and approaches—says, on the one hand, nothing about their source, and, on the other hand, he suppresses, more than anyone else to this time, any allusion to this universe in general. That is, he also suppresses any possibility for the latter to constitute a source, in whatever respect that might be. This strikes me as troubling in the extreme—whatever the pertinence, moreover, of his analyses of "onto-theology."

Does that mean that Heidegger would attribute to himself, as his own, that which he borrowed from elsewhere? Not at all. There is no gesture here of an author who refused to acknowledge his sources, but rather that of a thinker who recomposes history. For a peculiar inscription doubles the erasure. All the determinations presented above—whose extreme originality we acknowledged relative to what was then current under the name of "Western thought"—are precisely not presented as original [*originales*], but rather as "originary." In Heidegger's eyes, they constitute an outpost or advance, made by means of a step backward. That means that these determinations are presented as issuing from a memory, as referring to a source. But this source is, here as elsewhere, the Greek text.

Such a referral has nothing impossible about it. As we will see further on, when we present Heidegger's approach to interpretation,[67] nothing can forbid us crediting a given text as being a "prefiguration" or a "premonition." For, this credit, being always open, is inherent to any text as such, inasmuch as it is a reservoir of what is unthought. What is problematic here is not that certain determinations (which we might take to be absent from the Greek text) are referred to the Greek text in an after-the-fact movement; it is that they could be misread in the very text where they are nevertheless present and legible. In other words, what is problematic is that they are not recognized there, where they are *out in the open*, only to be set down *as covered over* in the Greek text. For in this case inscription functions as the completion of the erasure [*parachèvement de l'effacement*]: it does not bring to light those possibilities that would remain buried without it; on the contrary, the inscription obscures what was still legible before it. That means that Heidegger did not limit himself to passing over in silence the real historic source of the words he uses. Instead, he renders it indiscernible; he actively forbids its identification, since he immediately ascribes these words to the credit of another source, historial and secret.

A secret source can have its heuristic fecundity, but when it is *substituted* for the real source, its function is perverted: it henceforth contributes to a new covering over, and is no more than a necessary moment in a structure of erasure.

4

The Question of Interpretation

We have seen in the preceding chapters that the so-called originary essence, of language as also of thinking, was very distant from the dominant conception of them in our history, and that this essence presented certain analogies with an entirely other experience, set down in the Bible. Heidegger, as we know, refers the essence thus set forth not to the Hebraic heritage, but to Greek words, such as they resound notably in the Presocratic texts. That said, as it is impossible for him to assert that this essence was inscribed, in black and white, in those texts, he can only attribute it to them from an angle that entailed a *redefinition* of what a text is, in general. I would like to show that this definition, which allows Heidegger to credit everything to the Greek unthought [*impensée des Grecs*], comes to him from the non-Greek source of our history. That will be the final level of analogies. However, as the Greek and non-Greek sources have been intimately mingled in Western hermeneutics, it is fitting that we first consider the space of their encounter.

I. The Medieval Crossroads

If it is undoubtable that the philosophical hermeneutics that was constituted in the nineteenth century with Schleiermacher and Dilthey has its roots in a hermeneutic of the Holy Scriptures, and especially in a biblical hermeneutics, we nevertheless cannot reduce the latter to *Jewish* hermeneutics alone. In the questions we looked at earlier (language, thinking), the situation was different: we noted, on the one hand, a tradition of thought dominant in the West, whose fundamental traits had been clearly fixed, from their origin, by Greek philosophy. On the other hand, we noted a different experience, which was, to be sure, not totally foreign to Western man (which was indeed in many respects familiar to him), but which constituted, relative to the metaphysical order, a current at once parallel with it and underground. Thus we were able, without running too many risks, to identify the resurgence in Heidegger of the current hidden up until then, which had remained the prerogative of the Hebraico-Judaic tradition, barring a few exceptions. And if it had remained so, it was not only because this tradition had maintained it—from its origins up to modern times—but especially because the philosophical tradition, for its part, had in no way taken it in charge (and when the philosophical tradition did, at times, encounter it, it was only in an entirely indirect manner).

Things are otherwise with the theories of interpretation, where we approach a terrain much less clearly marked, and where it is an arduous thing to discern a dominant and a subterranean field. This is due to several factors. In the first place, the theory of texts is not philosophy's lot: it stands at the crossroads of all the disciplines having to do with written works in general, whether this be history, jurisprudence, or theology. Secondly (and consequently), its basic principles have been the object of a systematic development, but this development was not completed in the grand age of Greek philosophy. It takes form during the Middle Ages, at the crossroads of influences that mingled—at this time and around this question—as closely as possible: Greek, Christian, Hebraic, and Arabic.

For this reason, when Heidegger takes up anew the question of interpretation, he in no way claims that such a renewal would have been prefigured by the Greeks, and that one can just as well argue that it ought to be referred to a forgotten Hebraic legacy. Here, the heritages interpenetrate each other too deeply to warrant such cut-and-dried distinctions.

It remains nonetheless that in the complex fabric of medieval hermeneutics *specific contributions* remain discernable. It is still possible to identify, in certain cases at least, fully Hebraic motifs—in continuity with very old Jewish sources—next to other motifs, imported or evincing other influences. Now Heidegger, in his singular approach to texts (that is, in the renewal to which he subjects the interpretative tradition) remains, paradoxically, closest to those few motifs that belong only to Jewish exegetes. He isolates them and highlights them—as though he were following only the Hebraic thread within the hermeneutic weft.

Let us consider this weft more closely. The only place where the crossing of influences is, if not established by evidence, at least strongly probable, is that of the fourfold meaning of Scripture. This is a theory that does not appear in the oldest Jewish texts, but it arises in the *Zohar* in the thirteenth century and in certain contemporary kabbalistic circles (it is the garden of *pardes*),[1] in close relation to the dualism of meaning (external and internal) developed by Arabic authors in their exegesis of the Koran,[2] and above all to the earlier Christian doctrine, elaborated at the beginning of the Middle Ages with the Patristics.[3] Some historians have attempted to disentangle this complex scaffolding, in order to extricate the meaning of these filiations. Their interpretations diverge. According to Scholem,[4] on this point, the *Zohar* underwent the influence of two distinct "branches," coming from a common source: the first (Christian) branch, he argued, carried the imprint of the second (Arabic) one, but both of them referred back to Philo, in the last instance.[5]

Let us leave this question to the historians. Whatever the order in which these filiations were carried out, here we are interested in their outcome. We are interested, that is, in the Judeo-Islamo-Christian crossroads (in which the Greek influence participated, therefore, via the Neoplatonism of Philo and the Fathers), where the idea of a plurality of meanings of Scripture was elaborated, in its different faces. This idea will remain central in the later theories of interpretation, and we again find it, almost unchanged, in the twentieth century, in the four moments of the "hermeneutic itinerary" ["*parcours herméneutique*"], recognized as necessary to a "poetics of translations."[6]

Yet this doctrine of four meanings, as the site of encounter between the interpretative traditions, is not the sole or most essential component of Jewish hermeneutics, which is characterized by many other determining traits. Now, among these traits, certain have been extended into the Christian hermeneutic tradition where, combining with others, they mingled with Christian hermeneutics to the point of becoming imperceptible in it, while others remained, as it were, *marked* by their index of origin [*chiffre d'origine*]. This was either because they did not become the objects of a

"recovery" ["*reprise*"] in the later codifications, and so perpetuated themselves, as it were, subterraneously, only in the Jewish milieu; or because,
even "recovered," they kept something of their Judaic identity (even their
Hebraic one, since their tie to the Hebrew is sometimes so patent). It is
these that we must presently consider.

II. The Judaic Conception of Interpretation

The Jewish tradition constructed an entire hermeneutic apparatus,
aiming to regulate the relations between the text and its commentary. A
number of the rules thus set forth remain exclusive to that tradition; the
best known among them is the *Gematria,* or calculation of the numeric
value of the letters, whose interpretation, especially when it was of kabbalistic inspiration, was the object of continuous use. I will not get into a
presentation of these rules here; one can find them recapitulated in all the
studies treating of Judaic exegesis.[7] It seems more interesting to me to direct our attention to the ground that supports them, that is, to certain fundamental principles relative to the very *nature* of interpretation.

Among these principles, those we can consider proper to the Judaic
universe, without running too great a risk of error, are limited in number.
Beyond their specific conception of language—already presented above[8]—
one of the most remarkable traits is the *infinity* of interpretation [*l'infinité
de l'interprétation*]. To grasp the full meaning of such a notion, and the is-
sues implied by it, we must recall the context in which it is inscribed.

The point of departure is the fact that a text of a particular nature is
at stake: a *revealed* text. God has spoken, the text is there, each of its terms
is sacred, and none is modifiable. Under what conditions can this word,
revealed in an ancient past and venerated all the way down to its letters,
warrant a new word, that of interpretation?[9] Under one condition only:
provided the new word adds nothing to the text, provided it limits its pre-
sentations to *delivering* the text.

But as soon as interpretation finds itself thus defined (and it cannot be defined otherwise, given the status of the text), we find ourselves
confronted with a major problem: the impossibility of apportionment.
There is no longer any way to distinguish between the text and its reader, between the ancient and the modern (just as there is no way to distin-

guish, in Heidegger's discourse, between what must be referred back to the Greek unthought and that which ought to be acknowledged as Heidegger's thought).[10] How to know, in effect, whether the interpreter had limited himself to "lending his voice," or whether he used the support of the text, and the pretext of the commentary, to bring a new voice into being?

It is clear that the Jewish tradition, which is through and through an exegetical tradition, could not fail to encounter this problem. But it did more than encounter it; it resolved it, in its manner. It accounted for the impossibility of apportionment by contemplating, as no tradition had done before it, the *essential co-belonging* of the text and its interpretation. We must consider each one of the terms of this relationship.

In the first place, the *interpreter* adds nothing; yet, without him, the text would remain mute. That is to say that the interpreter occupies nothing like the classical position of the reader. He is the indispensable partner, the interlocutor of a text that speaks only in this dialogue. What takes shape here is an idea familiar to us today (which has become familiar to us thanks to thoughts like that of Heidegger, then of Gadamer): the idea that the interpretation belongs to the spoken word, to the point where this word is only properly fulfilled when the interpreter takes it up.[11] Without him, the word is not, or is nothing; it does not "speak."

This was an idea favored no doubt, at the origin, by the very structure of Hebrew itself. We know, indeed, that the Hebrew language, composed purely of consonants, demands of the reader that he himself perform the work of giving voice. The text of the Bible, left unread, would remain mute in the strict sense: "the score for a song, whose vowels determine the diction, always actualized, always taken up again and different from itself, the Torah is presented as a call by the text itself, which bears witness—even in its typographical 'blank white spaces'—to a 'void' in which the sense finds its inspiration."[12]

This void, with which language already weaves, will thus be treated as the warp and woof of the sacred text itself. The Jewish tradition goes so far as to refer commonly to two parts of the Torah: the written Torah (the five books of the Pentateuch) and the oral Torah (the set of exegetical writings, which attempt to bring to light the meaning of the written Torah). This oral Torah, as its name suggests, is considered as intrinsically part of Revelation.[13] How could it be stated more clearly that there is no pure revelation, cut off from its interpretation, and that the text lives only through the grace of an encounter?[14]

Clearly, this singular importance accorded to the reader cannot fail to reflect back on the definition of the *text* itself. If we want, in effect, the task of the interpreter not to be subjective, while being resolutely active, we must declare that there is nothing in the interpretation that is not already in the text. Yet, since interpretation is by nature unpredictable and plural, we must necessarily declare that the text already contains, albeit in a blind mode, all the elements that will be discovered in it.

Now there is only one way to account for this, which is to declare that what is essential in the text is the unsaid, which the interpretation must come to deliver. Understood as the silent heart of the discourse, this un-said has nothing negative about it. It is not that which escapes the saying, but that which crosses it through and through: "A proposition or a phrase or a chapter or a book does not end in the Bible because there was nothing more to say, but because the unsaid and the unsayable desire at that moment to be said."[15]

In order to render this dimension of the unsaid intelligible, or simply possible, the Jewish tradition insists upon the blanks in the text. We find in the Midrash, as well as in the Kabbalah, a multitude of parables, each of them turning around the same fundamental image: that of a text in which something is *lacking*, and which, in this sense, is not only subject to interpretation, but can only be properly accomplished or finished by interpretation. One of the best illustrations of this is the story according to which the Torah, which in its visible form contains only 340,000 letters, nevertheless would mysteriously contain 600,000 of them. This is because each individual in Israel possesses one secret letter that the text lacks; a letter that reveals to him what the other letters cannot grasp.[16]

Another text completes this idea, adding a supplementary dimension to it. It is no longer a question of saying that the Torah reveals itself otherwise to each of its readers, but that—even in being given once for all times at Sinai—the Torah is other at different moments in time. As the author explains, it is that, in the age of the universe to which we belong, one letter is missing—or it is incomplete, or invisible, which are other versions of the same parable. But the letter will appear in the next Shemittah [cosmic cycle in Kabbalah], at the same time that still another letter becomes invisible.[17]

I will not multiply examples here. Whatever metaphor is chosen, it always aims at illustrating a single teaching: it is through each of us that the blank comes to language and the text becomes legible. Thus the paradox is resolved: the principle of revelation does not forbid the renewal of signification; on the contrary, it requires it. "Moses had already been told everything on Sinai, and yet everything has still to be begun."[18] Everything is inscribed—white fire lurking under the black fire of the signs—and everything remains to be discovered. A text, by its very definition, is what "manifests its own expectation of an actualization still to come."[19]

That is why interpretation is, in the strict sense, *infinite*: this infinity is one of the traits most specific to the approach we are following here; it is that which, no doubt, most clearly marks its difference with all the other approaches to the interpretive act, though they might be related to it. All the specialists of Jewish thought, be it Talmudic,[20] or kabbalistic,[21] insist on this point. To speak of the many senses of Scripture is to place the accent on a process of knowledge leading from the material to the spiritual, from the outside to the inside, from the exoteric to the esoteric. Yet an apparently close image, like that of the seventy faces of the Torah,[22] opens onto an entirely different perspective: not an access to an invisible stratum, but the work of an infinite depth. "The meaning of the holy text cannot be exhausted in any finite number of lights and interpretations, and the number 70 stands here for the *inexhaustible* totality of the divine word."[23]

That means that Jewish hermeneutics is marked by a double "supplement." On the one hand, it is not a matter of making a sense appear that was, on first glance, hidden, but rather of giving oneself to an "inexhaustible quest,"[24] to a "perpetual movement."[25] On the other hand, this movement consequently is more than an act of knowledge, more even than a cast of mind. It becomes something like a way of existing. In this way the Jewish tradition can define itself (and this is the fine title of David Banon's book) as an "infinite reading."[26]

This infinity of meanings, accorded to Scripture, supposes a double conception: a conception of *interpretation as realization*, indissociable from a conception of the *text as potentiality*. This is a most singular conception, whose difference we are now prepared to measure. It is *neither* a matter of saying, as the Patristics had done, that the text holds within it a meaning hidden behind its primary and literal sense, *nor*, as modern hermeneutics asserts, that its meaning sees itself modified bit by bit or enriched by the tradition of reading that was constituted after it. Much more radically, we have here the idea of "a text that modifies *itself* in function of the degree of accomplishment of him who reads it,"[27] the idea, then, of a text that is open or wide open in its ownmost being, awaiting a future.

This is the most specific trait of the Jewish hermeneutic tradition. It is specific because, though it marks this tradition through and through (to the point of sufficing to define it, in its turn), it was hardly taken up, in its radicality, outside this tradition. No doubt excessive, it knew its full deployment only in the "midrashic novels" James Barr spoke about with a certain contempt.[28] Yet it is indeed this trait (as we will soon see, in light of the texts) that is at the center of Heidegger's definition of interpretation, and that forms the theoretic axis around which his own interpretive practice unfolds. But the filiation passes here by a major mediation, for this so specifically Jewish doctrine knew a remarkable incarnation in Western hermeneutics *before* its resurgence in Heidegger (and the first explains, no doubt, the second): the translation theory of the later Hölderlin.[29]

III. Hölderlin, or the Mediation

This theory is, to tell the truth, more than a simple methodology of translation. Let us recall its principal aspects.

In the first place, as George Steiner remarks, the temporal distance between the moment of writing (under the circumstances, Greece in the fifth century B.C.E., since he is dealing with *Antigone*) and that of translation (Germany in the nineteenth century) will be assigned a dynamic character. This takes place not in the sense that an evolution of reading would take place "in the meantime," but because time itself is thought of as the co-creator of the text. Time "leavens" the text the way leavened dough rises, and it shapes it into new forms: "The original text carries, in a latent fashion, truths, orders of meaning, potentialities that are only virtual in the form it incarnates initially. This incarnation is, in certain respects, only the intimation [*annonciation*] of forms of being to come. . . . The 'translator' has—for his sacred and paradoxical, even antinomic, task—to make these buried and sleeping seeds germinate, to 'surpass the original text.'"[30] Thus the text exists only as a call to its own realization in and through the time to come—and, Steiner continues, "it is these which empower the 'translator' to act as the legatee and, in the strongest sense, as executor of the antique poet's heritage and 'will.'"[31]

It is clear that this theory of translation—still judged "hallucinatory" today[32]—breaks radically with the habitual comprehension of what a text is. In the eyes of Hölderlin, reading *is not* the extrication of a meaning, hidden until then but nevertheless remaining immanent in the text and belonging to it from the origin. Reading is the fulfillment of possibilities to come, sunken deep in the *yawning* of a text, which, though perfect, remains nonetheless "unfinished" in its most intimate being. In this sense, Hölderlin rejoins—via filiation or encounter, we are not concerned with this here[33]—the definition of the text (as reserve of potentialities) and of the interpretation (as realization), which was continuously asserted in Jewish thought. For the one as for the other, the word is "pregnant with" meaning, and the work of interpretation leads to its "delivery."[34]

The two theories, which up to this point espoused each other so intimately, will nonetheless separate on one point: reading, in Hölderlin, is not "infinite." On the contrary, what lies in wait in the initial text (among the Greeks) finally finds its truth in the final translation-interpretation (into German). For, here, a shared conception of the text encounters a different philosophy of history. In the Jewish perspective, we are standing in a history entirely structured by waiting, oriented toward the future [*avenir*], a history that will find its closure only in the messianic era—hence the inexhaustibility of the text. It is because history is unfinished that interpretation is "interminable."[35] For Hölderlin, we are the "Hesperidians," men of the twilight of history at which dawn finally finds its truth;[36] hence the epiphany of meaning. It is because the Hesperides represent decline and completion—in which the inception is illuminated—that the work of interpretation can come to an end, and the text, so long open, can be closed again.

This specific comprehension of history reflects back on the theory of interpretation, to institute there a complex dialectic of the ancient and the modern, the past and the future. The text (past) is crossed through with possibilities that can be appropriately realized only in the translation (future). In this sense, it is open through and through, toward the time to come. But what this coming time brings to pass is, paradoxically, a return: "going back up" ["*remontant*"] the text, like going up a river, to its hidden source, the Hölderlinian translator is "led back" to his own past. That means that the translation quite surpasses the text. It is the *Verbesserung* [improvement] promised by Hölderlin to the editor of his *Antigone*.[37] But it surpasses toward *its* own, most intimate possibility, that possibility which the text, in taking shape, had denied.[38]

Such is at least the *formal* outline of the trajectory. It is this form that will be taken up again by Heidegger, followed anew by him in his interpretation of Greek texts. But Hölderlin says something else again. He advances to a site where Heidegger will no longer follow him, a site that brings him close, mysteriously, to those who preceded him in his theory of interpretation. If the Greek truth can be fulfilled only in being referred to a more archaic source, the latter is not only an original possibility in the order of meaning (the "aorgic," the "fire from the sky"—as counterpoint to Greek "sobriety"), but a dimension of history, that means, also of space: it is the "oriental," the "Asiatic." The Hölderlinian translation thus aims to go back into time prior to the Greek text, but this defines itself specifically as a return to the *non-Greek* element (which comprises the whole thematic of the "orientalization" of the original, such as it is presented in the letters to Willmans). Steiner gives us a limpid description of the entirety of this movement: "But Hölderlin can only generate this 'realization' by 'going behind' Sophocles, by proceeding 'upstream' and 'Eastward' to those archaic fonts of tragic meaning and of tragic gesture which Sophocles' continence, Sophocles' Periclean addiction to temperance, had, to some degree, stifled."[39]

In what respect is Hölderlin to be distinguished from Heidegger? In this: that when he orients himself toward the occult source, beyond the inception that is preserved there, he does not discover—as Heidegger will do—the pre-original morning, which is prior to the (Greek) source. Hölderlin discovers there, under the name "Orient," the *other* source toward which he will attempt to return, and to which he would like, perhaps madly, "to hand over" the Greek text. Let us listen to him discovering this Asia in the hymn "Patmos."

> Thus I prayed; a Genie then
> Rapid beyond my expectation
> And so far that never I might have
> Dreamed even to arrive there, outside my home

Carried me. In the twilight of dawn, beneath our flight
Are born forests charged with shadow
And nostalgic rivers
Of my fatherland; then came the unknown lands.
But soon, brilliant and dazzling,
Mysterious
In a steam of gold, at each
Step a sun more immense, in the perfume of a thousand souls embalmed,
You open to me like a flower,

Asia!
And with dazzled eyes, I sought
A place I might have known, for these broad avenues
Were to me something new . . . [40]

Everything resides here in the blank that separates the "flower" from its *name*, that is, from its identification: Asia. Heidegger, who takes up the general Hölderlinian movement, appears to me not to respect the displacement of the ground that is marked by such a blank. For him, the flower, mysterious and unopened though it may be, is not yet that which is reserved in even the most precocious fruit to come from Greek soil.

Let us summarize. An extremely unique theory of texts and interpretation finds itself developed by the Jewish tradition. This theory is nevertheless found, in very close terms, in Hölderlin's conception of translation. If Hegel, and especially Schelling, disregarded this conception,[41] a more informed reader of Hölderlin, Heidegger, will draw no small inspiration from him, as much in his comprehension of interpretation as in the practice deriving from it. Yet nothing in his text leads us to suspect that Hölderlin (and thereby Heidegger himself) would find his place here—if not in a relation of descent, then at least in a remarkable closeness—on a path already taken (and trodden over how many centuries!) by others.

There is more. This theory of translation is indissociable, in Hölderlin, from a conception of history of which Heidegger makes himself the attentive interpreter and, at least in part, the inheritor—yet only in part. Everything takes place as though Hölderlin—in the very act by which he gave life back to an ancient tradition that was not Greek—remembered in some fashion (if only mythically) the non-Greek source of the West.

Heidegger, on the other hand, draws sustenance from that same tradition *via* Hölderlin, but leaves without echo the entire oriental dimension in Hölderlin's text. But it was there that something of that tradition could still be heard.[42]

This entire analysis, it seems, can thus lead us to the following conclusion: Heidegger, inasmuch as he renews the Western interpretative apparatus, encounters (as he also does elsewhere) the Hebraic heritage. But on this question at least, the mode of transmission can be clarified: it passes via Hölderlin—a Hölderlin cut off from his "oriental" dimension. We must now consider more closely Heidegger's approach, which to this point I have only evoked.

IV. On Interpretation in the Work of Heidegger

Insofar as language in Heidegger is not the simple designation of things, but that which accords them being, thinking, as we have seen, cannot be defined otherwise than as a listening to language. In this respect, thinking is through and through hermeneutical. The Heideggerian notion of interpretation, therefore, does not only name a mode of accession to the text, a search for its signification; by reason of the "ontological" status accorded to language, interpretive listening is indissociably reading (of the text) and thinking (of the "thing itself"—since there is nothing, once again, except through the word). That means that, from the first, by way of the finality he assigns to interpretation, Heidegger goes beyond the framework of hermeneutics within the entirety of the Western tradition since Schleiermacher, to involve himself in a region infinitely vaster and stranger: a region where language *is* living presence, where reading is existence, and where the mere listening to words and the interrogation of texts, *is* thinking. This is a region that we have identified as that in which the Hebraic tradition moved, indefatigably, since its origins.

The ("ontological") function assigned to interpretation being thus set, of what does the interpretive act consist (or of what ought it to consist), what are the ways taken by it, and to what does it lead? The Heideggerian opus contains, at the same time, a *practice* of interpretation (which is set to work in three large domains: initial words or fragments, grand texts of the metaphysical tradition, and the songs of poets), and a *defini-*

tion of interpretation. It is this double aspect that I would venture to set forth here.

First, the definition. It is marked by three key words, which find their full resonance only in German: *die Erklärung* (explanation), *die Erläuterung* (elucidation), *die Erörterung* (emplacement).[43]

Explanation is the mode of thinking dominated by the principle of sufficient reason; a mode of thinking that finds its full development in modern science, but which reigns already secretly in metaphysics. Inasmuch as the latter, as onto-theo-logy, founds beings in their Being, and Being itself in a supreme being, the whole metaphysical quest for the foundation can be, as it were, "reduced" ["*rabattue*"] to the ontic explanation: it becomes "a technique for explanation by way of supreme causes."[44]

But it is clear that explanation, which aims at accounting for and justifying everything, can only miss, for this reason, that which by essence disappears and for which we could not provide an explanation: that which escapes all "foundations."[45]

This is why Heidegger opposes an entirely different thought to this explicative one, proper to metaphysics. The other thought does not aim— by going back up the chain of causes and effects—to master the thing [*la chose*], but rather to welcome it, to let it come.[46] And as it comes only in its word, this other thinking will necessarily unfold in the mode of listening, thus it will be presented as a hermeneutics. It is this hermeneutics that the two terms *Erläuterung* and *Erörterung* name.

Why two terms? Because language offers us two things in a single act: that which it says and that which it does not say, the formulated and the unformulated.[47] The interpretation that attempts to clarify the *formulated* [*le formulé*] in its variety, will be called *Erläuterung*. That which aims at situating the *unformulated* [*l'informulé*], in its unity (which is always on reserve beneath the variety of what is said), is called *Erörterung*. The two modes of interpretation are therefore not in a relationship of succession (as though the one abolished the other); they would remind us instead of the two faces of a medal or the two sides of a fold: they suppose each other reciprocally, just as the said refers to the unsaid and the thought to the unthought.[48]

These relationships between *Erörterung* and *Erläuterung* are very clearly presented by Heidegger himself. Let us recall the context of this presentation. From the first page of his lecture on Trakl—entitled appropriately "Eine Erörterung seines Gedichtes"[49]—Heidegger distinguishes between particular poems (*einzelne Dichtungen*) in all their rich variety, and the unique Poem [*das einzige Gedicht*],[50] which remains unformulated but is nonetheless the "source of the wave," the truth of what we recognize as "rhythm." It is this unformulated poem that, gathered together, constitutes the "site" (*Ort*) toward which the situation (*Erörterung*) will tend. How to accede to this site? On the basis of particular poems. The *Erläuterung* allows us to clarify these poems, while the *Erörterung* will question back toward the secret unity that is reserved there.

That is to say that the site (of the Poem) is by right prior to all the places it grants (the poems, in their variety); but the interpreter, for his or her part, cannot spare [*faire l'économie de*] the back-and-forth movement between the two. "A good elucidation already presupposes the situation. It is only on the basis of the site of the Poem that particular poems shine brightly and resonate. Conversely, situating the Poem already requires a precursory trajectory through a first elucidation of particular poems."[51] It is in this "back-and-forth play" [*jeu d'échange*] between *Erläuterung* and *Erörterung* that Heidegger sees what is essential in the "dialogue" between thinking and poetry,[52] with thinking leading what the poet said all the way back to the unsaid [*nondit*] that is its "site" and that thinking alone, as such, can "situate."

However, though the two modes of interpretation are, by right, not dissociable from each other, Heidegger's *accent* (and his effort) will always bear more on the second one (the *Erörterung*), to the precise degree to which his thinking seeks, ever further, to highlight the un-said and to clarify the unthought. In this sense, the *Erörterung* can appear, effectively, as the last word on interpretation. How to understand exactly what is in play in this word?

The *Erörterung* presents several characteristics, parallel to those of the *Ort* that is discovered there. We have already noted the priority of the site in relation to all that which it grants: the site is the provenance, the source, the *that from whence*. By this fact, the first trait of the situation will be that it is oriented toward the condition of possibility. This language— marked by the vocabulary of the transcendental—is that of the *Principle of Sufficient Reason*. Presenting the "principle," Heidegger writes:

We ought to consider it, as it were, in the other, opposed direction: not in the direction of his fields and domains of application, but in the direction of its own provenance [*Herkunft*], in the direction of *that from whence* [*von woher*] it speaks. . . . We call the site [*Ort*] of the principle of reason that from which speaks the call of the principle. The path that ought to lead there, and permits an initial exploration of it we call the situation [*Erörterung*] of the principle of reason.[53]

The same text offers us, moreover, a second indication concerning the nature of the site and, thereby, of the situation: its character as *gathering* [rassemblement]. "What we call the site is that in which the essential unfolding [*das Wesende*] of a thing is gathered."[54] Thus, situation will be an attention to the provenance, inasmuch as the latter is gathered together in the mode of unity [*recueillie en mode d'unité*].

If we follow this first formulation—which defines the *Erörterung* relative to a metaphysical principle and not, as will be the case elsewhere, to the song of the poet—it appears that situation is applied to "localizing" and "gathering" the unthought provenance or source of what is thought [*du pensé*]. By virtue of this, what is gathered together by situation *belongs to what is thought*—if only as that which escapes it or is held on reserve by it. It is clear, in effect, that the unthought has meaning only if it is called by what is thought, itself, if it is in some sense pretraced there, if it is harbored there "sunken" ["*en creux*"]. In a word, the unthought has meaning if it is that toward which what is thought [*le pensé*] leads (or leads *back*), when what is thought [*le pensé*] is questioned in view of that which, while holding itself in reserve in its unfolding, *permits* the thought [*le pensé*].[55]

In the text on Trakl, dating from a few years earlier, Heidegger's formulation is different (with a difference that is underlined neither by him nor by his interpreters,[56] but which seems to me extremely significant). The movement of *Erörterung* is not presented there as a passage from what is thought to the unthought, but rather as a passage from the said to the unsaid [*du dit au non-dit*]. This change is certainly called for by the nature of the text that Heidegger is "situating" or "placing": a metaphysical principle expounds a thought, which Heidegger refers to the unthought reserved within it; a poem sings or speaks, and it is this said that Heidegger refers back to the un-said [*non-dit*] harbored within it. He does so in order, as a thinker, to think it, that is, to make it "worthy of inquiry." The passage of the thought/unthought pair to the said/un-said pair seems thus to correspond to the passage from a philosophical text to a poetic one. The two pairs would say "the same thing" (as to the nature of the interpretation), and they would only say it in different terms because the supporting text had changed in the interim. But we must look more closely at this.

Heidegger's *first formulation* defines the *Erörterung* as a passage *from the thought to the unthought*. The unthought, by its very definition, is what has not been taken in charge by thought. If, however, it can be considered as *thought's* unthought, then this is because what is thought points doubly in its direction: on the one hand (by reason of its derived character), what is thought "lacks" its condition of possibility and in this sense *calls for it*. On the other hand (by reason of its linguistic character), it "harbors" that condition and in this sense *attests to it*. The unthought, in effect, is that which has not been contemplated *by thought*, remaining lodged meanwhile in the language.[57] One will say, for example, that, within *lógos* considered as logic, its "gathering" essence (which the verb *legein* already meant) lies in reserve, in the mode of the unthought. Or again, in *alèthéia*, considered as agreement or correctness [*concordance ou rectitude*], is reserved (in the mode of the unthought) its "disclosing" essence (which is what *a-lètheia* already says). In other terms, the "leap" toward the unthought does indeed leave the domain of what was thought, but not that of what was *said*. On the contrary, the leap finally reaches the ground of the said. If it leaps, it leaps *toward* the word [*la parole*], in order to hear it resonating in its initial nominative force, and ultimately to think that which thinking had not gathered up there, but which remained waiting in the "shelter" of the term.

To be sure, it is not *because* the word carries the trace of the initial essence that thinking is led to this essence (here, the etymology is not directive). But it remains nonetheless that, when thinking is directed to that essence, it cannot *fail* to encounter its echo in the word. If we break this parallelism, we miss the most characteristic trait of Heidegger's problematic, a trait that consists in granting to thinking (including his own) the double warranty of history (the "morning") and of language (the "words"). It is this latter warranty that interests me here.[58]

Let us consider, now, the *second formulation* of the *Erörterung*. It is presented as the passage *from the said to the unsaid*, from the formulated to the unformulated. In this case, the "situation" [*Erörterung*] deviates, not only from that which was thought over the course of our history, but from that which the language, or tongue, *says*. The second formulation deviates, to be sure, to the benefit of a dimension of silence that language itself contains. But this unsaid harbored in language is not that which "is lacking" in a determinate said; nor is it that to which such a said would attest. It is, purely and simply, *that which lies in reserve in all saying*. In this sense, Vattimo is not wrong when he compares the presence of the unsaid within the said to that of the earth in the work.[59] In effect, like the earth, the unsaid is the reserve, inexhaustible and permanent, from whence arises all opening and, in this case, all that is explicit. But if we accept this definition of the unsaid we should draw its conclusions. The definition means, in effect, that in the very act in which language speaks it reserves something of itself; and it is in drawing from this reserve (always anew and always in a different mode) that we can make the said resonate, each time differently.

There are therefore two orders of differences between Heidegger's formulations. *On the one hand*, the leap from the thought to the unthought would encounter a trace, lodged in language. In making this leap, the thinker would thus set his feet on a track unnoticed up to then, to be sure, but always already dug. The leap from the said to the unsaid leads beyond that trace, and thus acquires a new freedom. *One the other hand*, and above all, the passage from the thought to the unthought reaches the unthought-of-the-thought. That is to say, it reaches what is called forth by the thought [*le pensé*] itself, and which, by virtue of this, belongs to it. The passage from the said to the unsaid reaches an inexhaustible reserve (like the earth), a reserve from which it is certainly possible to draw, and to make new forms arise, but this reserve is not in a direct connection with *this or that* specific said, and in this sense it cannot appear as "that which the said is lacking."

In other words, in one case, Heidegger's interpretation goes back to the condition of possibility of thought, that is, to a determinate source, directly tied to what derives from it. In the other case, the interpretation moves forward within a permanent reserve of what is implicit [*réserve permanente d'implicite*], that is, in the dimension of night that all openings conceal, including the opening of discourse. Grasped according to this second figure, the *Erörterung* consists not in referring a thought [*une pensée*] to what supports it while forgetting about it, but in recalling that even the fullest of words (here, that of the poet) is forever incomplete: it is yet but a call, an opening in the direction of its own future.

Heidegger assimilates these two movements. For him, they are but two formulations of a single act, which is the act itself of interpretation, understood as *Erörterung*. I have tried to show that he used instead a single term (*Erörterung*) for two different actions. Now these two actions are both present in the *interpretative practice* of Heidegger. In effect, we must distinguish between the reading he proposes of the philosophers of the metaphysical tradition, and that of the initial words of the poets of the "morning." The first reading goes back from the thought to the unthought [*du pensé à l'impensé*]. In this sense, it "encounters" the texts of poets and thinkers. On the other hand, the second reading goes back behind [*en deçà*] these same texts, to enter into a region until then unknown, but properly traced out by Heidegger's thought, and, moreover, recognized as such by Heidegger himself.

We must here bring in again the evolution of his oeuvre. As long as Heidegger argues that he is letting himself be guided by Greek words, his gesture remains that of the *Erörterung* in the sense of a return to the unthought. From the moment he surpasses these words, in the direction not of what was unthought in them, but of what is fitting to think on their basis (and we have seen that the "surpassing" is effected, then, by the intermediary of the German language),[60] his gesture becomes that of the *Erörterung* taken in the sense of a return beyond the *said* itself.

Does that mean that this surpassing is effected, then, "in freedom," and that it would only be the purely external fixing of a meaning? Not at all. In question is indeed a horizon, to which the (initial) word, or the song (of the poet), *can* be referred. But it is henceforth impossible to assert that *they* do indeed lead, or refer us back to that horizon. It is rather the horizon (recognized as *our* site, different from that which opened originally on the basis of the word, and which was not "proposed" by it, even in the mode of the unthought), which can be projected onto the word in question, to allow it to be read in a direction other than that toward which it *was pointing*.

That is to say, in his interpretation of the great moments of the metaphysical tradition Heidegger goes back from what is thought (acknowledged as derived) to the (originary) unthought. Having come to the first saying (poetry and fundamental words), he begins to apply to this the same treatment, in order, finally in his late work, to "pass" beyond, into a region from which the unthought can certainly be derived (and thereby also the thought), but whence something entirely different can be derived as well.[61] It seems to me that this other region—more "ancient" than the Greek language itself, and therefore more ancient than the unthought of our history—is suggested in two determinate sites: on the one hand, in a certain formulation (not in all, however) relative to the nature of the *Erörterung*— that which utilizes the couplet said/unsaid; on the other hand, in a certain practice (not the only one) of this *Erörterung*. It is a matter, then, of a *late* reading of the poets and of the first words.

One of the sites in which this practice is the most visible is, once again, the precious seminar *What Is Thinking?* where Heidegger develops the hidden essence of thinking, following the thread of the *Gedanc*, that is, *on the basis of German*. He does this because he cannot develop it on the basis of the Greek *lógos*, even on the authority of its unthought. Once this path is followed, he turns toward the Greek texts, to bring them to resonate in this site that was opened up by wholly other paths. But he does not assert anywhere (how could he?) that this site would be *the* proper site *of the Greek texts*, or that the Greek words could lead us there, or that it could be summoned by those words. Once again, if that were the case, it would have sufficed to "go back to" the Greek words in order to find it, the way one finds the source. More subtly, Heidegger tries to show that this site, opened on the basis of other signs, can offer a new space of resonance to the Greek words. That is, this space does not proceed from them, but it can *become*, in some manner, one of their possible sites.

Such, in any case, is what can be deduced from the course effectively followed by Heidegger—and which he follows exactly in many other texts. But here he goes farther: he returns, in thought, to the movement thus accomplished, to thematize it *as the very movement of interpretation*. The text in which he does this is very interesting, and we should not hasten to understand it on the basis of other, similar formulations, which may seem familiar to us. Heidegger has just cited the beginning of Parmenides' Fragment 6 (*Khre to légein té noein t'éon emménai* ["That which can be spoken and thought must be"],[62] and he adds:

> We will attend to this saying while we are underway on the way of the ques-

tion [the question: what calls us to think?]. . . . But are we not forcing Parmenides' saying to enter, in advance, into a specific perspective, determined solely by the prospect opened up by the way of our question? It is indeed this that we are doing. But that is not a lack we must confess . . . [63]

We must indicate, on this occasion, an error into which one always falls too easily: one believes, in effect, that one approaches Parmenides' saying objectively and without presuppositions, if one comes to know it with no presentiment [*Ahnen*] of anything. . . . But this way of coming to know something, deprived of any presentiments and any questions, and apparently free of any prejudice [*Vormeinung*], is in fact the interpretation most burdened with presuppositions and the most biased one could imagine. It rests, in effect, upon the stubborn and widespread prejudice, according to which one could enter into dialogue with a thinker, when one confronts him on the basis of an absence of thought.[64]

Our principal task here is not to bring down what Heidegger says to what are, certainly, adjacent notions, but which are in no way equivalent. Heidegger asserts that we "force" the sentence to enter into a "particular," determinate view, through a "perspective" that is "ours." Two directions of reading (which perhaps form only one) are immediately excluded.

In the first place, it cannot be a matter here of a *return to the unthought*. It is clear, in effect, that if it were a matter of the unthought the "perspective" would be that of the text itself (we have seen above that it is what is thought that points toward its unthought condition of possibility). Far from being "forced" by us to enter into a "particular" view, it is this text, on the contrary, that would lead *us* to "that which it lacks." The movement of interpretation, such as it is presented here, could not be reduced to setting forth the unthought.

For this reason, the movement of interpretation also cannot be referred to the hermeneutic principle of *precomprehension*, understood as a moment inherent in every act of comprehension. To be sure, some of Heidegger's formulations (the "presentiment" or the "questioning" recognized as necessary to coming to know something) might lead us to believe that we have not left the ground laid since *Being and Time*. But it seems to me that Heidegger surpasses hermeneutic circularity itself. Here, it is neither a matter of the classical idea of a clarification of the part by the whole, and the whole by the part, nor is it one of the structure of anticipation in the comprehension that *Being and Time* brought to light.[65]

According to this structure, interpretation has a character of "violence"[66]—so it appears, at least, to the common understanding—because it projects upon the being interpreted (whether it is, or is not, of the order of the text) a precomprehension that was not there, in the open. But if this violence is not "arbitrary," this is because the project is a "liberation" of what was already there,[67] albeit withholding itself. For example, the interpretation "projects an entity [*étant*] toward the Being [*être*] that is proper to it," even if this entity [*étant*] (as is the case for *Dasein*) "goes all the way to withdrawing, in its guise of Being, the Being that belongs to it."[68] Outside of this affirmation of what is already-there, the act of projecting would lose all "guidance" and "regulation."[69] That is to say, by the same token, it would lose all legitimacy. Such is the sense, which is still maintained, of the "presupposition" inherent in the hermeneutic circle:

> Or does this presupposing have the character of an understanding projection in such a manner that the Interpretation by which such an understanding gets developed, will let that which is to be interpreted *put itself into words for the very first time, so that it may decide of its own accord whether, as the entity which it is, it has that state of Being for which it has been disclosed in the projection with regard to its formal aspects?*[70]

The definition itself of precomprehension thus demands that it be called for (even implicitly) by the text, to find itself confirmed, in return, by that text. Therein lies the condition of validity of precomprehension in Heidegger's vocabulary. In this sense, it is hardly important that an outside reader might judge that what Heidegger presents as an anticipation is not one, that is, that it is not "truly" called for by the text. What is important is that, in order to be able to speak of precomprehension, it is necessary that what is set forth of this term by Heidegger's interpretation be posited *by the latter* as pretraced, from the origin, in the text itself. And this is indeed the reason for which the structure of comprehending can be said to be "circular."

Now, in the text we have followed, this circularity is *broken*, despite certain appearances to the contrary. This is a breakage that is, to be sure, hardly perceptible in the way in which Heidegger *presents* his interpretation, but which is very clearly marked in the *use* he makes of it. Heidegger nowhere argues, indeed, that what he discovered on the path of "his" question should be the hidden truth of Parmenides' sentence, whose release waited there in reserve, from its origin. The relationship he establishes between "his" question and Parmenides' sentence is more complex than that: having taken a certain path (that which the German *Gedanc* opened), and having followed it through its "stations" (memory, gratitude, thanksgiving, etc.), Heidegger has come to a "thinking" (here, that of the essence of thinking); starting from there, he believes it possible to return to Parmenides' sentence, to make it enter into this "particular view," and to open a "dialogue" with it. However, if it is really thus that we should understand the relationship between Heidegger's question and Parmenides' sentence, then we do not find there a *circular* movement, leading *from* the sentence to that "proper" [*ce "propre"*] that belongs to it without appearing in it. Here, there is instead a breaking of the circle, by the entry into play of an *other path*, coming from a distinct point of departure—a path to which Parmenides' sentence can certainly be referred, but in order thereupon to find a *new* resonance in it.

I cannot say with complete certainty that that is indeed what Heidegger means when he speaks of a "particular view," determined solely by "our" question. It is perfectly clear, on the other hand, that that is what he *does*. Immediately following the "warning" we cited above, he considers the fragment of Parmenides where *légein* and *noein* are in question, and he interprets this question in the direction opened by the *Gedanc*. Now, I would again repeat, such a trajectory could not be innocent: if *légein* and *noein could have* been interpreted in this way on the basis of themselves (that is to say, in Greek), they would have been so interpreted. If it is the *Gedanc* that leads to the site where the *lógos* can resonate differently, this is because this site was not already that of the *lógos*; otherwise it would have sufficed, as *Being and Time* already said, "to allow to speak" the being (here, the *lógos*) "itself."

That is to say that Heidegger's conception of interpretation (such as it is defined in the term *Erörterung*, and more and more clearly practiced in the later works) is certainly remarkably original relative to the current "tradition," but it contains nevertheless two precedents in history: Hölderlin's translations (which "put back" the "oriental" element) and Jewish hermeneutics (which proceed on the authority of the "blanks" of the sacred text to make the interpreter the high priest of a "second revelation"). What makes for their unity is that, for all three (and for them *alone*), the work of interpretation is not the deepening of a dimension, hidden to be sure, but *inherent* in the interpreted material. In a quite radical way, the text is understood as *unfinished*, thus as open to a future that was not pretraced therein. This is why the interpreter can, in the strongest sense, *re*-create it.

If I were to venture a somewhat daring wager, I would apply the telling metaphor of hidden letters to Heidegger's conception of interpretation; that is to say, the stroke of translating Heidegger into Hebrew (just as he would sometimes translate German into Greek). The *Erörterung* would thus be stated in this way: because the interpreter holds, in some manner, the missing letter—a letter that is not given in the Greek alphabet—he can turn back to the dimensions of the text that remained mute until then, and make them sonorous. But if *this* conception of the text—as inexhaustible reserve, open to the future—is indeed Heidegger's, how can we not see that it is also, firstly, the Hebraic conception, and that, despite its closeness to many of the aspects of Western hermeneutics, it is not reducible to it?

We have come to the end of the first part of this work. Whether it is a question of language (as the opening of Being), of thinking (as memory and recognition), or of interpretation (as new revelation), Heidegger breaks with the "essence" dominant until then, in favor of a wholly other essence, called "more originary." In this radical renewal to which he subjects the leading notions of the Western tradition, Heidegger accompanies, with a peculiar steadfastness, the paths opened—and followed patiently up to our time—by the Jewish tradition. How could these paths, so long opened, still have remained secret? How could they belong by right to the history of the West and yet constitute for the West, an "unheard-of" future [*un avenir "inouï"*]? As we have seen,[71] if the West constituted itself on the basis of two distinct components (Greek and Hebraic), then it was by means of the path opened by but *one* of these [the Greek] that the West came to the *reflected* representation of itself [*représentation* pensée *de lui-même*]: that which took place in metaphysics. By virtue of this, the Western tradition always agreed, *thanks to the voice of its historians*, to recognize its dual source, Greek and Hebrew, which in no way kept it from asserting, at the same time, *thanks to the voice of its thinkers*, that it recognized but a single fundamental component, and thus but a single origin: the Greek. And how could it have been otherwise, since it was in (Greek) philosophy alone that (Western) thinking took the measure of its own essence?

Thus, paths of thinking other than metaphysical logic were indeed *there* in the West without being recognized as such. These were paths belonging to the tradition of Western thought, yet ignored by it; paths followed anew by Heidegger, and again ignored by him. They were ignored in the first case, *because* the Western tradition had reduced all thought to metaphysics; they went misprized in the second case, *although* Heidegger had led thought back beyond metaphysics alone. In his surpassing of metaphysics, Heidegger encounters the other current of thought, underscores its alterity, and unfolds it in its ultimate possibilities; in a word, he restores its rights in the field of thinking. Yet he does so without recognizing in it the source from which it flows, thus without ever bestowing on it an *identity* distinct from the Greek identity.

In following the conjoined paths of Heidegger and the Hebraic tradition, I wanted simply to cast light on this parallelism. It is a parallelism hard to contest in itself, which a thinker like Derrida, for example, emphasized in *De l'esprit,*[72] and which I have tried to unfold following the texts examined here. Therefore, it has been a matter of "reading" up to this point, that is, of following what each text elaborated in its way, and attempting to show their secret convergence.

What then remains to be done, now that this first task is accomplished? It remains for us to open questions posed *on the basis of this reading,* and these are numerous. Once the convergence is brought to light, it is a matter of making the questions that flow from it into problems, and trying to work them out. That is the objective of the second part of this work.

PROBLEMS

1

And How Is It with Being?

The above is the very first question that the preceding developments could not fail to raise. It is a question I have put off until now, for it does not participate in the convergence I was attempting to set forth, but constitutes, on the contrary, the principal site of *rupture* with the convergence. Now, this rupture is so radical that it seems, on the other hand, it must problematize everything I attempted above: if there is an abyss *here*, then is it not inconsistent to claim to find, *elsewhere*, any sort of community or neighborhood of thought?

With the support of this suspicion, we might say that the separation between Heidegger's thought and the biblical universe on a question as central as that of Being entails two immediate consequences. On the one hand, it implies that the one and the other share points of encounter or proximity only on the most minor points, which leave untouched the heart of Heidegger's thought (Being), as well as that of the Hebraic universe (God). On the other hand and above all, it implies that *even* on these minor points, the proximity may only be *apparent* in the final analysis. Heidegger's elaboration of some "peripheral" question (language, thinking, etc.) may only seem close to the Hebraico-biblical perspective on condition of being previously cut off from what alone gave it meaning: the question of Being, to which language, like thought, must necessarily be referred in order to find their properly Heideggerian dimension. Conversely, the Hebraico-biblical approach to these questions may only appear to admit an analogy with Heidegger's work on them on condition of being cut off from the God of the Bible—the same God without which language and thought would lose their specifically Hebraic meaning.

The question of Being seems thus to function, from the outset, as the most formidable objection to the enterprise ventured here. To give all its force to this objection—and to attempt at the same time to respond to it—amounts to the whole question of the relations between Being and God, which we must consider. We will do this not to close it off immediately with a definitive response, but rather to attempt to indicate the possible *site* of its elaboration.

I. Heidegger's Position: God or Being.
"The Two Paths"

"God and Being—Being and God: this constellation as old as Western thought," is presently recognized as the most tangible sign of our "dual belonging": "to the truth of Being disclosed by Parmenides, Plato, and Greek philosophy, and to the truth of the transcendent God, announced by Moses, the Prophets, and the Christ."[1]

Grasped in its greatest generality, the work accomplished by Heidegger relative to this founding pair consists in *unfolding* the question of Being in order to renew it, and in *situating* that of God in its relation to the former. This was a situation rendered complex by the evolution of his thought; between the courses of 1920 and the Zurich seminar of 1951, Heidegger certainly never stopped working this question out, but he did not always do so in the same terms.

Three notions allow us to sketch the general framework in which such an elaboration takes place: these include *theology, faith,* and *divinity* (inseparable from the sacred). Three notions that all gravitate in some way toward or around the relation to God, but that do not say the same thing about it and, perhaps, do not speak of the same God. Indeed, through these notions are sketched the three different figures of God, as Henri Birault recalls them:[2] the god-cause of self and without divinity (that of the philosophers), the redeemer God (that of believers), and finally the sacred god (that of the poet, and perhaps the future god of the thinker).

Heidegger's elaboration of the "question of God" will consist in taking account of these three figures, not directly, but through their methodical articulation in three key terms (theology, faith, and divinity). As to their evolution, it will consist in passing from a primary configuration wherein only the relation between theology and faith figures, to a second, later configuration wherein the dual motif of divinity and the sacred becomes prevalent.

The initial configuration is outlined in the first Freiburg courses (those of 1920–21),[3] crosses through *Being and Time*,[4] is thematically presented in the 1927 article "Phenomenology and Theology,"[5] and will only be modified toward the middle of the 1930s, seemingly under the influence of Hölderlin.[6] Globally speaking, it consists in going from theology to faith in order to make possible, on the basis of faith, another theology. That is to say, to the question What is theology? two answers may be given: a de facto answer (what theology was and remains, i.e., a part of metaphysics) and a de jure response (what theology could be, considering its proper object).

The de facto response is already sketched out in the first configuration, but it will be fully unfolded only in the rest of the work, when Heidegger comes to think the essence of metaphysics in its proper structure. Theology, in effect, claims to think of God, to think God, and it thinks God within a dimension of Being issued directly from Aristotle's metaphysics: "The interpretation of the being of God . . . has recourse to means provided by Classical ontology."[7] Understanding God in terms of Being, classical ontology is led in return to "take Being for God," an error that, according to Heidegger, "has slipped even into the Bible."[8] By virtue of this central "error," theology maintains a general confusion of registers, leading it, for example, to make use of the (Christian) idea of creation to claim to answer the (ontological) question of Being, whereas such an "answer" has "no relation to" and "can in no way have one" with what is asked in the "question."[9]

Is this to say that Christian theology might, at some point in its evolution, have been contaminated by Greek philosophy? Not at all. It is rather metaphysics that, from its birth and through its very structure, makes a place for theology.

The theological character of ontology does not rest, therefore, on the fact that Greek metaphysics was later adopted by the ecclesiastical theology of Christianity and modified by it. It rests, rather, on the manner in which, from the beginning, beings were disclosed as beings. It is this disclosure of beings that first made it possible for Christian theology to lay hold of Greek philosophy.[10]

Because metaphysics, from the moment of its constitution, aims at "beings as such in their generality and primordiality," at the same time as it considers "beings as such in what they have that is supreme and final,"[11] metaphysics is onto-theology in its structure.[12] For this reason, when (Christian) theology uses concepts from (Greek) ontology, it merely admits its fundamental belonging to metaphysics.

Why does this belonging pose a problem? Because it makes theology lose the object most proper to it. Transforming God into the supreme being [*étant suprême*], this fundamental belonging de-divinizes God radically, to make him the "god of the philosophers." Yet, if Pascal already recognized in the latter a relative kinship with the God of the Christians—whereby the one, though already surpassed, would be preserved in the second—Heidegger insists upon their insurmountable opposition.[13] The *ens causa sui*, as a "name conforming to the thing for the God of philosophy,"[14] can be the God *of the philosophers* only if this God ceases to be that *of the Christians*: "To this God, man cannot address his prayers, nor offer sacrifices. Before the *causa sui*, man cannot fall to his knees filled with fear, just as he cannot play music or dance before this God."[15] Inasmuch as it is "fundamentally irreligious,"[16] Christian theology thus misses the God it claimed to reach: the God of love and compassion, the God of the Christ.

If it misses this God, however, it is because this God absents himself, by nature, from all general ontological propositions, to give himself only in an *experience*, itself indissociable from a specific *mode of existence*.[17] It is this experience, and it alone, that is (or ought to be) the true object of theology, inasmuch as it remains given over to its proper essence. In this way we arrive, beyond the de facto (inappropriate) answer, at the de jure one. What is theology? It is not the ontology of a supreme being, but the science of this domain of beings that is Christianity or Christliness (*Christlichkeit*).[18]

From the one register to the other, the movement Heidegger makes is that of "destruction": the destruction of traditional theology, parallel to that of traditional ontology, which he carried out in *Being and Time* (the theological enterprise prior to the ontological one—that is, from the first courses in Freiburg—and serving the latter, perhaps, as its model).

This movement of destruction finds its impulse—and its legitimacy—in the conceptual pair, concealment/disclosure [*recouvrement/découvrement*].[19] Whatever the domain in question, Heidegger's task consists in "dis-closing" a conceptuality recognized to be inadequate, in order to reach "the experience that stands beneath it, and which must be delivered from the foreign language in which it is expressed."[20] From the traditional concept to the original experience, whether it is a matter of ontology or of theology, the same gesture is thus at work. Gadamer, recalling Heidegger's research during the Marburg period, describes this gesture in its greatest generality: "Whatever he read, whether the departure point was given him by Descartes or by Aristotle, Plato, or Kant, his analysis always opened to the most original experiences of *Dasein*; experiences that he brought to light (*freilegte*), behind the concealments accomplished by traditional concepts. And it was theological questions that, from the beginning, urged him from within."[21]

In the case of theology, the "destruction" is all the more imperious in that the conceptuality utilized is not only inadequate, but also foreign to the object it conceals. As soon as one sets about defining, as Heidegger does, what can (and must) be this object—considering what the science is that treats of it—it appears clearly that this could not be God (considered speculatively, from the point of view of his substance or his attributes), but exclusively the experience that one may have of him in the specific domain that is Christianity. Such an experience is called *faith*. It is therefore faith, and faith alone, that constitutes the given, the *positum*, of theology.[22]

But what is faith? Without entering into the entire analysis—such as it unfolds in the essay "Phenomenology and Theology"—it behooves us to underscore two of its characteristics, and to underscore them precisely because they do not go without saying and they constitute so many particularities of Heidegger's thought. In the first place, faith or *credo* is pure belief and is confessed as such. As the adherence to "the properly evangelical proclamation of the good news,"[23] faith is not presented as a form of knowledge, and consequently it does not imply any assertion of existence. As Henri Birault notes, "it is unto itself its first and last justification";[24] "its own light and its own warrant."[25] In the second place, and in conformity with the Lutheran orientation, it is primordially faith in Jesus Christ, the Redeemer.[26]

This implies for Christian theology (henceforth referred to its object, which is faith—itself understood as an act of allegiance to the crucified God) a double consequence. First, it has nothing to do with the question of Being, a question that does not belong to faith's proper domain of
unfolding [*domaine propre de déploiement*]: faith can neither make use of
Being nor in any way serve it. On the other hand, it is in its very essence a
Neo-testamentary theology.[27]

Christian theology is thereby torn out of the site in which it was,
from its origins, settled—a site foreign to its essence yet which had been
prescribed to it, so to speak, by the Greek constitution of metaphysics. It
gets referred back to Christian faith, understood as the constitutive mode
of existence of Christianity, itself recognized as the unique object with
which a scientific theology might be preoccupied.

Once this recentering is accomplished, what can philosophy's place
be, in regard as much to the pure experience of faith as to its conceptualization in theology? Heidegger's answer is perfectly clear: philosophy can
serve theology within the express limits of a formal (that is, ontological)
correction of the fundamental theological concepts. But philosophy and
theology remain no less opposed as to their ontic content, and this is why
faith is the "mortal enemy" of thought.[28] Of these two assertions, Heidegger will maintain the one (concerning the possible use of ontology by
theology) only as long as he believes it possible to work out a fundamental
ontology; it ceases to be evoked after his "turn." The other assertion (concerning the separation of faith and thought) will become the object of constant reaffirmations, all the way into Heidegger's latest works. We recall,
no doubt, his famous "little expressions," all of them aiming to underscore
the radical heterogeneity of the two domains. Faith has strictly nothing to
make of Being, and nothing to do with it. "If I were still writing a theology,
which I am sometimes tempted to do, the expression 'Being' should not
figure in it. Faith has no need for the thinking of Being. When it requires
Being, it is no longer faith at all."[29] Conversely, the thinker has nothing
fundamentally to say to the believer: "Within thought, nothing can be accomplished that might prepare or contribute to determining what takes
place in faith and in grace. If faith called to me in this fashion, I would
close up shop."[30]

As we can see, what was qualified at the beginning of this analysis as the first configuration is maintained, in a number of its traits, over the entire course of the work. If I chose to distinguish a second configuration,[31] it was not because the first was to be abandoned but because a new element appeared, which modified the general economy of Heidegger's work. Once theology is led back to faith—and to a faith clearly recognized in its independence in regard to thinking—Heidegger comes to reflect on what might be, *from the perspective of thinking,* the possible space of divinity. This is the meaning of the famous passage from the "Letter on Humanism." "It is only on the basis of the truth of Being that the essence of the sacred can be thought. It is only on the basis of the essence of the sacred that the essence of divinity [or of the deity, the *Gottheit*] can be thought. It is only in light of the essence of divinity that that which the word 'God' names can be thought and said."[32]

Referred in this way to the truth of Being, God again comes close to thinking. He is even recognized as bearing a more intimate kinship with thought than with faith,[33] and this is indeed the new trait, characteristic of the second configuration of Heidegger's thought. But we must be precise here. Which god is at stake, and which thinking? The god glimpsed here is no longer that of the philosophers,[34] but neither is it that of the believer: neither supreme being, foundation of all other beings, nor savior and redeemer God of the Bible, this god could not be the object of a theology, whether Greek-inspired (and so, inadequate) or Christic (and so, in conformity with faith). This god's principal trait is *presence,*[35] and it is because this god is pure presence that it is sung by the poet. In naming the sacred—that primordial gaping or abyss wherein all presence gleams in its immediacy—the poet creates a space for the divinity. This god alone, poetically announced on the basis of the "sacred chaos," will henceforth interest thinking. Heidegger emphasizes this himself very clearly: "The passage from the 'Letter on Humanism'[36] speaks exclusively of the god of the poet and not of the God of Revelation."[37]

Moreover, the thinking in question here is no longer ontology, to the precise degree that the "truth of Being" (whence "the divinity draws its origin") "'is' something other than the foundation and cause of beings."[38] The confusion between God and Being, brought about by the thinking of onto-theology, is found to be relieved or sublated [*relayé*] by a wholly other constellation, in which each of the terms resonates in a new manner, that is, nonmetaphysically. The clearing, or lighting, of Being [*Lichtung des Seins*] (which is no longer a foundation) appears as that in which the appearing [*ce où peut advenir l'apparition*] of the god may come (the god who is no longer the *causa sui*).[39] Because the sole task of thinking is to "keep watch" [*veiller*] over this clearing, this lighting [*Lichtung*], it does not close itself to the coming of the divinity.

It thus appears that the god that is divine and inseparable from the sacred, the one proper to Heidegger's second configuration, again finds a relation to thought. Yet this god does so only in the sense that it constitutes a possibility for thought. Perhaps it is thought's sole possibility; it is in any case thought's final one, as the following remark from Heidegger attests: "The sole possibility that is left for us is to prepare a sort of readiness, through thinking and poetizing, for the appearance of the god, or for the absence of the god in the time of foundering [*untergang*]."[40]

That is to say that the clearing or lighting of Being conditions at once God's appearing and the eventual experience that thinking can have of it—precisely *that thinking can have of God*, not that faith may have of God. We are no longer in the sphere of Christian, or even religious, life. It is, instead, a matter of the experience that a thought concerned with Being could have of a god to come—the one who would come after the time of "the gods that have fled," and this is why Heidegger no longer speaks of God, but of the god, even the gods . . .

Thus the second configuration completes the first by modifying it. Having started from theology (of Greek inspiration), only to go back to (Christian) faith and to recognize it as foreign to thought, Heidegger ultimately opens thought itself to the possibility of another god. And it is because this god is no longer the God of faith that the welcome given it, even the invocation addressed to it ("Only a god can save us now"),[41] changes nothing in Heidegger's "verdict" on the radical separation between the thinking of Being and the dual domain of faith and theology. It is in the very text in which he evokes the possibility of a god to come that Heidegger, in one and the same movement, "refuses any meaning of philosophy for theology" and "likewise contests the thesis of an essential influence of Christian faith upon philosophy."[42]

What comes out of this analysis, taken as a whole? Whichever "configuration" we consider, Heidegger's position in regard to the question of

God remains characterized by a triple separation. (1) "Being and God are not identical":[43] there is no possible confusion between the one and the other except in metaphysics, because God was misinterpreted there as the supreme being [*comme étant suprême*], at the same time that Being is misinterpreted there as the foundation of beings. (2) There is no possible compromise between faith and thought. These are two "paths,"[44] equal in dignity, no doubt, but irreducible to each other. Whoever lives in faith cannot think *stricto sensu*;[45] whoever dedicates himself to thinking is obliged if not to a necessary "atheism"—as Heidegger asserts at least once[46]—then in any case to the suspension of belief, since what is asked in the question of thinking is "madness for faith."[47] (3) Finally, there is no possible assimilation between the gods to come (offered to thought as one of its ultimate possibilities) and that which the Western tradition called God—whether we mean with this the God "of the Christians" (revealed to faith) or that "of the philosophers" (contemplated by reason).

Far from maintaining some sort of relation of dependence in regard to God, theology, or faith, thought (inasmuch as we understand it in a rigorous sense and not as the vague sphere of "worldviews") would be indebted only to Being such as it was illumined in the morning of the Greek world. Thinking owes everything to this world, since it is in its essence the thinking *of Being*; to God, theology, and faith it owes nothing, and cannot owe anything. The Bible and the God revealed therein are for thinking a *foreign land* [*terre étrangère*], which it does not encounter, or believes it encounters only by a misunderstanding. The sole tie with divinity that thinking finally accepts to acknowledge is, on the contrary, the dependence of the god, whatever it might be, in regard to this Being [*cet être*] that thinking guards.

Such is at least Heidegger's position, outlined in its most general traits, which seems to me to require examination on one particular point. Assuredly, the question of Being was opened by the Greeks and remains the exclusive prerogative of philosophy. The question does not penetrate—proximally or distantly—the biblical world, which is the world of Revelation. As to God, he can be linked to Being, even identified with it, only inasmuch as he is no longer the biblical God of Revelation, but still—and forever—a Greek figure. On this point (that of the onto-theological structure of metaphysics), no return "prior to" Heidegger seems envisionable.

Being is thus found carefully maintained at a distance from the entire universe of Revelation. *But what being is in question here?* This seems to me to be the principal problem. Being, such as metaphysics unfolded it? Or Being itself, the *Seyn*, such as Heidegger rethought it? It is to this Being, never thought by metaphysics and reconsidered in a radically new light by Heidegger, that we shall have to turn.

II. Heidegger's Renewal of the Question of Being

Over the course of these pages, it has never been a question of forming some sort of amalgamation of the two so radically distinct universes, that of the Hebraic tradition and that of Greek thought. My sole concern was to question the way in which Heidegger's work is situated in relation to these universes, and especially the way in which it can be situated in regard to the Hebraic pole.

I will not proceed differently concerning the question occupying us here. The preceding developments indicate well enough that we cannot confuse, or even compare, the (biblical) God and (Greek) Being. The problem is not there, however: it consists, rather, in asking ourselves whether Heidegger stands, without recognizing it, at the *crossroads* of these two heritages, and whether he brought about their intersection in some way (which remains to be defined). Now this is a gesture that, were it to be confirmed, would prove paradoxical in the highest degree, insofar as it was precisely Heidegger who most radically separated the two poles in question, even forbidding their synthesis. Yet between what Heidegger *says* relative to the dual, antagonistic couple God/Being and faith/thinking, and what he *does*, identity does not go without saying. It is, in any case, worth subjecting to examination before being asserted.

The question posed here is thus the following: is it not the case that the fruitful renewal that Heidegger brings about in regard to the question of Being is due, at least in part, to categories of thought or apprehension [*catégories de pensée ou d'appréhension*] that originate precisely in the biblical approach to God—to the hidden God who reveals himself in history, who takes shelter in the word [*parole*], and who is at every moment in danger of being forgotten, and so on? That is, in no way is it a question of comparing the God of Israel to Greek Being, but rather of investigating whether Heidegger is or is not using categories of thought inherited from the Jews, to think a question-content [*teneur-de-question*] he inherited from the Greeks. If this were the case, then this question of Being, opened by the Greeks, would be reworked thanks to a perspective opened by the biblical approach to God. This amounts to a perspective *doubly* ignored by Heidegger, inasmuch as he did not deny all Christian influences (whether a matter of faith or of the Revelation that supports it) on thought, but instead amputated Christianity itself from its ineradicable tie to the Old Testament text. Thus the Hebraic dimension finds itself twice covered over.

Such, at least, is the hypothesis I am proposing to test here. To support this hypothesis, it is worthwhile considering some of the major moments of renewal to which Heidegger subjects the question of Being. In the first place, there is his point of departure, meaning that which motivated the young Heidegger to consider the Greek understanding of Being as problematic or insufficient, and which led him to consider Being, at the end of his long maturation, entirely otherwise than had the ontological tradition issuing from Aristotle.

1. The Point of Departure in the Questioning of the Greek Understanding of Being: The Experience of Christian Faith

It is very interesting to note that, though Heidegger's thought, once constituted, shakes Greek ontology by referring it to the initial experience of the first thinkers, the young Heidegger in no way followed this path: it was on the basis of a renewed meditation on faith that he was led to discern the insufficiency of ontology.

Did Heidegger realize this? Yes and no. As Jean Greisch has pointed out, if Heidegger's debt is patent in regard to theology, his attitude to theology is at the least ambiguous. "It is at once a debt explicitly recognized and a debt which Heidegger does not want to know about."[48] The debt was explicitly recognized, in effect, because Heidegger does not fail to recall on numerous occasions that he "comes out of theology," "has preserved an old affection for it," and "understands something of it."[49] On one occasion, at least, he goes even farther and recognizes that "without his theological origins, [he] would never have come to the path of [his] thinking."[50]

Often cited since he made it, this admission was nonetheless considerably minimized by the same Heidegger. Minimized, in the first place, by the very context in which it took place, which we too often neglect to recall. Heidegger only recognized the importance of his theological origins in regard to the notion of hermeneutics; he did so to indicate immediately his abandonment of this notion after *Being and Time*. Thus the theological influence is recognized on a specific point, only to be indicated as surpassed: it will have been merely "a way-station along the way."[51] Again, as Jean Greisch puts it, "things unfold as though the 'Dialogue on Language Between a Japanese and an Inquirer' consisted essentially in a new staging of this problem."[52]

An influence minimized thereafter, and above all—and it is in this sense that we can say that, in regard to this debt, Heidegger "does not want to know"—because the admission remained purely isolated or occasional, and without any resonance. The avowal does not constitute an axis for a self-reflexive interpretation of his oeuvre [*axe pour l'auto-interprétation de l'oeuvre*], in which regard the late Heidegger was nonetheless anything but sparing, as we know. The selective reconstruction of his own path of thinking did not incorporate the above-mentioned admission (which thus becomes a simple "biographical" detail). In a certain sense, the reconstruction goes so far as to annul this admission, since the path as a whole will be reoriented a posteriori toward the single question of Being, coming out of Greek readings. "If every past contains an element of reconstruction, then in Heidegger's reconstruction of his own philosophical past, Aristotle's is the unique word of origin."[53]

It would assuredly change nothing of the interpreter's ever-open freedom, if this reconstruction had not set its mark [*fixé sa loi*] upon the *publication* of Heidegger: the first Freiburg courses went unpublished until the 1990s. Jean Greisch speaks on several occasions about the "decision to exclude these texts from the *Gesamtausgabe*." He sees in this "one of the most massive symptoms of the interpretive violence at work in the publications: everything must be oriented toward extricating the question of Being; the 'mental burrowing' [*travail de taupe de l'esprit*], which must have stirred up a lot of ground to arrive at this question, must in a certain sense be forgotten."[54] Other sources indicated that these texts were duly foreseen in the *Gesamtausgabe*, but scheduled, according to Heidegger's wishes, for the final part of the publication. Whatever the case may be, the contemporary reader who desires to consider Heidegger's initial theoretical orientations long found himself confronted with a double difficulty: he must not only go against the principal lines of force traced by Heidegger's self-interpretation, but also work on the basis of secondhand accounts.

The course summaries at our disposition are fortunately the work of the best, and most rigorous, of Heidegger's disciples: Pöggeler, Gadamer, and more recently Lehmann.[55] The interest of these different works lies in the fact that, providing largely convergent information, they complement each other remarkably.

These texts will be analyzed more closely in the chapter that follows. If I evoke them here, it is because they furnish a preeminent clue into the initial context that led to Heidegger's decision concerning the renewal of the question of Being. Heidegger constantly asserts that faith is foreign to thought and can in no way influence thought's course: the thinking (of Being) is separated from the experience of faith by an "abyss."[56] Yet, on at least one occasion—and, not the least of them—it turns out that the thinking (of Being) let itself be *guided* decisively by the experience of faith: precisely at the time of its elaboration by Heidegger during the years immediately after World War I. In the courses from this period, if Heidegger goes back, from "bad" (theological) thinking to *faith* (such as it was given, as experience, in original Christianity), he does so to *let himself be taught, by faith, something relative to thinking*. All the witnesses of that period confirm this claim: it was starting from a renewed meditation upon the experience of faith in primitive Christian life that Heidegger was led to problematize the metaphysical conception of Being (notably, Aristotle's conception).

How, then, can we assert that the two paths are lacking any relation to one another? All we can assert is that the two "currents" from which Heidegger alternately drew sustenance from around 1907 onward (on the one hand, *life*, with Dilthey, Saint Paul, Augustine, Luther, Kierkegaard; on the other hand, *Being*, with Brentano, Aristotle, and the ontological tradition) were effectively without relation *before* they came to cross and interpenetrate each other in Heidegger himself. Yet if Heidegger used "witnesses of the faith" like Paul or Luther to reread Aristotle in a different way, then how can one assert that the Being, *of which Heidegger speaks* (and which is no longer that of Aristotle), still remains without the slightest relation to the teachings of Luther or Paul?

We must consider this more closely. The course from the winter semester, 1920–21, is entitled Introduction to Phenomenology of Religion.
Heidegger there attempts to discern the "effective experience of life," such
as it is expressed by the apostle Paul, in order to set forth the characteristic of fundamental historicity—a historicity to which he will return in the
course of the following semester, entitled Augustine and Neoplatonism.
Lehmann and Pöggeler both recognize, in the Christian experience of history (or of life, inasmuch as it is recognized as historical), the "fatherland"
of *Dasein's* historiality,[57] as well as the historical character of Being.[58]

In effect, what Heidegger discovers, as much in Christian evangelical *life* as in the subsequent Christian *faith* (so long as it is not unduly the-
ologized), is an experience of temporality in light of which he is able to
reread the ontological tradition in a critical fashion and cultivate the suspicion that "Being as constant presence is not adequate to the temporality
of life."[59] This is why Pöggeler proposes to show "how Heidegger taught
himself the experience of history through Dilthey and the experience of
life in Christian faith, in order to *transfer* it thereafter to the metaphysical
doctrine of Being."[60]

Lehmann adopts and develops the same interpretation. As his work
is not translated into French or English, it does not seem to me otiose to
cite large segments of it here: "The experience of the comprehension of
history in originary Christianity is the sole possible site from which the
limitation of the prior ontology could be noted, in its comprehension of
the meaning of Being. It is here alone that Heidegger found the Archime-
dean point on the basis of which . . . the interpretation of the meaning of
Being as *Vorhandenheit* [the Presence-at-hand] could be brought to a crisis
point."[61] "The 'evidence' and 'naturalness' of the orientation to the Greek
comprehension of Being could only have been perceived and broken up by
a *radically different or other* interpretation of Being. Without such a confrontation between Greek ontology and the experience of history proper to
originary Christianity (*urchristlicher Geschichtserfahrung*), the question directed toward the *meaning* of Being could simply not have been posed."[62]

This is why Pöggeler could legitimately conclude that the orientation toward factical life, effected at the beginning of the Freiburg period,
was in no way "an abandonment of the question of Being,"[63] such as it concerned Heidegger early on, but on the contrary, one of the decisive conditions of the deepening of this question.

Naturally, all that does not mean that the young Heidegger himself *shared* the Christian faith. But the problem is elsewhere. No one has ever argued that he drew his motivations for thinking out of personal religiosity. Simply, Heidegger considered the experience of faith as rich in lessons for a thinking to come. This is why he endeavored, in the first place, to extract the experience of faith in its purity, delivering it from inadequate conceptualizations liable to caricature it (those that Augustine borrowed from Neoplatonism,[64] or those of the later Luther).[65] This is why, in the second place, he strove to make the experience of faith explicit,[66] that is, to bring to light the teachings it harbored. Heidegger rendered this faith explicit as an experience of factical life, that is to say, of temporality and of history.

In possession of these "lessons," which came to him from primitive Christian religiosity, Heidegger turned anew toward the question of Being, to work it out differently. This is to say that the experience of faith, at least in this period, by no means appeared to him as foreign to the question of Being. If it had remained so up to that time, it was precisely by a *misunderstanding.*[67] Heidegger's arrival in Freiburg marks, in this sense, the end of that secular misunderstanding. His first three courses can be understood, Lehmann rightly remarks, as an attempt to "set these two interpretations of Being in relation to each other":[68] one interpretation sheltered, in a nonconceptual mode, in the experience of faith; the other interpretation worked out in ontological thought. The best proof that this connection was reestablished is found in that the *limits* of the one can only appear *in light* of the other.

What is the upshot of this first analysis? Simply this: if Heidegger was led to consider critically the Greek comprehension of Being and, consequently, to attempt a "deepening" of it in the form of a "renewal," it was on the basis of elements that he found, initially, in the experience of Christian faith. This means that the latter carries teachings *for thinking* (contrary to the claim that the one is the "mortal enemy" of the other and could exert no "influence" upon it),[69] and *for Being* (contrary to the claim such that the question of Being, even to the point of its reelaboration by Heidegger, should have no other source than the Greek one). Being, such as ontology grasped it, is certainly Greek. However, if Being "is" other than as ontology understood it, and if this other could be confusedly sought at first and then in some sense revealed by Heidegger, it is because Being inhabited, if provisionally, a different ground than the Greek one. And, contrary to what he will argue later, this different ground was not "foreign soil."

2. Nothingness

We have seen that an early interest in theological questions could have incited Heidegger to cast a critical gaze upon Greek ontology. The impetus thus given, he will devote his work to "deepening" the question of Being—all the way to renewing entirely the way it was worked out. One of the principal foci of this renewal consists in underscoring a difference: Being is not constant presence, and still less a supreme being. Being—properly speaking—"is" not; it is not an entity. What then is it? The first step toward answering such a question consists in saying: with and within the entity is divulged, in some way, the Other of all entities, this other that is Nothing—a nothing [*cet autre qui n'est Rien—un néant*]. It is only when man passes beyond the entity in its entirety, to withdraw into the inside of this nothing, understood as active nihilation, that he can relate to the entity.[70] Thus, nothing appears, in the years surrounding *Being and Time*, as the condition for the revelation of beings. Far from being reduced to a pure negation, nothingness gets referred to the "Being of beings,"[71] although the nature of this reference is not yet clearly established.

Later, that which the 1929 lecture was still calling Nothing [*Nichts*], albeit sensing already its quality of plenitude [*caractère de plénitude*], will be recognized not only as participating somehow in Being, but also as constituting its proper mode of unfolding, that is, its very essence: "That which is never a being discloses itself as that which distinguishes itself from all beings and which we are calling Being."[72] And it is this "nothing that is not nothing" that, still later, Heidegger will hear resounding in Hölderlin's "sacred Chaos,"[73] identified with the primordial gaping from which all openings arise and, thereby, all beings. In brief, one of the essential traits of Being, such as Heidegger endeavors to think it, is its character as nothingness, which will be specified later on, in a more complex movement of thought, as an abyss (that is, the groundless [*Abgrund*]) and as withdrawal (that is, self-concealment). That such a conception of nothingness could have given rise (notably, in its initial formulations) to so many misinterpretations, tells us to what point it was unheard of, in regard to the traditional mode of thinking in the West.

What was understood, in effect, by nothingness? Heidegger himself drew up a brief review of it in his lecture of 1929. Simplifying to the extreme, it might be said that scarcely anything other than *Chaos* and *Nihil* were known: *chaos*, in opposition to *kosmos*, is above all magma and disorder. Chaos is not nothing, but it is without form or face, matter deprived of *eidos*, therefore it can produce nothing. Thus conceived, nothing is not pure nullity, then, but it could in no way be endowed with power or creative energy.

With Christianity there appears a wholly other idea of nothingness: nihil is the radical absence of any being, absolute nonbeing. Considered within the perspective of creation, nihil becomes the pure absence of all things, starting from which (*ex nihilo*) God created all things. It is this conception that will be carried thereafter, as much by philosophy as by theology, including certain currents of Jewish theology insofar as the latter (like any theology) made use of imported concepts.

Yet what is the situation of nothingness in the Bible? The first two verses of Genesis amass a series of related terms to describe the "before" of all creation: *toho-va-vohu*,[74] *tehom* (abyss), *hoshech* (shadowy chasm)—all of which will be commented on at length by Jewish exegetes. It is this specific conception of nothingness that will occupy our attention here.

The point of departure is that, rather than conceiving this "before" from the outset as "nothing," the "Masters of the Midrash and the Kabbalah penetrate into the closed garden of Nothingness."[75] Immediately engaged in this direction, they discover, on the one hand, the living presence of nothingness ("The Being of Nothingness lives and has an existence, which, though detached from that of the created universe, is nevertheless real"),[76] and, on the other hand, the persistence of this presence. Nothingness is not simply pre-liminary, its tumult is not extinguished with creation but accompanies creation continuously, like a reservoir of forces always ready to rise up again: "ready, also, to respond to the call of Being were it suddenly to remember its original kinship with nothingness."[77]

It is not enough to say that this nothingness, out of which all things arise, is endowed with reality. Grasped in all its depth, "it is infinitely more real than any other reality."[78] That means that Jewish exegetes did not limit themselves to attributing to nothingness a kinship with Being, they sometimes went so far as to identify nothingness with Being. The Ayin, the no or nothingness, is then deciphered—as the letters of its name allow—as *Ani*, the "yes," or Being. "The *Ayin* is the whole, and yet he is unapproachable. The Ayin is immediately present and yet cannot be found. He is near, and yet far away."[79] There are many attempts to illustrate this primary assertion: "Far from being the negation of essence, nothingness is the essence of Being."[80]

Such theses are already found in the Midrash. However they will find their fullest extension only in the masters of the Kabbalah. It is the Kabbalah that develops, in effect, beyond the mere idea of an existent and active nothingness, a truly mystical conception in which nothingness, identified with what is most intimate and absolute in Being, comes to be understood as God himself. This means, conversely, that God will be understood *as nothingness*. He is hidden and eternally unknowable only because he has withdrawn "into the depths of his nothingness."[81]

Such a bold perspective will lead kabbalists to reinterpret the doctrine of creation *ex nihilo*: for them, this no longer signifies the creation of all things *on the basis of* nothing, but creation *out of* God, on the basis of that Nothing that is God himself.[82] A number of texts will thus be reread in the same perspective. For example, according to the *Zohar*, the traditional prayer of Psalm 130:1, "I have called unto Thee from the depths," does not mean, "I have called unto Thee from the depths [where I am]," but rather "From of the depths [in which Thou art] I call Thee up."[83] The nothingness, recognized as unfolding its presence, not only within existence but also in God himself, then becomes the Ayn Sof, the infinite, source of all emanations or manifestations, and "root of all roots."[84] If people have misinterpreted this idea, it is because, unable to recognize the wealth of the nothingness and inapt at comprehending its infinite fullness, they have called it Nothing [*Rien*].[85]

We thus find ourselves confronted with three radically distinct conceptions: the Greek nothingness-as-confusion; the nothing-as-negation of metaphysics; the nothingness-as-power [*néant-puissance*] of Jewish mysticism. Now Heidegger, as we know, attempted to render to nothingness its fullness, recalling its intimate kinship with Being itself.[86] In this sense, he subscribes to the third of these conceptions, if only with a view to renewing it. Yet, in his work, the recourse to the concept of nothingness was as yet but a provisional "station," something like a first approach, still negative, to Being—the same Being that will find its proper essence only later on, once it is recognized as Withdrawal.

3. Withdrawal

At the end of his oeuvre, Heidegger considered that the "fundamental experience" providing an impetus to his entire reflection was that of *Seinsvergessenheit*:[87] the forgetting of Being, that same Being that he acknowledged very early as not "being" in the way of an entity, that is, that it was the Other of all entities. But it remained for him to account for this forgetting. If the latter was first attributed to thinking, it was subsequently recognized as proceeding from Being itself: thinking is only characterized by forgetting because Being unfolds its essence as withdrawal. The passage from the problematic of forgetting to that of withdrawal was made possible by the *Kehre* or turn. To be sure, the turn, such as it was outlined at the beginning of the 1930s, was not yet an acknowledgement of withdrawal, but it already takes history seriously. And it is on the path opened by this new point of departure that the thinker was able, from 1935, and above all in the 1940s,[88] to locate the "remaining-absent" of Being over the entire course of its history: an absence that was quickly recognized to be the sole modality of Being's dispensation. Thus appears the idea of the clearing or lighting *as* withdrawal, whereby access to the essence of Being and of the truth is finally made possible.

Let us consider more closely this withdrawal, as essential origin and foundation of the forgetting of Being. The act by which Being withdraws or eludes us is recognized as constitutive of its unfolding. It is in withdrawing that Being can give rise [*donner lieu*] to beings; in concealing itself Being can make possible every disclosure, and thus, properly speaking, "be" itself. Whence Heidegger's decisive formulation: "Being proffers itself to us while at the same time withdrawing its essence, concealing this essence in the withdrawal."[89] Because Being only proffers itself in withdrawing, we must hold its two traits together (which are, in truth, but "one and the same"),[90] and recognize that the entire history of Western thought lies in *this* paradoxical dispensation, in the form of an absence. Because beings can appear only in the light of Being, Being is always already given in every revelation of beings. Yet, because Being only gives itself in concealing itself as such, it has always already withdrawn for the benefit of beings alone—which appear thanks to Being—precisely *in order to* make their appearing possible.

Whence the forgetting. The withdrawal underway, forgetting can be resituated within the essence of Being [*à l'intérieur de l'essence de l'être*], to which the withdrawal gave us access. "The forgetting of Being, which constitutes the essence of metaphysics and was the impetus for *Being and Time*, belongs to the essence of Being itself."[91] The circle thus closes: Being was forgotten only because it slips away, and it slips away because in evasion lies its unique manner of "being."

There is therefore no other being than that which withdraws for the benefit of beings. And there is no other God, in the Bible, than the *hidden* God. The theme of the hidden God, as Stanislas Breton has pointed out,[92] is not reducible to that of the unknown God, with which it was sometimes confused. If Psalm 65, "Unto Thee, silence alone is fitting praise,"[93] recognizes that no language reaches the height of the unpronounceable Name, the exclamation in Isaiah 45:15 ("Verily, Thou art a God that hidest thyself") is an affirmation of the proper mode of the presence of God. This is the presence that determines man's attitude in regard to God: it is an attitude of confidence *despite* the mystery, one of waiting despite silence and the night, as we see again in Isaiah 8:17 ("And I will wait upon the Lord, that hideth his face from the house of Jacob, and I will look for him").[94]

Although it crosses through all of Christian theology to the point of becoming central to its mysticism, in the specifically Jewish reading of the Bible the theme of the hidden God nevertheless finds a wholly surprising incarnation, surpassing by far—even inverting—the classical idea of a God who hides himself in his creation. This was the doctrine of Tsim-tsum, developed by Isaac Luria, the kabbalist of Safed, around 1550.[95] Originally, the problem for him was to determine "how there can be a world if God is everywhere."[96] An early Midrash ventured the idea of a "concentration" of all God's power, that is, of his presence as well, into a single point (the holy of holies). It was on this occasion that the term *Tsim-tsum* was first used. But the great value of Luria's doctrine lies precisely in the fact that he invokes this text only to reverse its perspective radically: as Luria presents it, Tsim-tsum "designates not the concentration of God *into* a single point, but rather his withdrawal *far* from a point."[97] To Luria, this withdrawal alone seems to be such as to permit the resolution of his initial question. Originally, God was everywhere, yet to make the world possible, it was necessary that he contract, that he withdraw into himself as it were. This represents a radically innovative interpretation of the "eclipse" of God: God is in no way hidden in the world, but withdrawn or folded back into himself, literally "engulfed" [*abîmé*],[98] *in order* that the world might be.

We can thus see that far from insisting, as the tradition was wont to do, upon the act by which "God comes out of himself, communicates and reveals himself," Luria's Kabbalah directs our attention paradoxically to the act by which "God limits himself, pulls back into himself, and contracts his essence."[99] The God that reveals himself is then replaced or sublated by the God who withdraws. But the second God does not simply replace the first: the second makes the first possible. The very movement of creation, up until then seen as a unitary phenomenon, finds itself separated into two acts: the one, an exile or withdrawal into self, the other a coming out of self, a donation or a giving of self. These two acts must necessarily be held together, and all the analyses of Tsim-tsum endeavor, each in their way, to make this paradoxical unity audible. "While it withdraws into himself, the Infinite leaves behind himself an empty space. In this way, he creates a lack, comparable to shadows."[100] As these shadows are the source of all light, Betty Rojtman defines brightness itself, with a superb expression, as "the residue that [God] left as the trace of his infolding."[101]

Luria's school thus makes a drama of creation, having the form of "combat" or "tension," like an incessant struggle in which all that is is engendered: "Every stage involves a double strain: i.e., the light that streams back into God, and that which flows out from him, and but for this perpetual tension, this ever-repeated effort with which God holds himself back, nothing in the world would exist."[102]

In this way God is not limited to "concealing his face." In the perspective of Tsim-tsum, God, properly speaking, "is" only through hiding himself for the benefit of his creation. Again, as Rojtman says, and I will leave her the last word in this analysis: "the very existence of the world rests upon the first withdrawal of the In-itself [*l'En-soi*], whereby creation becomes possible in the gaping void of contracted light, and reality shapes itself in its very distance from the focus." At the end of this singular process, "what remains in our hands is a vibration, the perception of a relation."[103]

4. Provisional Conclusion

What, then, have I tried to demonstrate? Did I intend to prove that Heidegger had read the *Zohar* because he conceives nothingness as a reserve and as a certain richness? Did I mean to show that, when he comes to reflect on the domain of Being's withdrawal [*dimension de retrait de l'être*], Heidegger "is inspired" by Isaac Luria and the Safed kabbalists? By no means. The question of knowing *whether* and *how* certain elements, characteristic of the Hebrew cluster, might have been carried by the Western memory and transmitted to Heidegger will be examined in the following chapter. It could in no way be resolved by the simple notion of "influence," and still less by that of a "borrowing."

I have simply sought to show that, from his earliest approach (at once fascinated and critical in nature),[104] to the Aristotelian problematic, up to his last reflections on the *Lichtung* as the "clearing left by a withdrawal," Heidegger's thought remains focused on a single question, which incontestably opened *as a question* in Greece. Yet I have tried to show that he works the question out differently than the Greeks, perhaps entirely differently than it could have been elaborated in the Greek language. For this reason, it is fair to say that the Greeks were the first and only ones to pose the question of Being as such. It is likewise fair to affirm that the comprehension of Being qua being of beings, that is, as the (constant) presence of every present, is also Greek. However, though it came out of the question thus opened by the Greeks, Being, as Heidegger understood it, can in no way be reduced to the Greek understanding of it. The "truth of Being," of which Heidegger speaks, like the topology for it he proposes later on, are together a new and unusual development (one that we may consider to be "properly Heideggerian") of a question initially posed in the Greek world.

Now this development was effectuated thanks to categories that, while lacking any Greek equivalent, are nevertheless not without precedent. A number of the most innovative traits guiding Heidegger's approach *to Being* find something like an echo of anticipation in the universe of Hebraic thought, where traits (if not similar to Heidegger's, then at least proximate) served, over the course of the history of biblical commentaries, in their approach *to God*. The most marked of these traits—at least with regard to Heidegger—were examined above; but it would be necessary to supplement these with all those noted earlier (recollective thinking, the welcoming, recognition, etc.), at the same time as we examine later ones (the *Ereignis* or "enowning" and the problematic of donation). All these traits contribute to Heidegger's approach to Being, even as they find their response on another scene.

This certainly does not mean that Heidegger had direct knowledge of that other scene. Neither does it mean that the Being of which he speaks might simply be equated with the biblical God. Every attempt to reduce the former to the latter—or to perceive in Heidegger's Being a transcription or secularization of God—has ended in failure—it could hardly be otherwise given the great distance between the two registers. But that perhaps means that (this is the line I would be inclined to follow) if Heidegger so radically renewed the Greek comprehension of Being, he did so on the basis of thought forms drawn from another source, a source initially related, like the entire biblical universe, to God. That means that we find ourselves before the reappearance in Heidegger's work of *categories* closely tied to a certain heritage, aiming to reflect on a *question* come straight from an other heritage as well.

But, naturally, using these categories to renew a question foreign to them amounts to taking them up in an exclusively formal manner, that is, on condition of abandoning their biblical meaning. The form/content distinction is facile, to be sure. It is no doubt only half-adequate, moreover, to consider the problem that occupies us here. Yet, it may indicate at least a direction, which remains to be clarified, and allow us to situate the site of a problem, if only in still inappropriate terms. The adaptation of forms of thought of Hebraic origin to a Greek question-content (Being) implied the abandonment of their Hebraic contents. Their contents, that is, God, are given up, but so too is the domain indissociable from God in the biblical universe—the Law and, thereby, ethics.

This may lead us to understand why Being—such as Heidegger thinks it—which is, in a certain sense, *closest* to the Hebraic universe, can also be seen as constituting the *most distant*, most foreign pole to everything that Jewish memory cultivates, and more broadly, to everything biblically inspired traditions preserve. This extreme proximity and this equally extreme distance are not as contradictory as it might seem. Perhaps they are but two aspects of a single relationship. In effect, if the proximity concerns forms—or precisely because it concerns *only* forms—then it amounts to an authentic negation of the Hebraic universe, which could not sanction such distinctions. To retain of this universe only that which is liable to permit us another approach to Being is to retain nothing of it. For the biblical lesson may not be "utilized"; form and content therein are indissociable. To utilize it while tearing it out of the Law that is its focus and meaning is no longer to follow this lesson, but to combat it, so far as this is possible for humans or for thinking.

This is what the work of Emmanuel Lévinas attests, in an illuminating fashion, and is, at the same time, what explains his position regarding Heidegger.

III. From God to Being: The Abandonment of Ethics. The Debate with Emmanuel Lévinas

It is no doubt the work of Lévinas that has contributed the most to awaking contemporary philosophical thought to the possibilities built up within the Hebraic universe. The work could only make this contribution because, as indefatigable mediator, it had first allowed the Hebraic universe to "enter into philosophy" by drawing from "Jewish wisdom" [*sagesse juive*] all the elements needed for a dialogue with "Greek wisdom" [*sagesse grecque*].[105]

The "Athenian moderation," and the "paroxysm of Jerusalem,"[106] thus find themselves articulated one to the other in Lévinas, whose entire effort consists in bringing about their juncture without erasing their differences. To "express, in Greek, those principles of which Greece knew nothing,"[107] is to cause a rigorous thinking to arise, within the field of philosophy, even though it was not Greek-inspired.

Such a thought—the same one that Lévinas's oeuvre endeavors to work out—would be a thinking *of the Other*, understood as "Wholly Other" [*l'Autre comme "tout-Autre"*]. To be sure, this is an Other that has not ceased to concern philosophy, yet, barring exceptions,[108] it is one that philosophy has never been able to find without reducing it, because philosophy remains the thinking *of Being*, in conformity with its primary Greek orientation. Now, the thinking of Being is fundamentally a thinking of the Same [*pensée du Même*]: "Western philosophy coincides with the disclosure of the Other [*l'Autre*], wherein the Other showing itself as being loses its alterity. Philosophy is stricken, from its infancy, with a terror of the

Other who remains Other [*l'Autre qui demeure Autre*]; it carries an insurmountable allergy to it. It is for this reason that it is essentially a philosophy of Being."[109]

"Something," nevertheless, resists the hold of the same, something that is precisely not reducible to any thing: the other person [*autrui*]. The appearance of the other person [*autrui*] comes to interrupt, or to trouble, the order just described. This appearance keeps the Same from being a principle, from resting upon itself in peace. It is thus on this precise point that everything hinges. Thinking can find there a new point of departure, aimed at a wholly other constellation, as yet unexplored. "If the Same does not rest, in complete peace, upon itself, then philosophy may not seem so indissolubly linked to the adventure that encompasses every Other in the Same."[110]

This means that as long as philosophy defines itself as ontology—which it did from its initial, Greek constitution, even though the word had not yet been coined—it seeks the Other untiringly, but without ever being able to reach it, since philosophy never leaves the ground of Being, which is the ground of the Same. Yet a thinking nourished by the double lesson, biblical and Talmudic, is able to find the Other as such, that Wholly-Other that philosophy sought in vain. And this thinking finds it *philosophically*, although it does not encounter the Other in ontology (where it always sought the Other), but rather in ethics (where the Other remained ignored): "The absolutely Other is the other person."[111]

On condition that we do not reduce it to the familiar *alter ego*, the Other is the other person finally recognized in its irreducibility, that is, as Face [*Visage*]. The Face, in effect, because its nudity is pure expression, "*is* by itself, and is not by reference to a system";[112] because it is outside every system, that is, also outside all totality, the face "reveals the Infinite."[113] That is, what the Lévinasian vocabulary calls the Face proceeds from the "absolutely absent":[114] exceeding all presence, but also all that is contrary to presence, it interrupts the order of the Same. As Maurice Blanchot says, endeavoring to translate the enigmatic mode of appearance of the Face, "it is that presence that I cannot dominate with my gaze, which always overflows both the representation I can conceive of it and every form, every image, every view, every idea in which I could affirm it, or fix it, or simply let it be present."[115] It is therefore by way of a phenomenology of the Face,

understood as the trace of the Infinite, that Lévinas's first great work places at the heart of philosophy the concept of *alterity*. In this way, Lévinas
has worked back from the order of the Same to the Wholly-Other, who
escapes him absolutely, in the sense that the Other can no longer be integrated into the Same, or go from a "logic of Being" to a "logic of the face,"
as it has been called.[116]

Yet, by the same token, this other—finally preserved as Wholly-Other, and who, as such, marks the limits of the reduction to the Same that
is the thinking of Being—affords us access to the region called the "otherwise than being."[117] If *Totality and Infinity* still saw in the immediacy of
the face an entity that comes before the disclosure of Being and unseats its
privilege ("the notion of the Face . . . signifies the philosophical priority of
a being [*de l'étant*] over Being [*sur l'être*]"),[118] *Otherwise Than Being* takes a
decisive step: no longer limiting itself to thinking otherwise the relationship between Being and beings, it endeavors to open the field to "meanings beyond the ontological difference."[119] From the one to the other great
work of Lévinas, a single movement is underway, in search of itself in the
first work only to come to its end in the second. *Totality and Infinity* discovered the Face as that which interrupts the order of the Same. *Otherwise
Than Being* discovers, in the radical decentering characteristic of subjectivity, that which exceeds the very register of Being, *considering* its difference
from beings.

Yet, if the otherwise than being is announced in subjectivity, inasmuch as the latter is initially structured through its exposure to the other
person [*autrui*], then the thinking oriented toward that other person, that
is, ethics, is not a branch of philosophy. It is that which shakes all ontology
from within. It is that which is found, from the time of the Greek dawn,
covered over by ontology without ever being able to be erased by it. It is
stricto sensu "first philosophy."[120]

Thus, the trace of the Infinite, such as it is marked on the face of the
Other, finds itself placed at the foundation of ontology itself. But where is
this trace preserved? What text remains crossed or marked by it, functioning as the shelter of pure alterity? Certainly not the philosophical edifice,
nor even those "anti-Scriptures" that the pre-Socratic texts have become,
according to Lévinas,[121] but rather the Bible, and more specifically that
which the Talmudic reading retains of it. The heritage of Jerusalem, far
from being reduced to a set of beliefs or religious utterances, finds itself in-

vested with an eminent function in the order of thought: as guardian and guarantor of the Other, that is, of that which concerned Athens itself, although the philosophy born there was never able to do it "justice."

In recognizing in the other person the paradoxical presence of the Wholly-Other—and, thereby, the invitation to pass "beyond" Being—Lévinas has "expressed, in Greek, the principles of which Greece knew nothing."[122] Throughout the problematic of the Other and the Face, the Trace and the Good, Lévinas has "brought to mind" [*il a fait "venir à l'idée"*] the proper ground of the Hebraic tradition, and shown that it could function, even within the philosophical field, as the most decisive alternative to the up until then dominant problematic of being and presence, mastery and reason.

Now, if Heidegger, as I have attempted to show in this study, has indeed also contributed in some way (albeit in *another* way) to bringing this ground to our thinking, Lévinas's problematic ought to have and to acknowledge a certain closeness to that of Heidegger; and this, at the same time that Lévinas ought to acknowledge a certain closeness to the common "ground" [*fonds*] whence both thinkers drew inspiration.

Yet it is precisely Heidegger whom Lévinas places at the greatest possible distance from both his own thinking and from biblical teachings. The reading of Heidegger that Lévinas proposes is peculiar. Far from distinguishing between the ontological tradition and the radical critique Heidegger presents of it, Lévinas considers the latter's work as the site in which the entirety of that tradition is gathered and aggravated. Heidegger "does not destroy, he *sums up* a whole current of Western philosophy."[123] But even this claim is still insufficient; and we read a few pages later: "Heidegger does not only sum up a whole evolution of Western philosophy. He *exalts* it."[124] Effacing the "leap" Heidegger accomplished—or taking no account of it—Lévinas has him participating in the wandering that Heidegger continually criticized.

The matter is especially striking in regard to the word that is central to Heidegger's work: *Being*. Far from acknowledging Heidegger's Being as that which was *forgotten* throughout all of the ontological tradition (or, as that which withdrew from it, was not taken in charge, thought, or even glimpsed by that tradition—in a word, the tradition's radical unthought [*son impensé radical*]), Lévinas sees in Being the *recapitulation* of all that philosophy thought under its name, which is why, moreover, Lévinas persists in speaking of Heideggerian "ontology."

This is in no way a pure quarrel of words. It is *every aspect* of what Heidegger called Being that must be crossed out, or resolutely neglected, in order for Being to be reduced to the Being of ontology. But how could it be otherwise when the Being that Heidegger tried to make us find again in our memories "is," precisely, only thanks to its difference from what ontology had called "being," which itself was, in truth, only the being-ness of a being [*qui n'était . . . que l'étantité de l'étant*]? Because the least of Being's aspects bespeaks this difference, we cannot dismiss the difference without effacing all that which characterizes "Being itself" in Heidegger's work. And it is just that which comes about in the reading Lévinas proposes of Heidegger. What of the irreducibility of Being to mere "constant presence"? It is held to be negligible in light of the "perseverance" supposed to define Being.[125] What of Being's withdrawal in history? It is denied for the sake of its exclusive and manifest domination within this same history.[126] What of Being's radical resistance to all phenomenality? Denied in favor of the "regime of appearing" ["*l'apparoir*"] that would be "the very movement of Being."[127] And what of Being's difference from beings, finally, and the Fold that separates it from them? These Lévinas interprets as an "amphibology," that is, as the perfect reversibility "in which Being and beings can be understood *and identified with one another*."[128]

Lévinas's constant reduction of Heidegger's thought to the tradition from which it diverges, like the assimilation of Being, its central term, to the mere being-ness, on which ontology focuses, finds its principal incarnation in the word by which Lévinas "translates" Heideggerian Being: *essence*, a word that likewise will allow Lévinas to confuse Heidegger's Being with its other. From the preface to *Otherwise Than Being*, Lévinas insists upon the fact that what his book calls essence, which he will later write *essance*,[129] is indeed Being in Heidegger's sense. "The dominant note necessary to understanding this discourse and even its title must be emphasized at the opening of this book. . . . the term *essence* here expresses *Being*, as different from *beings*, the German *Sein* as distinct from *Seiendes*."[130] One could hardly speak more clearly. Yet, at the same time, the word *essence* encompasses the entire ontological tradition (where Being is precisely not different from beings), that is, the entire theme of constant presence, whose meaning and limits Heidegger showed precisely.

Having thus disburdened Heidegger's Being from those principal traits by which it was Other (than any being or entity, thus likewise the Wholly-Other), Lévinas brings forth—facing this Being that has been reduced to the Same—an Other that would be radically opposed to it. The "otherwise than Being" is thus presented not as merely the other of Being such as ontology intended it (that would be the precise definition of Heidegger's Being, which could only be thanks to its separation from what was always called by this name), but as other than Heidegger's Being itself—Being in Heidegger's sense having been cut off from its difference, and then reduced to that against which it defined itself, the Being of ontology.

I have attempted to show the strange alchemy that Lévinas performed on the Heideggerian text. It seems to me to amount to filling an abyss on one side, in order better to mark a separation on the other. The abyss that separates Heidegger from the ontological tradition is narrowed to the point of erasure, in order to bring forth better the gap between Heidegger and the thinking of the Other, such as Lévinas elaborated it, recalling the Jewish tradition. If I have thus endeavored to rehabilitate another reading of Heidegger's text, I did not do so only to recall everything that separates Heidegger from traditional ontology, but also to make possible an understanding of all that draws him close to the biblical universe. More specifically, I have ventured to show all that brings Heidegger's Being (insofar as we leave its true nature) close to the Lévinasian Other. For, it does not suffice to say that Being, such as Heidegger conceives it, is not reducible to the reading Lévinas proposes of it. In truth (though this is just the other side of the same move), the Other such as it is thought by Lévinas, presents close analogies with the Being he insists it surpasses, but he surpasses it only after having distorted it, at least in part.

In effect, if it is a matter for Lévinas of "thinking the possibility of being uprooted from essence,"[131] then this uprooting could not be realized once and for all; strictly speaking, it can never be "realized." This uprooting takes place only as the memory of a *difference* (always already covered over in some way by the very thing from which it differs),[132] as the concern for an *asymmetry* (always already erased within the reversibility of an equivalence),[133] as a nonsynchronizable *dia-chrony*.[134] The uprooting from essence (that is, from the order of Being) can thus reach subjectivity (understood as absolute alterity), but the uprooting only reaches subjectivity by not itself "being," which is the sole way of not reducing it "to the annexations by essence."[135]

This means, by the same token, that the Other as thought by Lévinas through the concept of subjectivity is only as "a hither side, a pre-original, a non-representable, an invisible,"[136] and, thereby, as an irreducible "enigma."[137] It is that which, in the very order of presence and of Being, exceeds this order—yet which can only exceed it in being inscribed within it, because it has no separate positivity. It is therefore that which is only by erasing itself for the benefit of what it makes possible, and which, in thereby erasing itself, calls for forgetting.

How should we not see in this astonishing structure, which governs the entire problematic of the Other, traits already characteristic of Heidegger's Being? The proximity is so evident that Lévinas's most faithful interpreter, Jacques Rolland, could not avoid noting it. At the time of the Conversations of the Centre Sèvres (Paris, 1984), Rolland not only recognized "the twisting or deformation to which Lévinas subjected what is conventionally called the second Heidegger"[138]—that is, he underscored all that Lévinas refused to grant to Heidegger's Being—he also points out all that Lévinas's thought *owes* to Heidegger.

It remains the case that the three concepts through which the discourse of the "otherwise than being" passes only function . . . according to a formal scheme such that the concepts include in themselves the moment of their withdrawal before that which they let be and which is thought as present, covering and denying and confining to oblivion that from which it comes or which lets it be. In this sense, the concepts of *Otherwise Than Being* function according to a scheme formally identical to what governs Being in Heidegger's sense of the term.[139]

We thus arrive at a double remark: Heidegger is closer to the biblical universe than he says he is, and Lévinas is closer to Heidegger than he believes. Does that mean that Emmanuel Lévinas could have "misread" Heidegger's texts, that he might "not have seen" the proximity between Heidegger and his own thought, and the ground from which the latter drew its nourishment? Lévinas was, doubtless, less familiar with the later texts than with *Being and Time*. But this explanation is far from sufficient. It seems to me that Lévinas knows very well—better than anyone, no doubt—all that connects Heidegger with the thinking of the Other, such as it was developed by Lévinas and sheltered in the Jewish tradition. Yet it also seems that, through an immense and decisive *foreshortening* [*raccourci*], Lévinas also knows that this proximity (however great it might be) is *nothing*, that it is absolutely negligible considering the distance that separates them, which is radical. This distance is radical because, whatever the structures of alterity that pass through Heidegger's oeuvre (donation, welcome and passivity, memory and gratitude, promise and salvation, etc.), the Other in all its concreteness is effectively absent from this oeuvre. That Other who is God, in his transcendence, but also and primarily its trace in the face of the other person. This is the immense absence that Lévinas discovers from the first in Heidegger's oeuvre, leading him to deny to Heidegger any right to speak in the name of alterity, since the only possible site of alterity is decisively misunderstood—even erased—therein.

We can thus say that Lévinas "forgets" all that which in Being, in Heidegger's sense, might be liable to approximate it to the Other, and, more broadly, all that which, in Heidegger's work, could evoke the biblical universe. Yet this forgetting is a decision, a considered decision that takes a *precise measure* of a distance, while foregoing any calculation [*renonçant à faire nombre*], in order to "count" only the "essential." Now the essential in the heritage that comes to us from Jerusalem—in any case, the essential as it appears to the inheritor who is Lévinas—is precisely not pure structures, but rather the Other incarnate in them, who alone gives them their meaning. And the essential in Heidegger's work is that this Other is misprized or unknown there, even if its structures are maintained or even underscored. For these structures are *nothing*; there is no shared vicinity, no proximity that might be worth noting or even glimpsing, since they are empty.

Forgetting in the form of a decision: this is how I would be inclined to grasp the apparently "deformed" reading Lévinas proposes of Heidegger's work.[140] But Lévinas himself gave an explanation for it on at least one occasion. Without speaking directly of Heidegger, or of the strange interpretation he proposed of Heidegger's work, Lévinas stated, it seems, the *rule* that governs and legitimates his interpretation. It is a matter, he says, "of hearing beyond essence the subjectivity of the subject, as starting . . . from a forgetting of Being." What does this singular forgetting—singular because assumed and insisted on—mean? Let us listen to Lévinas: "Not of an 'unregulated' forgetting [*un oubli sans contrôle*] . . . but a forgetting that would be an ignorance in the sense that nobility ignores what is not noble, and in the sense that certain monotheists do not recognize, while knowing, what is not the highest. Such ignorance is beyond consciousness; it is an open-eyed ignorance."[141]

We comprehend thereby why even those occasional proximities noted by Lévinas are immediately denied by him as not stating the same thing, appearances to the contrary. But what about the whole thematic of passivity in Heidegger? It is recalled only to be immediately set aside: the passivity of the subject would be "more passive than any passivity."[142] And freedom, which Heidegger conceives as always already given over to obedience? Lévinas accepts it, only to add immediately, "obedience makes [freedom] arise and does not put it into question."[143] And Being as mystery? Heidegger *says* this; but in the final instance "Being is equivalent to phosphorescence, to light, it is converted into intelligibility."[144] And transcendence? Pure appearance "for, once Being has been disclosed, even partially, even in Mystery, it becomes immanent."[145] Finally, and above all, there is this expression, apparently paradoxical, which sums up the double movement that we find at work in all the preceding texts: "even if Heidegger conceives the comprehension of Being as gratitude and obedience . . . [he] lightens Being of its alterity."[146]

In this way Lévinas is led to mark a distance, even to exaggerate it deliberately, not in order to caricature Heidegger's thought, but on the contrary to disclose that which is most proper to it. And what is most proper to it is the absence of the only Other that might give meaning to the concept of alterity. In this sense, Heidegger's work stands *farthest* from the Lévinasian endeavor, as also from the heritage to which the latter claims to be faithful.

So far and yet so near. Lévinas brings to light all that separates Heidegger from the Hebraic heritage. I have tried to set forth all that approximates him to it. The two positions are, nevertheless, not as contradictory as it might seem. Yet they can only be reconciled by turning to the form/content distinction I ventured to propose above—not, it is true, without hesitation.[147] Following this perspective, we may grasp the possible (and no doubt necessary) double reading of Heidegger's work. We may understand it as called for, in some manner, by that work itself. For we indeed find in Heidegger the double gesture: at the same time as he takes up formally a certain number of structures proper to the biblical universe, notably all those evoking a radical alterity, he abandons all that constituted, for this universe, the alterity of this Other: the ethical dimension. In this sense, Lévinas is perfectly justified in discerning in Heidegger's work a radical opposition to Jewish memory, and to his own thought that claims to follow it. Nonetheless, it remains that this opposition is brought about within strikingly similar structures. Let us go farther: it is to Heidegger's credit that—though he abandoned what is for Lévinas, and probably also for all those who claim to follow the Hebrew Bible, the essential part of the message—he nevertheless transmitted something of this message to philosophy, and perhaps even to the philosophy of Lévinas.

This is why I am inclined to think that, among the various formulations Lévinas put forward, some are more appropriate than others to the Heideggerian oeuvre. To reduce Heidegger to a thinking of the Same is after all rather difficult, as such a qualification goes against the avowed intention of the text and, in the final analysis, against the letter of the text itself. But to understand it as a thinking of the Neuter—as Lévinas did in his first great work as well as in more recent texts[148]—is much more evocative. It is, in effect, undeniable that the Neuter is found everywhere in the late Heidegger: whether it is a question of *the* god (who no longer has a proper name), of donation (which is faceless and comes from nowhere: *Es gibt*, it gives), of serenity (which, to be sure, is awaiting and welcoming, but which has nothing of hope, for this awaiting is without content),[149] of the call (which still calls, whatever it says),[150] and even of language (which, in a sense, says effectively nothing other than itself—or which, if it says Being, only says it in a tautological mode, since Being is already language)—in all these cases one form is operative. It is at once coercive and remarkably anonymous. This neutrality is not necessarily proof, as Jean-Luc Marion suggested, of "idolatry."[151] Maria Villela-Petit has shown that it is found in a number of mystical texts that "carry not the slightest trace of a divine, experienced as personal,"[152] without thereby being apt to be labeled "idolatry" (Marion) or paganism (Lévinas). My concern is thus not to "criticize" the neutrality of Being, as with Heidegger's other main terms. But I am interested here in its value as a *clue*: the clue to a *disidentification*, the clue that what was initially provided with a signifying identity, with a name, a place of origin, finds itself taken up formally and—because the appropriation remains formal—is condemned to neutrality.

This way of situating the Neuter is certainly no longer that of Lévinas (nor that, moreover, of Marion). In effect, Lévinas sees in the Neuter a primary ontological structure, which would not yet have been "awakened," as it were, to the Other. Just as signification is understood, in the final pages of *Otherwise Than Being*, as a process of "deneutralization,"[153] so subjectivity appears as the "stakes of a conquest over that which at once precedes and denies it: Being in the neutral, or the *there is*."[154] More sensitive to all that which, in the Heideggerian problematic (and right to Being, which constitutes its heart), *comes from elsewhere*, I am inclined instead to understand the neutrality of Being as itself having been *conquered* or *won* through the disidentification of an alterity that was initially "full." In other words, I conceive of neutrality as coming (at least partially) out of a movement of formalization applied to structures that spoke first of the Other, in its simultaneously religious and ethical dimension.

Whatever the order in which we find it appropriate to read the relationship between the Neuter and the Other, the theme of neutrality would confirm, in some sense, the analysis attempted in the preceding pages, on the basis of the couple: form and content. For, if Heidegger indeed utilized a Hebraic and biblical ground as a reservoir of forms, to think a wholly other question, then he had no other choice than the Neuter. Neutrality would thus derive, in all necessity, from this singular retrieval that, because it only took up the structures, was destined to anonymity.

Let us conclude. Being is indeed a Greek question, the development of which Heidegger thoroughly renews, using categories of thought that belonged initially to another heritage. But he only uses these categories to think Being and all that which was opened on the Greek ground. This amounts to saying that he only uses these categories after having emptied them of what constituted their weight of truth in the same heritage. In this sense, he keeps himself at an extreme distance from the Hebraic universe—if we take this universe seriously, that is, as Lévinas does. It remains true nonetheless that Heidegger rethought Being, like everything else that opened on Greek ground, by way of these categories. These thus find a new relevance in the field of thinking and, more broadly, in the West. Now, just as Lévinas may perhaps not always recognize all that approximates him to certain structures of Heidegger's thought, so too Heidegger—in a much more radical manner—does not always recognize what he owes to the sources from which Lévinas's work comes. Both men are right, no doubt: they are not speaking of the same thing. Yet one would understand them better, and one would grasp more clearly all that separates them, and which they emphasize, if they agreed to recognize that in some ways they use the same language. As always, it is a question of debt.

2

The Problem of Transmission

The preceding analyses all endeavored to show that something of the Hebraic heritage can be found in Heidegger and that it was probably transmitted to him without his ever saying anything about it, perhaps without his ever knowing anything about it. The question then becomes one of grasping how this heritage could "pass" into Heidegger's text, that is, how the transmission was brought about.

If this question was not posed from the beginning of our itinerary, that is because it was not decisive for it. Not primarily historical, our inquiry intended to set forth a *proximity* that could continue to teach us lessons even if it could not be interpreted in terms of filiation or descent. Only when this proximity was brought to light could we attempt to *explicate* it, that is, to advance certain hypotheses aiming to reconstitute its origins. The examination of the sources of Heidegger's work, therefore, could not give rise to the question we are studying here. Yet it may make a useful contribution toward resolving that question, by casting light on certain access routes by which the Hebraic legacy could come down to Heidegger.

Clearly, this cannot be a matter of direct influence. If, by his training and initial theoretical interest, Heidegger was well acquainted with theology, this was essentially a New Testament theology. And the biblical text itself, such as Heidegger calls on it—either to comment on it at length in the courses of his youth, or to evoke it periodically in the later work— seems to be reduced to the Gospels and the Pauline letters. To be sure, he occasionally names the prophets or, more often still, the God of the Old

Testament. But he always does so on the basis of Greek etymologies. This is what Bernard Dupuy notes, deducing (legitimately, to my mind) that the Bible to which Heidegger refers, and the only one he knows, is the Septuagint. "Heidegger is a reader of the Greek Bible. He encounters the word God in the Bible on the basis of its translation."[1] In other words, if we determine his readings based on the traces they left in his work, Heidegger knew Neo-testamentary texts and theology well, no doubt less well the Old Testament, no Hebrew, and still less the specifically Hebraic tradition, including the Talmud and Midrash, whose existence he did not even seem to suspect.

We could hardly speak of an influence, then, in the classic sense of the term. Would it thus be a matter of a coincidence pure and simple, one of those fortuitous encounters that take place sometimes between currents of thought that nothing, however, connects? The overlappings here are too numerous, too regular (perhaps even too resolutely *ignored* by him, as paradoxical as such an argument might seem), not to attest to a filiation. Yet this remains a necessarily underground filiation: since Heidegger's thought could not have been directly inspired by the Hebraic tradition (which it did not know), but since it also could not have developed independently of that tradition (so considerable is the vicinity it shares with the tradition), the sole means by which we can resolve the aporia is to admit that Heidegger drew unawares from a heritage he never acknowledged.

How was such an act possible? The first, and most essential, point of passage seems to me to be constituted by his theology studies, which form in effect the principle of a double dependency: (1) A dependency of Heidegger's thought (including the late thought) in regard to certain New Testament notions; this dependency was partly evoked in the previous chapter, and we have seen that it was formally acknowledged by Heidegger even as he neglected it in the reconstruction he proposed of his oeuvre.[2] (2) There is the dependency for these Neo-testamentary notions on their Hebraic and Old Testament soil. Now, *this* dependency goes radically unacknowledged, even occulted, by Heidegger. In this way, definite lines of thought can "pass" into his work, while being marked from the outset by a forgetfulness of their source.

Yet if Christian theology formed the first point of contact between Heidegger's thought in its early formation and the Hebraic heritage, it was not the only such point. My hypothesis is that, beyond just theology, it is the history and thought of the West, taken as a whole, that carries this heritage, if quietly. And, as a particularly vigilant witness to this history, Heidegger was able to discern in it not merely that which it admitted as its own, but also that which was held there in reserve.

Before unfolding this hypothesis for itself, we must go through all the facts. That is, we must attempt to set forth, using a few examples (those at our disposition in the present state of Heidegger's *Gesamtausgabe*), the double movement characteristic of the above-mentioned filiation that began to take shape in the 1920s: how a very ancient heritage could be transmitted while remaining masked in some way, and then taken up again, without being *identified* for all that.

I. New Testament Concepts in Heidegger's Early Courses [*de jeunesse*]: The "Formalization" Hypothesis (According to Lehmann)

Let us take up again the two Freiburg courses, about which we have sufficiently consistent information. What are the New Testament concepts that interested Heidegger at that time, and what becomes of that interest in his later work?

The principal part of the 1920 course is devoted to reflecting on two letters of Paul: the first, to the Thessalonians, and the second, to the Corinthians. From the Letter to the Thessalonians (he comments on chapters 4:13–18 and 5:1–11), Heidegger retains essentially the concept of *kairos*.[3] Let us recall the context in which it appears: the question Paul is treating is that of the coming of the Lord, or Parousia. After having expressed his desire not to leave the disciples "in ignorance" (1 Thess. 4:13), Paul adds nevertheless that they have no need to be informed "of the times and the seasons" (5:1). Heidegger points out that Paul gives no temporal indication,[4] nor even any concrete indication about the return of the Lord. He only emphasizes the *mode* of its coming—its suddenness—as attested in verse 2: " . . . the day of the Lord so cometh as a thief in the night." To this sudden character of the Lord's coming corresponds the human behavior of vigilance [*veille*]: "Ye, brothers, are not in darkness such that this day should surprise you like a thief. Yes, you are the sons of the day. . . . Let us not sleep as do the others, but keep watch and be sober" (5:5–8).[5]

This pair, formed by the suddenness (of what is to come) and vigilance (of those who await it) is what interests Heidegger. In effect, he sees in it a specific determination of time—"kairological" rather than "chronological"—at the same time that he perceives an equally specific determination of existence: its determination as vigilance and availability [*vigilance et disponibilité*].

Let us consider first the determination of time such as it can be set forth from the Pauline experience. In the first place, to insist upon suddenness is to characterize the temporal event by the way in which it is given, rather than by its content. This is a difference that Heidegger deepens to the point of creating an opposition: "If man tries by means of chronological computations or content-orientated characterizations to define the inaccessible event, which suddenly bursts upon the scene, the event upon which his life is based, he then eliminates that which should determine his life as the always inaccessible and replaces it with the secured, the accessible."[6]

In the second place, this suddenness amounts to an advent, a coming in essence unforeseeable. The present gets placed "under the threat that comes to it from the future."[7] Every event arises from the future, unknown and undecidable, to surprise the present. "The *kairos* can neither be awaited (*erwartet*), nor grasped (*ergriffen*), for the importance of its ungraspable quality would be broken in the representation of a present prolonged into a future that we fundamentally already know."[8]

Consequently, in the third place, this threat coming from the future makes the present into the moment of *decision*, at the same time that the decision is the affair of the moment. In the moment, "everything" is in play,[9] although nothing of it may be calculated. The *kairos* "places it on the razor's edge in the decision,"[10] and thus signals the failure of representation and mastery: "the thinking which computes time and turns toward accessible 'objective' contents, thereby disguising for itself its relation to the inaccessible future, will not escape ruin."[11]

This kairological experience of time, which excludes all anticipation and every appropriation, leads to a determination of existence—which Heidegger still calls "life" in this period—as *openness* and *resoluteness*. Only he who is constantly "available" to the unforeseeable temporal event can welcome, in the moment of decision, that which comes to meet him. The two determinations are naturally indissociable from each other: "If the *kairos* can come suddenly, then man's resoluteness is necessary at each instant."[12] Through his resolute openness, man does not only live *in* time, he lives time itself in some manner; he experiences its unavailable truth.[13]

The same perspective is developed in the 1921 course devoted to Augustine. Augustine conceives the blessed life not in light of what it contains, but according to the way in which it is realized. It is this realization that holds Heidegger's attention. And he emphasizes its double character as historical and nonobjectifiable—nonobjectifiable precisely because it is historical, which is to say, temporal.[14]

What is therefore retained from the Christian experience of time— through the Pauline texts, then in those of Augustine—will mark, as Lehmann and Pöggeler both underscore, the entirety of Heidegger's work.[15] It is not only the existential Analytic that remains marked by the memory (and the vocabulary) of vigilance and awakening, by that of the imminent future and the unavailable, and by that of availability and openness. Even after the *Kehre* [turn], the imprint of the eschatological *kairos* remains perceptible in the notion of destiny, in the being able-to-wait proper to serenity.[16] It extends finally into the *Ereignis* [event, or "en-owning"], which, as Jean Greisch notes, "inherits the structural traits of the instant, starting with that which makes the moment into a space of encounter."[17]

Did Heidegger recognize such an imprint? And if so, how did he interpret it? To my knowledge, such a trace is hardly mentioned in the late work. Outside the periodic remark cited above on the role of his theological "origins" of his (passing) interest for hermeneutics,[18] we find no example after the *Kehre* of a connection acknowledged and commented on by Heidegger between elements of his own vocabulary and biblical conceptions, even New Testament ones. If we limit ourselves to the questions raised above, nowhere are the *Ereignis*, destiny, or more broadly, time in its essential futurition referred to the Pauline *kairos*.

Things are otherwise in *Being and Time* and those texts immediately contemporary to it. Everything unfolds there as though Heidegger, still quite close to his initial theological interests, endeavored to *situate* these interests, considering explicitly the relation between his own concepts and the corresponding Christian notions. For example, the lecture entitled "Phenomenology and Theology" confronts the ontological concept of the fault [*faute*] with the specifically religious and Christian concept of sin.[19] To be sure, the one and the other come out of two distinct "sciences." However, to the degree that every theological concept preserves a pre-Christian content—surpassed from the ontico-existentiell point of view, but nevertheless determinant within the ontologico-existentiell order—the ontological clarification of the concept of the fault may serve as a "guiding thread" for the theological explication of sin.[20] Philosophy thus appears—this is the whole thesis of the 1927 lectures—as "the formal ontological corrective to the ontic, that is to say, pre-Christian, contents of the theological concepts."[21]

Such an interpretation of the connection between theology and philosophy was obviously made possible by what was earlier established in *Being and Time*, and notably by the idea of a fundamental ontology.[22] By securing the relation between ontic contents and ontological structure, Heidegger set up the general framework of interpretation, allowing him to account for the connection between the existential Analytic and all the existentiell experiences of *Dasein*[23]—and thus also Christian experience, inasmuch as it is considered not as Christian but as experience. In a word, fundamental ontology, without allowing us to rule on the (ontic) content of this experience, would allow us to set forth its (*formal*) *condition of possibility*.

In this way, Heidegger imposed in advance norms of reading for all the proximities we could highlight here. These have been effectively raised, systematically, in Lehmann's study; he shows the repercussion, within *Being and Time*'s thematic, of the principal concepts present already in the lessons of 1920–21, the same concepts that were forged on the basis of originary Christianity. With this filiation established, Lehmann proposes an interpretation. In so doing, he surpasses the letter of the Heideggerian text, but he does so simply by utilizing the means proposed by that text, that is, by following a direction Heidegger himself opened up: that of *formalization*, understood as a reference to its formal condition of possibility. "Heidegger is said to have 'formalized' the original Christian experience of life. He takes no position relative to the contents, but pursues the conditions of possibility that support such a behavior."[24]

While it poses a number of problems (excellently set forth by Lehmann),[25] this schema may be considered as operative as long as we go back from an existentiell behavior to the existential structure in which it is inscribed, that is, to the essence of *Dasein*. On the other hand, it is no longer applicable once Heidegger abandons the field (and the ambition) of fundamental ontology, in order "to turn" toward Being itself, such as it is destined in history. That is, it is no longer applicable when Heidegger turns toward the trace that subsists in the *Grundworte*, wherein thinking, language, or truth were spoken from the beginnings of this history.

From that moment, in effect, the perspective is transformed. The previously established connection between the formal structure and its condition of possibility sees itself broken. To be sure, Heidegger's thought remains oriented, as before, toward setting forth that site "starting from which." Yet it cannot claim access to some formal ontological condition in its difference from ontic contents. This is quite simply because the ontic experiences of *Dasein* are no longer the point of departure for Heidegger's investigations. These now move entirely in the domain of essence in its verbal sense, which is deployed, while holding itself in reserve, in history and language. And it is in this domain of essential deployment that Heidegger henceforth takes his "step backward" toward a more originary region, a step backward allowing the "thing itself" to be thought more adequately than in its ontological essence (or nonessence).

This means that we indeed remain in the order (modified, moreover) of conditions of possibility, but no longer in that of the *formal* structure of existence that supported that possibility. How do the Neo-testamentary determinations function, then, in this new perspective? I already indicated that Heidegger no longer mentions them, as though they had deserted his work and were no longer worth situating in it. Yet, if they still hold repercussions for it, as I think they do, then we must attempt to define their mode of presence and action. Now it seems to me that, contrary to the direction of interpretation Heidegger opened up, it is precisely these determinations that function as a (formal) corrective in regard to the earlier ontological conceptions. Far from referring the content (albeit pre-Christian) of Christian experiences to their ontological condition of possibility, Heidegger would use this content contrariwise as a formal corrective to yet another content, that is, as that "in light of which" the questions arising from the Greeks could be subjected to a new development.

The problem we are touching on here is quite difficult, and I do not claim to master it completely. The hypothesis I am advancing is scarcely more than the outline of a direction for the answer, which merits a more ample development. To make this understandable [*audible*], let us simply tackle a few examples. Conceiving the concept of the fault as an existential determination of *Dasein* meant setting forth the ontological structure that alone made possible the "region of Being" in which the existentiell concept of sin should necessarily take place.[26] Fair enough. But, to conceive language as the appearing of the thing *and no longer* as signification, or thinking as memory and no longer as logic, or Being as the historial donation of a withdrawal and no longer as eternal presence, amounts to conceiving a characterization of the "thing itself" in its proper content, an essence (understood in the active sense of the self-unfolding of the content).

Lehmann sees the problem clearly. But he resolves it—and herein lies the entire originality of his interpretation,[27] which he moreover emphasizes by grasping essence itself as a pure *form*. In the verbal sense of the term, essence, or Heidegger's *Wesen*, should be in each case "not a content, but a condition of possibility."[28] It should be understood as the "formal" substructure [*soubassement "formel"*] that makes possible "any material fulfillment."[29] Yet it seems to me that such a definition is only applicable to the essence of *Dasein* such as it is presented in *Being and Time*, *that* essence can certainly be understood as a purely formal structure, which "supplies no empirical generality, but rather relates to its unconditioned and aprioric generality."[30] After the turn, things are no longer the same. The verbal essence of every question, such as it appears in the rest of the oeuvre, has lost this character of pure formality. Moreover, the new essence is, properly speaking, neither form nor content: it is the unfolding of the "thing itself." Yet, if we must absolutely translate this unfolding into the vocabulary of form and content, then we must acknowledge that it is indeed the very substance of the thing considered, which "reigns" in essence and unfolds there.

Now, when he thinks appearing, memory, or historial donation, Heidegger unfolds the essence (of language, of thinking, etc.) by means of categories that belonged initially to the biblical world. Because they were taken into another context and served, certain of them at least, in the approach to an entirely different question, these categories were charged with an entirely different meaning—an ethical meaning, notably. Heidegger abandons this meaning. He leaves behind their biblical substance in order to retain only the structures. In so doing, he gives himself over to a work of formalization.[31] But this work is no longer to be understood in the sense of formalization, such as Lehmann developed it and Heidegger accepted it in his fundamental ontology period. Therein lies the entire difficulty. Far from Heidegger's thought providing the formal ontological corrective for the ontic content of the concepts considered, it is rather this content (once unburdened of its weight of faith and its ethical-religious meaning) that serves him as a corrective in regard to the earlier ontology and the "essences" dominant in it.

We see this clearly in the case of the *kairos*. The experience to which Paul's texts bear witness marks Heidegger's work in a lasting way. That much is generally acknowledged. It remains for us to know how to interpret this. Setting about to do so, Lehmann poses the right question: "Given the repercussions, in *Being and Time*, of the experience of history proper to original Christianity, does the surprising and inaccessible structure of the *kairos* come to light in the existential-transcendental Analytic, or are its moments repressed in the Analytic?"[32] To this question (limited to the field of *Being and Time* alone), Lehmann only provides (and perhaps because of this limitation) a partial reply: "*Being and Time* keeps open, in its *formal* structure, the space for the appearing of the *kairos*."[33]

Such a response is not in error. It is true that the existential Analytic allows us to account for the formal possibility of the *kairos*. It unfolds a structure in which the *kairos* can find its place and starting from which it can possibly receive (though this is no longer under the jurisdiction of ontology) a Christian content. That is why Lehmann adds immediately, "*That* which comes to pass in the 'that' long prepared by the moment, that must be left free by thinking."[34] A "freedom" of content, but also its elevation to its condition of possibility: this perspective is perfectly suited to Heidegger's intention, that is, to the order of reading he proposed. And the majority of his readers, including the most critical ones, ultimately follow him on this path, if only to reproach him for it. Heidegger would thus have set forth a primordial ontological (or Neuter) structure, considered prior to any fulfillment by an ontic (or ethical) content.

Yet the impact of the *kairos* goes much farther than this interpretation would have it. It is Heidegger's entire conception of time—and, thereby, of Being itself—that remains marked by it, as we shall see more elaborately in the following pages.[35] It is not enough, then, to say that Heidegger understands the essential structure of *Dasein* in such a way that an experience such as the *kairos* might find in it its condition of possibility. We must add that Heidegger's thought uses the *kairos* to *rethink the very essence of time*, an essence that, as we have seen, is no simple form but rather a plenary determination of content.

Let us conclude. It is indeed in order to think this essential substance (e.g., that of time) that Heidegger draws inspiration from the New Testament experiences (e.g., that of the Pauline *kairos*). In this respect, he does not limit himself to setting up a place for such experiences within a formal ontological structure (that of *Dasein*). Instead, he draws from these experiences material by which to rethink the questions encountered. That, however, he does not tell us.

But there is more. The kairological essence of time, which thus "passes," in his oeuvre, right into the heart of the Heideggerian concepts, only enters it after having been cut off from its source. The New Testament marks the oeuvre, but only after having been cut off artificially from the Old Testament. It is this singular break that we must consider.

II. From the New Testament to the Old: The Forgotten Connection

The majority of his commentators have raised Heidegger's curious reduction of all theology to the single, New Testament theology.[36] Yet this reduction is just the outcome of a foregoing restriction, qualified as "Christo-centrism,"[37] of the entire field of Christianity. For Heidegger, there is no God other than Jesus Christ; faith is faith in the redeemer Christ; Scripture is wholly condensed into the New Testament. Therein lies the precise context of and justification for his remark about theology: "If faithfulness [*fidélité*], however, is attested in Scripture, then theology is in its essence a neo-testamentary theology,"[38] a remark that would have no sense if what Heidegger calls Scripture encompassed the Old Testament. And, if Scripture is condensed into the New Testament, then Greek is the language of Revelation.

This specific delimitation of Christianity brings with it a double consequence. In the first place, Heidegger only considers New Testament texts (and this is his right). In the second place, he considers these as though they formed an absolute beginning, as though an Old Testament ground did not support them, finally and above all, as though the Greek of the Gospels maintained no relation of any sort to the Hebrew of the Old Testament.

It is the second point that poses a problem. It is clear, in effect, that the New Testament could not be so radically isolated from the Old. From Pascal, who saw "the Christian religion as founded upon a preceding one,"[39] to Paul Beauchamp, who strives to explore this foundation in a fine work entitled precisely, *L'Un et l'autre testament*,[40] it cannot be denied that the connection between the Old and the New should be, as Origen already pointed out, "a primary given of Christianity and its certificate of birth, so to speak, renewed indefinitely in our spirits."[41] At times neglected in the history of Christian theology, this was a gift that was nonetheless never completely lost; one that, in our century and, notably, since the expansion of what James Barr calls biblical theology, appears as an indisputable point of departure.

Heidegger's choice is thus strange at the least, considering what has been generally admitted—and what was already underscored by authors with whom he was familiar, such as Pascal and Kierkegaard. Yet we know that paradox never frightened our philosopher, and it is not because he is alone in defending a position that it is unacceptable. There is, nevertheless, something more serious here: such a conception as Heidegger's leads in itself to multiple difficulties. These have been very clearly presented by Maria Villela-Petit in a brief study that starts from a double perspective, both exegetical and doctrinal.

First, the *exegetical* difficulty: to dissociate the Testaments, as Heidegger does, one must resolutely ignore the "fact of citation,"[42] constant, for all that, in the New Testament. Through these referrals, the second Testament acknowledges itself as leaning on the first one,[43] and develops (albeit in its novelty) through interpretation of the Old. Consequently, it cannot itself be interpreted outside this relationship that crosses through it and that constitutes it, at least to a certain degree.

Next, the *doctrinal* difficulty: if Jesus is indeed "the central event of the history of salvation," then this history begins with the creation, which the New Adam "renews" by his Passion. As the Son is indissolubly tied to the creator God, one cannot separate the faith in one from the faith in the other. Hence the decisive question: "Can we envisage the question of God on the basis of the New Testament alone, without creating exegetical misconceptions that lead to restricting the theological significance of the Christic event itself?"[44]

One might say that the doctrinal aspect did not interest Heidegger directly, since he did not share its faith perspective. To be sure. But it is not the same for the exegetical consideration, which, on the contrary, interests him to the highest degree, and to which we must return. It is not simply the fact of *citation* that is obliterated by the Heideggerian conception, but perhaps more important, that of *translation*. It is utterly remarkable that Heidegger treats the Neo-testamentary text as a univocal point of departure, which would have no *background* at all. This leads him to comment on Paul's Greek without ever inquiring about what it was carrying, and what would come to it from a possible *background language* [*arrière-langue*]. Now, the existence of this background language is here much more than a possibility, much more even than a simple historical source. It is *constitutive* of the Neo-testamentary language itself, which is a language that precisely finds its meaning only as a sort of cauldron in which the difficult synthesis of Hebrew and Greek is brought about. There is no exegete who is unaware of this articulation; how could they be, moreover, since it constitutes the very condition of any reading of the New Testament? The *Theologisches Wörterbuch zum Neuen Testament* reposes entirely upon this condition.[45] This is why James Barr, summing up its orienting principle, was able to limit himself to recalling the assertion of Friedrich, Kittel's successor:[46] "the essential lexical task is the investigation of the way in which Greek words are vessels for a content of Semitic thought."[47] This was an investigation to which Boman devoted himself systematically and with a rare linguistic precision,[48] and which Rudolf Bultmann takes up in a new way when he endeavors to set forth the effects of the influence he calls "oriental" upon the thought and the language of the Gospels.[49]

This undervaluing of the effects of translation and reference is not only strange in regard to what the New Testament manifestly is. It is above all strange as regards Heidegger's own positions. What would already be remarkable in any other thinker takes on a singular relief, here, by virtue of the attention constantly directed, from his seminary years onward, to the dimension of the *originary*. Far from being disavowed later on, this attention was only exacerbated in the subsequent work. It is, doubtless, one of the most authentic constants of Heidegger's thought. In his first philosophical efforts, the young Heidegger already seems guided by a veritable horror of "covering over": to un-cover, to deliver, to work back from the derivative to the hidden source—these are even then his key words. Yet everything, or virtually everything, from this perspective can be taken as "derivative." Theology covers, with inadequate concepts, the pure experience of faith given in *primitive* Christianity (*Urchristentum*). So we must return either to the direct testimony of the first Christians, in which the experience of faith is not obscured (Paul), or to those thinkers who endeavored to return to this experience themselves, those seekers of the source and artisans of the Christian renaissance (Luther, Kierkegaard, and Augustine to a certain degree). But even these "discoverers" participate in the covering over, whatever their efforts may have been. We should note that they participate in this covering over not from the moment they begin their effort, but always over the course of it. Christianity is only purely itself at the beginning, and those who seek to return to it arrive at it authentically only at their own beginnings, when they are young. Every forward step covers up other things; that seems to be the rule. Thus, Augustine, who nevertheless saw decisive things, becomes at a certain moment "untrue to himself."[50] As to Luther, Heidegger credits him with having rediscovered the Christian faith in its original nature. But it was only "in his youth" that he made this discovery.[51] The later Luther partly closes off what he had opened up; he is once again the victim of the "tradition."

We know what will become of this quest for the original in Heidegger's subsequent work. It will lead him to abandon successively all those registers in which a discovery (and thus a return to the initial) had first appeared possible to him. It all unfolds as though, after having striven to reach the ground by way of a deconstruction of the edifice, he noticed each time that the ground already served a covering function [*fonction de recouvrement*] and had consequently to be left behind, for the benefit of an underground, and then, of an abyss. I have already evoked this movement.[52] If the Marburg courses endeavored to work back from the metaphysical "edifice" to the act of its inauguration (Plato-Aristotle), it will then be metaphysics itself (including its inauguration) that is recognized as derivative in relation to the Greek dawn. Now this means not a return to some prior thinking, but to that which *supports* it, language and the experience sheltered within language. Nevertheless, this experience can only be revived if language is deconstructed in some manner. For every language, even Greek, gets worn out; it covers over its own significations and truly resonates only on condition of being undone, like the rest, toward its proper initial purity. Then comes the final act. Heidegger will finish by renouncing this language itself, complete with its intact weight of an unthought [*charge intacte d'impensée*], at the same time that he gives up Greece. Neither Greece nor its language is ultimately the shelter of the "most originary." Greece itself—that radiant morning of the West—is already derivative. The authentic sunrise is for tomorrow. It will dawn in Hesperidia, and in the German language.[53]

We thus find in Heidegger, to the end of his path of thought, the fascination of the originary [*vertige de l'originel*], which leads him to detect something derived in the place where others had nonetheless agreed to perceive something initial. And it was this way for him from the beginning, in his attempt to return to the evangelical experience, to the point where it is not impossible to consider that his very first step was already—even before he declared its norm—a step backward in the direction of the purity of an "inception."

Now, it is in such a context that Heidegger takes the Greek of the Gospels as a beginning,[54] though it is clearly (and even outside of any quest for the original) a composite, in which the direct imprint of the Old Testament Hebrew is set. This is tantamount to saying that it is within such a general project of discovery of the initial—though it were the best hidden of origins—that Heidegger brings about (or simply perpetuates, though the paradox would be no less great) the covering over of *a* determinate and manifest initiality [*initialité déterminée et manifeste*]. This is not the place to ask ourselves about the reasons for so singular an exception. What alone counts is its consequence: how could Heidegger measure what was transmitted to him through *that* language (i.e., Neo-testamentary Greek) and *that* text (i.e., the Gospels), since he abstained from questioning them in the perspective of the other language and the other text that still spoke within them? How could he recognize himself as their inheritor?

Such is the overall problem posed by the dissociation of the two Testaments. With this framework established, it is fitting now to explore it more rigorously. In the preceding paragraph, I chose as my guiding thread the principal concept of the 1920 lecture course: that of the *kairos*. It was then a matter of showing how a Neo-testamentary experience "passed" into Heidegger's thought, thereupon filling a function much more central than that which had been acknowledged for it. We will presently see that the term *kairos*, in its Pauline sense (the same sense that is taken up and developed by Heidegger), is unintelligible outside of the Hebrew concept of time, which he goes to great lengths "to make pass" into the Greek language.

To understand this we must go back a bit further, firstly in history. The confrontation, on this matter, of the two traditions, Greek and Hebrew, has become a commonplace. If the Greeks had great historians, Israel was the first to give a *meaning* to history by making it the theater of Revelation, which is to say also that of the encounter between man and God. It is this question of the meaning of history that, with the Enlightenment, will leave the sole, Hebraic-biblical terrain where it was born, to invest philosophy. Starting from Kant, history will no longer be a "determinate domain" that could be situated by philosophy, but rather that which situates philosophy itself.[55] It is what situates philosophy without losing its biblical traits. And this is why the Bible finds itself at the heart of philosophy, to the point where we can see in Hegel and Nietzsche's conception of history the secularization of Old Testament, and then Christian, conceptions; in a word, a lay eschatology.[56]

The meaning of history to which Israel bears witness, which passes through the Bible and finally invests philosophy, is opposed to the entire Greek universe by virtue of two major characteristics. On the one hand, the Bible acknowledges history as a "true reality,"[57] living and productive, the very site, in fact, of reality inasmuch as reality is precisely historical in its essence. On the other hand, above all, the history to which Israel bears witness is entirely determined by the *future*, which projects its radiance even backward onto the past, hence the messianism, such as it is indefatigably articulated by the prophetic word. Rudolf Bultmann, whose ties with Heidegger are well known, insists on this point: "For the Greeks, all historical research is oriented toward the past. . . . The conception of history that is at the basis of eastern messianism, and the consideration of the past that flows out of it are, on the contrary, oriented toward the future."[58] This is a future, "starting from which," Bultmann adds in another essay, "the entire past is revealed to be a unity."[59]

This so focused a sense of history was made possible by a specific approach to time, for which we find no equivalent in Greek thought.

In the first place, time does not have its being in the succession of "now" moments, and the metaphor of the line—fundamentally spatializing in character—is inadequate to this time. All the interpreters agree on this point:[60] Hebraic time is understood on the basis of the event, understood as "that which comes to pass," and it is indissociable from it. This means that the event cannot be detached from Hebraic time to become the regular and purely quantitative movement of "chronological" time. This insistence on a happening that cannot be measured chronologically marked, as we have seen, Paul's First Letter to the Thessalonians. But could we fail to see that what resonates there, for the first time in the Greek language, had previously crossed through the entire Old Testament? We might compare, for example, the way in which Paul speaks of the Day of the Lord ("as a thief in the night . . . ") with Proverbs 7:22–24;[61] or again with this passage from Ecclesiastes 9:12: "And a man cannot even know his time. As fishes are enmeshed in a fatal net, and as birds are trapped in a snare, so men are caught at the time of calamity, when it comes upon them without warning."

In the second place, Hebraic time is marked—like the history that was nourished by it—by an essential futurition. This leaves its trace even in the language itself. Whereas the Indo-European languages situate the future before us and the past behind us, Hebrew uses the same metaphor but in the reverse direction: it is the future that is "behind" us,[62] and the past that is "before" us. And it is precisely because the past stands before us, and in some sense awaits us—our forefathers being our precursors— that Hebrew time authorizes simultaneity. Past events can be lived in the present; I can be the contemporary of my ancestors. It is even possible to live future events in the present, to weep today over the ruin to come, as the prophets attest.

This is the source of the third and no doubt principal characteristic of Hebraic time: the present has nothing in common with a pure now; it is the site in which *all* of time is destined to me in the modality of unity. We grasp this from the way in which Hebrew presents the idea of the smallest space of time, the instant. The instant is precisely not a space, not even a point, but rather a sudden *stroke* or *blow*; it is the *stroke*, or better yet, the "pulsation" of time. Two words serve to express this. The first is *regha'* "the rapacious, violent, stormy suddenness with which something takes place." The second, *petha'* (from the verb *pathakh*: to open), "signifies that something arrives imperceptibly, surprisingly, and unnoticed, and when the eyes are raised unexpectedly, it is suddenly there."[63]

Something is suddenly there, not as an object of pure contemplation, but always as a call, or more precisely still as an *address* concerning me. The present is this encounter between the injunction with which the temporal event is charged and the welcome I give it. This is the time in which I must respond, decide, and resolve. In this response it is not just the present instant that is at stake, but time as a whole, which through that instant comes to me: it is on me that the face of the future depends and even, in a way not less essential, the face of the past as well. This is why the present is the time of responsibility and decision. We know that this will be one of the principal traits of Bultmann's theology. And if he uses a conceptuality inherited from *Being and Time* to formulate it, this is because it seems to him best adapted to render the specificity of the Hebraic experience. "That history could bring man into a specific domain of existence, making the present into a time of decision in which we must take hold of our responsibility for the future and thereby, too, for the past—this is what remained hidden to the Greeks."[64]

Let us sum up. That which comes from the future illuminates the past and assembles itself in the present understood as the instant of responsibility. Yet, by virtue of this fact, it is time as a whole that is illuminated on the basis of the instant thus understood, in order to appear as *a decisive or critical time*, that is, a time a thousand leagues removed from the indifferent regularity of chronological time. Therein lies all the originality of the Hebraic and Old Testament conception of time, and it is this conception that Paul takes up anew.[65] To be sure, he takes it up anew to modify it on one crucial point (the conception of the "new aeon," foreign to the Hebrews,[66] and which Heidegger does not seem to have broached in his commentary). But if he is able to modify this conception of time, it is precisely because he had firstly made himself at home in it, in clear opposition to the Greek mode of thinking, whose language he nonetheless spoke.

It will be said that already in classical Greek the word *kairos* signified the "right time" [*le "bon moment"*], the propitious or favorable instant, as opposed to the *chronos*, centered on duration. But the immense difference between the Greek and Pauline conceptions lies in the fact that in Greece, the essence of time is not thought *starting from* the *kairos*; the present is neither modified by it, nor is history transfigured by the *kairos*. All that comes only with Paul. After having "weighted" the Greek word with a resonance at first sight foreign to it, Paul uses the now overdetermined *kairos* to redefine time itself, to make of it the theater of the encounter and of the responsibility issuing from it, and finally to open the term to the awaiting of the Day of the Lord, as the first day of the new aeon.

The First Letter to the Thessalonians thus speaks Greek on the ground of a Hebraic content of thought. It does so to open a new direction, which will be that of Christian eschatology. In meditating and prolonging what he calls the "kairological experience of time," Heidegger makes himself, through Paul, the direct inheritor of Old Testament language and thought.

III. The Forgotten and Its Intensification

Over the course of a term taken as our paradigm, we have followed the two moments of transmission: Heidegger's thought is durably marked by a Neo-testamentary concept, which is itself marked by a Hebraic content of thought. Ultimately, the legacy has indeed been "passed on," all the while remaining unrecognized.

We must now ask about what it was that could make possible such a misprision. I have spoken frequently of a "dissociation" between the two Testaments, that is, of a "forgetting" of the Old Testament origin of the concepts under consideration and, more generally, of the absence of any reference to the Hebraic heritage. Nevertheless, it is not certain that these different operations may be attributed to Heidegger. One of the reasons (and not the only one, no doubt) for his singular ignorance in this regard resides clearly enough in theology, such as it was taught in Freiburg at the beginning of the twentieth century. It is not Heidegger, then, who isolates one Testament from the other: it is this Testament that, by the time it reaches him, has already been cut off from its roots.[67] More generally, it is not he who forgets the Hebraic heritage. This heritage was already covered over *in the very act through which it was passed on to him.*

If we follow this perspective, Heidegger's position should appear in its quasi-necessary character. It is in one and the same movement that he received, at the same time, the heritage *and* the forgetting of its identity. Resituated this way, Heidegger would only be continuing a long tradition, which was precisely that of a certain Christian theology.

Yet is this tradition *only* that of theology? This inquiry contains a double question. On the one hand, is it only theology that carries a certain legacy without taking its origin in charge? On the other hand, is it only from theology (or a certain theology) that Heidegger received this masked heritage? In the one as in the other case, it would not seem to be so. The question is delicate, for, if other sites of "passage" between the Hebraic heritage and Heidegger may be envisioned, they cannot be so clearly isolated as in the theological edifice by itself. It is the entirety of Western history, in effect, that bears the traces of this heritage and carries it on. Now, in a few elegant pages, George Steiner recalls to what degree we depend on the Greeks for all the landmarks of our identity. It is to the Greeks that we owe the "wine-dark of the sea" and the "green flame of the laurel"; "our lion's heart and our fox-cunning are theirs."[68] But we should add that our revolt is Job's; our children are called Judith or Daniel or Matthew; we are as old as Methuselah and afflicted like Jeremiah; and the lips of our brides are always the color of pomegranates and bear the taste of honey. Our thinking bears witness to a conception of the Word inherited from the Bible. Our morals were born at Sinai—unless it was on the Mount of Olives. And finally, is it not philosophy itself that carries, in a minor mode, whole swathes of Hebraic memory?

We should follow the lines of descent here. We should show how German Idealism—especially Schelling, whom Heidegger read so assiduously—is impregnated with the spirit of Romanticism, which itself took up the heritage of the Kabbalah through Jakob Boehme. Habermas has sketched such a project.[69] Concerned to show "to what extent it is fruitful, on the basis of the experiences of the Jewish tradition, to illuminate certain core themes of the philosophy of German Idealism, marked essentially by Protestantism,"[70] he has set down a number of markers. Yet he did so without pushing his essay beyond a simple evocation.

And how, in truth, could it be otherwise? The strict division of the heritages would be an impossible thing, whatever its intention moreover. That is, whether it were a matter of proving that one owes nothing to one of them, or whether one sought to establish, on the contrary, that which properly belongs to it. The interlacing of the two is too complex here, and the interpenetrations are too ancient, for us to legitimately claim to disentangle them one from the other. We can only recognize the complex character of this unity that is Western culture, or trace broadly the most manifest lines of force of each of the two components. But it would be illusory to claim to be able to do more than this.

Let us conclude. The Hebraic legacy "passes" no doubt all the way to Heidegger, following a double path: in a privileged manner (which we can thus describe quite rigorously) by way of theology; but also in a larger and more diffuse fashion (and we can no longer claim, then, to describe it with precision), through all of Western history and culture, of which Heidegger was a particularly watchful observer.

And, no doubt, the paradox that marks the transmission in the first case must be applied straightaway to the second one. If the Hebraic heritage was transmitted by theology only in being, from the outset, already misunderstood by it, this is because the West in its entirety, though carrying this heritage, never ceased to misunderstand it.[71] Thus, the misunderstanding in question would in no way be Heidegger's unique prerogative.[72]

Hence the question of his precise role here, and of the specificity of the act he accomplished within the global domain in which he is inscribed. If the West, in its entirety, is forgetful, can we still speak—and in what sense—of a forgetfulness proper to Heidegger's work? Everything we have just said amounts to recognizing that Heidegger in no way *instituted* the dissociation of the two Testaments (it was already established by a certain theological tradition), nor did he cause, more generally, the forgetting of the Hebraic cluster (this was already patent in the West): Heidegger simply *perpetuated* them.

Such an act, however, is not innocent: first, by virtue of the context of thought in which it is inscribed. What Heidegger has taught us to recognize is precisely that traditions may remain blind to what made them possible and that they can unfold around the forgetting of their own source—this, along with the lawlike quality of such forgetfulness for Western thought. Yet the fact that Heidegger could himself take a place in this movement, and so massively perpetuate the above-mentioned forgetfulness, is what is peculiar at the least. I have already expressed my own astonishment over this and will not come back to it here.[73]

That much said, it is above all through its effects that the act in question contrasts with its context. In perpetuating something that certainly came to him from elsewhere, Heidegger does more than continue it, in the sense in which one may confine oneself to transmitting to others a torch one has received. He actively placates it; it perfects the work of forgetting, and impedes any resurgence of memory. For Heidegger is a thinker. As such, he does not limit himself to *neglecting* the Hebraic heritage, as did theology in its own fashion. Heidegger erases the trace of it; he removes any possibility that this heritage be recognized as such. Henceforth, to restore Western thought to one of its essential sources demands, in advance, an extensive work of deconstruction of Heidegger's work.

We thus see that Heidegger is, in a sense, a perpetuator. He is a man who was taken up in a history and who, on one determinate point, could not cast light on what was transmitted to him. But in another sense he is indeed the founder of a new and different process: Heidegger redealt the cards of history and modified its meaning to the point of rendering undecipherable that which, hitherto, had been merely undeciphered. This is why it is fitting, by way of ending, to reconsider this history from the point of view of the status that is liable to be assigned to the Hebraic heritage. To put it clearly: it is fitting to consider the status that could be acknowledged it if, rather than following what Heidegger *says* about such a heritage, one took account of the way in which he *utilizes* it.

3

The Hebraic Heritage and
Western Thought

We have just recalled a few of the access routes that permitted certain Hebraico-biblical elements to come down to Heidegger. It remains for us to account for their mode of presence. Two questions shall therefore be considered. On the one hand, how did this unrecognized heritage mark Heidegger's work? A possible response to this question is provided by Jacques Derrida's 1987 work *De l'esprit: Heidegger et la question.*[1] I propose to examine this work in Section I.

The other question is this: what does Heidegger's work teach us about the place that *could* be accorded to such a heritage at the heart of Western thinking? If we are to have a chance of responding to this question in a way other than approximate, it will be necessary to come back to what can, strictly speaking, be called "Western thought." This will lead me to reopen a second debate, outlined some forty years ago: the debate in which Heidegger confronted Paul Ricoeur and, later on, Jean Beaufret at the Cerisy Colloquium (see Section II).

I. Heidegger, or the "Supplement of Originarity"?
Jacques Derrida's Interpretation

Derrida is the only one, at least to my knowledge, who has noticed the double relationship between Heidegger's text and the Hebraic refer-

ence. This is a relationship that consists at once of forgetting *and* of remembrance, of exclusion *and* of resumption [*d'exclusion et de reprise*]. The
first of these dimensions—his silence in regard to the Hebraic cluster—
was too patently clear to remain utterly unnoticed for long: although this
dimension first concerned only Paul Ricoeur,[2] it was raised with increasing frequency by the critics and the last decade has seen a growth of this
concern among Heidegger scholars, from George Steiner to Jean-François
Lyotard.[3] Derrida is a part of this movement.[4] He takes note of Heidegger's
"forgetting" [*l'"oubli"*],[5] and interprets it as "avoidance" and "foreclosure"
[*"évitement" et "forclusion"*].[6] However, Derrida does much more than this.
He underscores—and is alone in doing so, at least in so ample and con-
vincing a fashion—the whole extent of the *resumption* [*reprise*] of the Hebraic reference. Because his analysis leads him to conclusions nonetheless
different from mine, it is useful to recall the positions face to face and to
open the debate.

1. Heidegger's "Trajectory"

In following the trace of the ostensibly minor theme of spirit, Derrida presents the different figures taken by the latter over the course of Heidegger's intellectual journey. Let us consider one fragment, here, of this
journey—that which goes from the Schelling course in 1936 to the lecture
on Trakl in 1953—as Derrida recalls it. Having first distinguished the *Geist*
from the Latin *spiritus*, in order to refer it to the Greek *pneuma*,[7] Heidegger
ends by differentiating *Geist* from *pneuma* itself—that is, from breath—in
order to refer it to a more originary determination, which could only be
properly stated in German: the spirit-in-flames [*Flamme des Geistes*].[8]

We must pause a moment at this point. If we recall what we established at the beginning of this study, it is obvious that the structure Derrida brings to light around the question of spirit can be set into a more
general structure that we noted earlier as constituting the "rule of interpretation" [*règle de lecture*] constantly adopted by Heidegger.[9] The latter included two principal traits. On the one hand, there occurs a *splitting* of the
question between metaphysical determination and an "original" essence.
On the other hand, there is an *evolution* in Heidegger's thought relative
to the second pole of this *split*; that is, there is an evolution in relation to

the site to which the so-called originary essence should be referred. Initially identified with the Greek word [*parole grecque*], it is thereafter sought beyond the Greek language itself.[10] Such a movement was presented in its most general characteristics from the very first chapter of this work. There, it could only remain formal. Now Derrida, in showing that this movement governs Heidegger's elaboration of the question of spirit, studies *one* of its incarnations. Yet *all* the questions we encountered in the course of this study obey the same law; that is to say that they constitute so many *figures* of a single, fundamental structure.

The first of these figures is that of *truth*. It is first not in the sense of the time or history of Heidegger's oeuvre (taken up in its overall configuration, truth is, on the contrary, one of the latest of the figures). Rather, it is first because truth is the sole figure in regard to which Heidegger does not limit himself to *accomplishing* the movement in question: he *thinks* it, renders it explicit, and states its law. This is the reason why, without examining here the question of truth for itself, I used it as a *model* to bring to light the structure that was to serve as the guiding thread in our examination of the other questions.[11]

This structure, such as it takes shape in the question of truth, contains two major moments. Though Heidegger initially works back from *veritas* (understood metaphysically as agreement or conformability) to disclosure (which is indicated in the *alètheia*), he recognizes at the end of his work that *alètheia* "arises from the outset in the perspective of *homoiōsis*."[12] Now, it is not that he relinquishes the necessity of thinking truth as disclosure, but he recognizes that this originary essence never belonged to the Greek experience, not even in the form of something unthought; consequently, this essence does not belong to the name-giving horizon [*horizon de nomination*] of the Greek language [*parole grecque*]. That is to say that Heidegger is led to surpass *alètheia* itself toward a more originary land: the clearing in which the very possibility of all presence is sheltered, and whose essence is indicated in the German *Wahrnis* [safeguarding, preservation].[13] In this term more than in any other, the truth is itself said in its essential proximity to safeguarding or preserving. The passage beyond the Greek word is thus thematized here (this is, moreover, the only place where it is so), but the recourse to German, albeit present, remains extremely discreet. At most, it functions to punctuate the path.

The situation is reversed in the case of *thinking*, where, in a first moment, Heidegger indeed moves back from thinking (understood metaphysically as logic) to the initial *lógos*. Thereupon, he turns away, in a second moment (though this is presented as provisional), from his meditation on the *lógos*, to let himself be led into the original region of thinking by the German term *Gedanc*. But the relationship between what is said in the *Gedanc* and what is reserved in the *lógos* remains undecided: Heidegger nowhere asserts that the grasp of the originary essence would require surpassing the Greek word, or a leap beyond what it names. Instead, he is inclined to present the set of meditations on the *Gedanc* as a detour, permitting us to rejoin the unthought of the *lógos* (in any case, this is what the very last lecture of *What Is Called Thinking?* allows us to conclude).[14] Yet in another sense, if Heidegger makes such a detour, if he gives it so much breadth (and we can not deny that his recourse to the German is particularly massive and patent here), then this is no doubt because it was unavoidable. This unavoidable character is nowhere *stated*, but it can be legitimately *deduced* from the actual trajectories Heidegger takes. And so, if the detour through the German word is unavoidable—if Heidegger could not spare it, considering what he intended to set forth—then that is because the word *lógos* did not say enough.[15]

The question of thinking thus presents a structure comparable to that of the truth, although its *accents* are displaced: whereas, in the case of truth, the surpassing of the Greek was explicitly underscored while the recourse to the German word remained discreet, in the case of thinking, the surpassing of the Greek is not asserted, while the recourse to the German becomes prevalent. The German language thus sees itself *treated*, in fact, as though it were the repository of the last word (the word of the origin), even if it is not *presented* this way. Conversely, the Greek language no longer *functions*, in fact, as the royal road leading to the unfolding of the origin, even if this status is formally maintained for it.

The same structure, and same hesitation, is found in the question of *language*. From language grasped metaphysically as a set of significations, Heidegger goes back to the originary *lógos* as gathering. Nevertheless, language, such as it is named by the Greek word, still only appears "in the light of Being."[16] This is a decisive originarity, to be sure, by comparison with its metaphysical model—wherein it will be grasped only in its relation to beings—but the originarity is not final. A step remains to be taken between the "unthought," sheltered in the Greek word, and "what is to be thought" concerning the essence of language. This is the step leading from a *proximity* (of language to Being) to an *identity* (of Being and language).

In effect, in the Greek term, the word is indeed referred to the reign of Being itself: such is the unthought, meaning that which is sheltered in the Greek language and which remains, awaiting our listening. But, on that basis, there remains more to be thought, and farther still to go: that is, that Being itself must be referred to the reign of the word,[17] and that the ultimate essence of language resides only in this referral. Now it is in German—and no longer in Greek—that such a referral can finally be properly named. The *lógos* is but the opening of a path, whose endpoint leads to what Heidegger designates as *die Sage* [*the Saying*, though usually "the legend"]. The *Saying* is the ultimate essence of language; it is the finally stated unfolding of its "highest reign,"[18] in which the supreme lesson is given: Being comes to pass only through the word.[19] It is this essence that Heidegger endeavors to make resonant, as if starting from itself, by listening closely [*en se tenant à l'écoute*] to the poems of George or Trakl, and especially to the final line of George's poem that is entitled, precisely, "Das Wort" [The Word].

We see that the Greek word finds itself surpassed, even if this happens, as always, in a direction opened by that word. The original essence is finally stated only in the term *die Sage* [*the Saying*], which appears as the site in which language specifically *names itself.* Relative to the *Saying* understood in this way, the *lógos* itself remains "only the fore-name of all language,"[20] as Heidegger himself put it admirably.

Thus, a remarkable structural consistency is confirmed, a structure with the form of a cleavage between the "metaphysical" and the "originary," containing an element of indecision concerning the site to which the so-called originary essence should be referred. In this indecision, the difficult problem of the relationship between Greek and German is played out. If the first Greek words (and, thereby, the Greek language itself) are first considered as wholly legitimate repositories of the figure or code of origin, then they are treated subsequently in one of two ways: either they are recognized as already derivative and thus sent back to the side of metaphysics (in the case of truth), or they are formally maintained in their status of originary words (in the case of language and of thinking). Yet, the original essence having been sought and, in the final instance, named, more and more often (although not systematically), by way of the detour through the German, such a path allows us to think two things: that this essence can only be reached "beyond what is Greek," and that the German language is indeed vested in the final work with a "supplement of originarity" by comparison with the Greek itself.[21]

This cleavage, and simultaneously this evolution, is what Derrida brings to light relative to the question of spirit, neglected up until then. He shows how Heidegger, having moved back from *spiritus* to *pneuma*, finishes (in the 1953 text) by crossing the limits of the pneumatic breath itself, toward the fire: in this fire of the spirit [*feu de l'esprit*], Derrida recognizes "the border, or dividing path, which should pass, according to Heidegger, between a Greek or Christian determination (even an onto-theological one) of *pneuma* or *spiritus* and a thinking of *Geist*, which would be other and more originary. Grasped in the German idiom, *Geist* would lead to thinking, rather, and earlier [*plutôt, plus tôt*], the flame."[22] Thus, concerning the problem of spirit, Derrida brings to light, all at once, the originary/derivative division and the displacement of the so-called originary essence over the course of Heidegger's work. If this essence first presents itself as a return to the Greek term, beyond the derived (Latin and Christian, notably) interpretations, it thereupon becomes a crossing over the Greek toward the German. Not that Heidegger explicitly emphasizes the "dissymmetry,"[23] which interrupts the Greek-German "twinning,"[24] it is rather that he completes it. This is why Derrida feels authorized to set forth its outlines, and to present it as irreducible: "German is thus the only language, at the end of the day, at the end of the race, to be able to name this maximal or superlative (*geistigste*) excellence which in short it shares, finally, *only up to a certain point* with Greek. In the last instance, it is the only language in which spirit comes to name itself."[25]

Yet, while Derrida insists, following Heidegger, upon the difference that separates the two approaches to spirit, he does not fail to emphasize that this difference, albeit radical (since it is a matter, here, of nothing less than the distance between air and fire), is referred by Heidegger (as we have seen in the other cases studied) to a link of *derivation*. "Heidegger does not simply reject the determination of spirit as *spiritus* and *pneuma*

. . . he instead derives it, he asserts the dependence of the breath, the wind, of breathing, inspiration and expiration, and of the sigh, in relation to the flame. It is because *Geist* is a flame that there can be *pneuma* and *spiritus*. But spirit is not *firstly*, not originarily, *pneuma* and *spiritus*."[26]

Thus the flame—Heidegger's "final reply,"[27] in 1953, to the question "What is spirit?"—is the originary essence attained at last, although it is recognized as not yet opened in the Greek inauguration of *pneuma*. As "an origin before the origin,"[28] this essence is this "more than vernal initiality, the kind which comes even before the first day of spring [*Frühling*], before the principle of the *primum tempus*, comes the day before the day before [*l'avant veille*]."[29]

That then is Derrida's first move: recalling Heidegger's course, or rather—for, this is more than mere recalling, and Heidegger's is perhaps more than a course—the minute plotting [*relevé*] of a *course* [*tracé*]. This course composed, sometimes faintly, of the complex movements of the Heideggerian text relative to the question of spirit. Yet this first move is inseparable from a second one. Not confining himself to bringing this course to light, Derrida makes it appear in its problematic character. We must follow the different moments of that problematization, as it is essential for the problem we are treating here.

2. Derrida's Objections

The first moment obviously does not consist, for Derrida, in opposing some kind of "outside" to Heidegger's text, that is, something Heidegger would have neglected (for example, Jewish thought). It consists rather in recalling that what is thus left out of play belongs by all rights to the "inside" of the text and that, in this sense, not to name it is purely and simply to avoid it. Derrida picks up this "avoidance" on two levels.[30] Firstly, Heidegger failed to recognize, in his spirit as flame, a determination effectively more originary than *pneuma* and *spiritus*, but which occupies a no less definite position in language and history: the Hebraic *ruah* (and thereby, more broadly, that of "a whole tradition of Jewish thought as an inexhaustible thinking about *fire*").[31] But, secondly, if this is possible, then it is because Heidegger had previously misunderstood the intrinsic tie (notably, that of translation) between the Greek and Latin determinations, which he rightly deems derived, and the Hebraic determination that preceded them and upon which the derived determinations depended, at least in one respect. Derrida recalls, for example, how numerous is the "evidence [in the Gospels] of a pneumatology, which has an irreducible relationship of translation with *ruah*"[32]—the same *ruah* that "the Greek, then the Latin Scriptures, *had to* translate by *pneuma* and *spiritus.*"[33]

A double misunderstanding [*méconnaissance*], then: first, the misunderstanding of what the languages Heidegger considers (i.e., Greek and Latin) owe to the Hebrew language, and at the same time, what the West itself owes to this other, never mentioned language. Second, a misunderstanding—less explicitly emphasized by Derrida, but deriving necessarily from the preceding point—of all that is owed to the Hebrew (and to the universe of thought that flows from it) by the determination Heidegger himself unearthed. This double misunderstanding leads Heidegger to assert that a certain essence of spirit, more originary than its Greco-Latin essence, remained unnamed in history, and that it comes only to be said in German, whereas it had already found a name and a site in that history, since it began by being spoken in Hebrew.

The *ruah*, however, is but a symptom here. If it is not recognized as a word (and still less as a word of origin) for the spirit, this is more generally because Hebrew does not appear as a language (and still less as a language of origin) of thinking. It is not taken up within the "historial triangle,"[34] in which the destiny of the West is played out—the same triangle sketched by the three languages Greek, Latin, and German.

That Heidegger thus closes this triangle, whereas by right it is open, means that "it is only closed, it seems, by an act of brutal foreclosure."[35] To speak of foreclosure is to indicate that the Greek-Latin-German triangle *is not* history: it sketches out Heidegger's conception of history. That is, it sketches the structure of what Heidegger presents as historiality in general. But at the same time, this course in the form of an enclosure is paradoxical to the highest degree. For, Heidegger—developing as he does the essence of spirit as fire—indeed left a place for a determination that belongs to history, even as he exceeds the limits of what he posits as historiality. That is to say, Heidegger closes up what he nonetheless contributed to opening (though Derrida does not state this so clearly). Heidegger unfolded, from the point of view of thinking, that which he nevertheless closes up from the point of view of attribution, in other words, as soon as he contemplates history.

Let us conclude. Derrida has recalled the course Heidegger followed on the theme of spirit. This is a course that Derrida resituates, broadly, within the "triangle" by which Heidegger thinks all historiality in general. Derrida has shown that this course (and thereby this triangle itself) included an act of "avoidance." And the term is justified by the fact that what is here never named (the Hebraic dimension), is nonetheless "incorporated" in that which Heidegger recognized as history (the Greco-Latin determinations),[36] at the same time as in that which he unearths as the originary determination (the essence that remains to be thought). Thus, Derrida is able to enlarge the debate, at the end of his book, and evoke, in the prosopopoeia of the theologians,[37] the full extent of what can be found in Heidegger from the Hebraico-Christian. We cannot take up, here, the entirety of this prosopopoeia. It must suffice to draw up the recapitulation of the different themes that the theologian highlights in Heidegger's text, and based on which he legitimately asks, "Do you realize just how close to us you are?"[38] These include the promise, the earlier dawn and the end of history, the fall and the curse, spiritual evil [*le mal spirituel*], the word of God ("his *Sprechen* [. . .], when you accord it with a *Zusprechen* [speaking-to] or to a *Zuspruch*—instruction [*mandement*], consolation, exhortation— which calls us to the *Entsprechung*, to correspondence"),[39] as well as the resurrection to come from the dawn, salvation, and the stroke that saves [*coup qui sauve*], and praise. And the theologians (or at least one among them, apparently open to ecumenicism) might continue: "At this point, especially when you speak of God, of *retrait*, of flame and flame-writing in the promise, in accord with the promise of return toward the land of the pre-archi-originarity, it is not certain that you would not receive a comparable reply and similar echo from my friend and coreligionary, the Messianic Jew."[40]

Derrida thus emphasizes clearly the erasure and the renewal. He accentuates the two dimensions that the present study has endeavored to think, calling these a denial and a taking in charge.[41] Up to that point, I agree with him, all the more readily in that he brings to light, around the theme of spirit, a structure that I had attempted to lay out, starting from other themes, and which I supposed could be rediscovered—if only it were sought out—in all the questions broached by Heidegger. However, once that structure is recognized, Derrida is led to a conclusion I cannot share: we find this in the very last pages of his book. It is Heidegger's response to the theologians themselves, the second prosopopoeia.

3. A Critical Perspective

To be sure, the word "conclusion" is much too firm, or too definite, to account for Derrida's extremely cautious propositions. His is a caution not only of formulation but truly of thinking. "Once this immense problem has been pointed out,"[42] our author does not hasten to conclude, and we readily grant him that De l'esprit closes with an exchange in the form of an opening. But at the same time, Heidegger's prosopopoeia is too Derridean in content not to carry the mark of a certain assent from Derrida himself. That he allows the theologian to speak again at the end means only that the exchange, in his eyes, is *indefinitely* open. It means that the theologian may recognize himself indefinitely in a discourse that repeats the exchange even as it nonetheless "withdraws" from it, that is to say, while exceeding it by a "step taken toward the 'earlier' [*le 'plus tôt*']",[43] in which the "origin heterogeneous" is marked.[44] But that withdrawal, such as Derrida presents it, is precisely what seems problematic to me.

Let us take this up more minutely. The *second moment* of Derrida's reading consists in "imagining" how Heidegger could respond to the critiques formulated earlier.[45] A first possibility would be to contest any rapprochement with Christianity, and to maintain that Heidegger's text *says* something wholly different. This is a "trail" ["*piste*"] that Derrida acknowledges as "scarcely passable,"[46] and which Heidegger only attempts to take "with reference to a quite conventional and doxical outline of Christianity."[47] Hence, the second possibility that, far from opposing the discourse of the theologians (which underscored Heidegger's recovery of the Hebraico-Christian determinations), on the contrary, would take it on. That is, it would recognize that Heidegger indeed says "the same" thing—but a same thing marked by a subtle difference, which, precisely, Derrida strives to set forth. What does this difference consist in? That Heidegger, while not thinking anything else, thinks "that *on the basis of* which all this is possible."[48] All this—which means the very thing that the theologian recalled:

the fall and the curse, the promise, salvation, and so on; all this—which means metaphysics, eschatologies, messianisms, and apocalypses⁴⁹—taken together. In thinking *that on the basis of which* this "all" becomes possible, Heidegger advances toward a *Frühe* [early time] that remains to come, and remains so in a double sense. Firstly, it remains to come because it shelters a morning that has never properly come to pass; secondly, because, on the basis of that morning, a whole other day becomes thinkable.⁵⁰ Therefore, Heidegger *could* assert:

> The thinking of this *Frühe* to come, while advancing towards the possibility of what you [the theologian] think you recognize, is going towards what is quite other than what you think you recognize. . . . This is why, without opposing myself to that of which I am trying to think the most matutinal possibility, without even using words other than those of the tradition, I follow the path of a repetition which crosses the path of the entirely other.⁵¹

We can see the strategy Derrida adopts. It consists in crediting Heidegger with an "originarity" greater than all the traditions, whether metaphysical or religious. That said, however, we see less clearly how this strategy can be *deduced* from what was brought to light earlier by Derrida himself, relative to the theme of spirit. If we follow his reading, in effect, Heidegger first surpasses the Latin (*spiritus*) toward the Greek (*pneuma*), then surpasses the Greek itself toward a more originary essence (the *Geist* as flame), an ultimate gesture whereby he *encounters*, without *recognizing* it, the Hebraic determination (*ruah*). We can therefore justly say that Heidegger goes farther, or farther back—earlier—than the Greek dawn, and that he advances toward a daybreak still more precocious. But *precisely* in what sense does it surpass the Hebraic determinations (here, for example, the fire of the spirit, which Derrida recognizes in the *ruah*)? Starting from the same premises, I am inclined to think, on the contrary, that Heidegger *settles in* [*s'installe*] these determinations without recognizing them as such, in order, each time, to give them the status of pre-originarity, that is, the status of a dawn never yet come to pass in history and earlier still than the morning itself. This status is eminently logical, considering what was posited at the beginning: as the Hebraic dimension was from the outset excluded from history (escaping the triangle by which Heidegger sketches and encloses the historiality of that history), that which it carries cannot be taken up, and recognized as "more originary," without, by the same token, being displaced *outside* history in a prehistoriality *from before* the origin (since the origin, in such a triangle, is necessarily Greek).

Yet Derrida does not take account of the subtle discrepancy that marks these hierarchies of originarity. After having shown, in an initial moment (this was his extremely minute analysis of *Geist*), that Heidegger encounters the Hebrew (*ruah*) by surpassing the Greek (*pneuma*), Derrida comes suddenly, in the last three pages of his book (and this is Heidegger's prosopopoeia), to present the Hebrew itself as that which is surpassed, *in the same way as the Greek was*, in the step back toward the *Frühe*.

It is on this point that Derrida's otherwise masterful discourse seems to give way to a singular acceleration, and to become hasty at the least. Not only does he not show *in what way* the fire of *Geist* could be said to be more originary than the fire of the *ruah* (whereas he showed clearly in what sense it was effectively more originary than the pneumatico-spiritual breath), but he also takes a step back relative to what he had so rigorously established earlier on. He had pointed out the "immense problem," constituted by the avoidance of the Hebraic cluster, and had interpreted this as violence and foreclosure. At present he treats it as a trivial forgetting or oversight, something like a simple lapse. We can judge as much from the following few passages from Derrida's (imaginary) discourse of Heidegger: "I am opposing nothing, especially not Christianity, nor all the discourses of the fall, the malediction, of the promise, of salvation, of resurrection, nor the discourses on *pneuma* and *spiritus, nor even* (*I had forgotten that one*) *on ruah.* I am simply trying, modestly, discreetly, to think that *on the basis of which* all this is possible."[52] And, as we read further on, "I did not say that the flame was *something other or opposite* than pneumatological or spiritual breathing, I said that it is on the basis of flame that one thinks *pneuma* and *spiritus, or, since you insist, ruah, etc.* I simply said, *Geist* is not *first of all* this, that, or the other."[53]

Now we saw above that Derrida (rereading Heidegger) asserted that the *Geist* was *firstly* flame, and that he pointed out (this time, against Heidegger) that this flame was written—in fiery writing—in the *ruah*. If we bring together these two "moments" of Derrida's analysis (the one where he comments on the thinking of *Geist*, recalling what it forgets; and the one in which he rules more generally on Heidegger's gesture, showing how it goes back farther, or earlier), their reconciliation appears difficult. In effect

Derrida asserts, *at the same time*, (1) that in the *ruah* the fire of the spirit is already said;[54] (2) that this fire, which Heidegger recognizes only in Trakl's *Geist*, is the condition of possibility of the "immense semantics of breathing" or the breath;[55] (3) that this *Geist* in which the essence of the spirit as flame is said is in any event more originary than all the other determinations of spirit, *including ruah* (though the *ruah* may have been accidentally "forgotten" by Heidegger). But it is clear that one has to choose. Either the flame is "that on the basis of which" the pneumatico-spiritual breath is possible, and in this case, *ruah* no less than *Geist* must be acknowledged to be more originary than *pneuma* and *spiritus*. Or, *Geist* is that "on the basis of which" the *ruah* itself is possible, and in this case we must indicate, if only cursorily, what it is that separates Heidegger's determination from the Hebraic determination.

Now, Derrida does not make this demarcation; he does not even sketch it. And, it seems to me that he fails to make it not through some kind of negligence, but because Heidegger's *text* does not authorize it. That means that the text not only does not invite this gesture of demarcation, but that, in the final analysis, the text forbids it. *It does not invite us to it*: we have just pointed out that it would be necessary, to complete the reading sketched in the final prosopopoeia, that we be able to measure clearly the distance between the Hebraico-biblical determination and the arch-originary one proposed by Heidegger. Now how could the text permit us to establish the measure of such a distance when one of the poles, far from being delimited (even in its insufficiency), is on the contrary bypassed, passed over in silence, denied? We may legitimately endeavor to measure all that separates Heidegger's *Geist* from the Greek *pneuma* and the Latin *spiritus*—because Heidegger defines the former on the basis of the latter—by deconstructing these, bringing to light their derived character, and passing toward what makes them possible. But how should we measure—otherwise than by way of a completely external gesture—that which separates *Geist* from a *ruah* that Heidegger never contemplated or even glimpsed?

But supposing that one were resolved to proceed in this way, resolved to confront Heidegger's text with a pole that remains external to it. We then notice that *it forbids* any rigorous demarcation and, further still, any hierarchy of originarity. *For, how can one be more originary than that which one has forgotten?* This is a question that is not simply good common sense, but one that is imposed by the status of the originary in Heidegger's problematic itself. How can one think the abyssal condition of possibility, the "that on the basis of which," how can one make a step backward toward the "earlier," if one does not start from finally disclosed boundaries, and from the already derived character of what comes "afterward"? It is only by a movement of rupture with the very system of his thought that we could accredit to Heidegger's thinking an advance toward a site *more originary than that which it had forgotten*; such a gesture falsifies the meaning of the originary and, finally, the very idea of deconstruction.

One will say that it is Heidegger, nonetheless, who claims he accedes to this site more originary than any history, more auroral than any dawn, and that Derrida is limiting himself, on this point, to remaining faithful to Heidegger. To be sure. But the passage to the pre-originary is coherent, and legitimate, only in relation to the Greek dawn (which Heidegger unfolds, toward a still more initial daybreak). So this passage could not be applied to what Heidegger had not unfolded. In other terms, Derrida accords to the determination Heidegger unearthed (that of the spirit "in flames") the status of pre-originarity, to which the latter had, in effect, laid claim—*but to which he could lay claim only because he had, previously, "effaced" the Hebraic determination*, by excluding it from the historial triangle characteristic of the West. Derrida, on the contrary, recalled this determination; he reintegrated it into a historiality that was no longer a triangle, since it was recognized as "legitimately" unable to be closed.[56] Yet should the mere fact of recalling it—and of insisting, as he does, on the tie that binds the Hebraic determination to the Greek and Latin ones—not have led Derrida to problematize the status of *pre*-originarity that Heidegger accorded to the spirit "in flames"? Now, Heidegger *had* to accord it, in fact, the status of pre-originarity, from the moment he limited history to the Greek-Latin-German triangle, but it is one that *can* no longer be accorded it, once the triangle is opened.

What I am attempting to make audible here is that one cannot denounce the closure of the triangle—asserting that the latter is "open from its origin,"[57] to that which Heidegger unearths at the end—and maintain the pre-originary character (that is, ante-historial) of what is thus unearthed. In the last instance, there are but two coherent moves: either one ignores the Hebraic dimension, as Heidegger does (thereby expelling outside history that which exceeds the Greek morning), or one takes account of it, as Derrida does, and resituates it in history—which must necessarily lead us to show not only the limits of Heidegger's conception of historiality but, at the same time, *the already historial character of what Heidegger presented as the pre-originary.*

At the beginning of this analysis,[58] I said that Derrida was the only one among Heidegger's readers to remark on the double relationship of Heidegger's text to the Hebraic reference: a relationship of forgetting *and* of memory—Derrida would say, a relationship of "avoidance" and of "renewal." But we have also seen that *De l'esprit,* in its last three pages, took a direction in which we could not follow him. It all happens as though, after having pointed out Heidegger's avoidance, Derrida strove to think the renewal (to think it in its plenitude as "that which crosses the path of the entirely other") in such a way that the previously indicated avoidance could not find its place in such a structure.[59]

Rather than privileging one move over another (whichever it might be, moreover),[60] should we not attempt to grasp them *together,* as the two sides of a single act? Should we not grasp them together, not only on a particular question (that of spirit), but also as characteristics of Heidegger's questioning as such? In effect, we have seen, beyond the one theme Derrida followed, a number of other questions governed by an analogous rule. How shall we think the singular articulation revealed there: the thinker who, more amply than any other, *restored* to Western thought the determinations central to the Hebraic universe is precisely he who never said anything about the Hebraic as such, who, more massively than any other, effaced it from thought and, more broadly, from the West itself?

To such a question there is no ready-made answer. It remains to be worked out, and requires great caution. Yet, whatever the sort of elaboration that might be proposed for this, it must account for the frequency and the *regularity of appearance* of the double gesture I have attempted to bring to light over the course of the questions broached by Heidegger. Such a regularity forbids us, it would seem, to see therein merely a minor attribute. It invites us to seek out the *logic* of so highly a paradoxical articulation.

It is this logic that I will endeavor to set forth at the end of this book.[61] But it is fitting, firstly, to clarify the general domain in which it is inscribed.

II. Western Thought and Metaphysics

We have seen that the Hebraic heritage, having accompanied the course of Western history (in a mode one might call minor), found in Heidegger a new status—paradoxical to the highest degree. It is, in Heidegger, more forgotten than anywhere else, even made completely indiscernible. And yet, at the same time, it is more present than ever, carried to the front of the stage of thinking, wherein it finds for the first time, both resonance and legitimacy. To be sure, it is not called there by its name (whence, the forgetting). But it is indeed this heritage that is presented there, and in broad daylight (whence, the memory or remembrance).

If this is the case, if the Hebraic heritage indeed finds itself deployed, in some of its principal aspects, by Heidegger, while also being misprized *as* Hebraic, then what would it mean to put an end, on this point, to the forgetting? We must understand this question properly. It is not a matter of turning away from Heidegger, to reestablish the "real" place of the Hebraic heritage in the West. It is a matter of determining the place that may be assigned to it, *considering the way in which it functions in Heidegger's text.* That is to say that Heidegger remains our sole guide. Given the use to which he put the Hebraic dimension, to renew thinking and render it "more meditating," what does he teach us about it and about its possible relation to thinking as such?

An answer to this question requires a certain number of preliminary demarcations. To situate the Hebraico-biblical contribution in Western thought, it is advisable that one agree about what may be called "Western thought," as well as about its precise relation to "metaphysics." It is only when these expressions—whose definitions, all appearances to the contrary, are not self-evident—have been clarified that we shall have a chance to know whether there remains, in the domain Heidegger assigned to "thinking," a possible place for a dimension that would be neither Greek nor metaphysical.

As these questions are not totally new—fortunately, they were actually posed to Heidegger himself—the framework of their discussion has already been traced. I am speaking of the debate engaged at the time of the Cerisy Colloquium of 1955, between Heidegger and Paul Ricoeur, a debate taken up twenty-five years later by Jean Beaufret. The different parts of it are presented in Beaufret's invaluable essay "Heidegger and Theology."[62] It is these that I propose to reexamine here, as minutely as possible.

Let us first recall the different positions present there. Heidegger has just presented his lecture "What Is Philosophy?" Paul Ricoeur then expressed his objection about the "Hebraic heritage," astonished as he was that the inaugural lecture could have passed over it in silence. To get a sense of Heidegger's response, we must reread the objection; it contains in effect *four* distinct questions: (1) The Hebraic heritage treats neither of Being, nor of beings, but rather contains a call: "Can one exclude such a call, which is not Greek, from philosophy?" (2) "Is not the translation of the Bible into Greek, called the translation of the Septuagint, an unfathomable event at the basis of our culture?" (3) "Is the surely 'equivocal' relationship between the Greek world and the Jewish world not that which, within philosophy itself, sustains a questioning address?" (4) "Can Being be so [*l'être peut-il l'être*], without being the first being or entity [*l'étant*]? Or, conversely, is not the first being [*le premier étant*] strictly its own Being [*l'être*] and the center from which radiates the Being of beings [*foyer de l'irradiation de l'être de l'étant*]?"[63]

Of these four questions it is clear that the first three concern the relation, within philosophy (first and third questions) or more broadly within culture (second question), between the "Greek world" and the "Jewish world." The fourth question (of different inspiration) concerns Heidegger's own thought—more precisely, the distinction it makes between Being itself [*l'être même*] and the supreme being—and attempts to problematize it.

To this set of questions, Heidegger responded in the following way (according to what we know through Beaufret, who remains on this our only witness):

You are touching here on what I have called the "onto-theological" character of metaphysics, which I have quite often treated. Must we really link the philosophers to the prophets, as you propose? I am convinced that, to those who examine these things closely, Aristotle's questioning—whether it be ontological, as it will be said much later, or theological—takes its root in Greek thought and bears no relation to biblical dogmatics.[64]

This response calls for two remarks. On the one hand, Paul Ricoeur only "touched" the onto-theological character of metaphysics in his fourth question, not in the preceding ones. That is, unless one has decided from the outset that the mere fact of mentioning the Bible, according to any one of its dimensions (including the literary, etc.), should immediately bring forth, like a specter, the onto-theological structure of metaphysics. But who could fail to see that so automatic a referral can no longer claim to belong to thought? If one wants to preserve the rigorous meaning of words (the same rigor accorded them by Heidegger himself), we must recognize that metaphysics has an onto-theological structure to the precise degree that it makes a place for God, conceived as the supreme being. By virtue of this fact, any attempt to identify Being and God can legitimately be said to fall within the scope of onto-theology. In this sense, Ricoeur's fourth question indeed concerns this problematic and is effectively apt to find an answer in what Heidegger has "quite often" treated.

That is not the case for the three other questions, however. In effect, these evoke the biblical contribution, not from the point of view of God understood as supreme being, not even, quite simply, from the point of view of God (in whatever way he might be conceived), but rather in consideration of several *events*, in regard to which Paul Ricoeur judged, rightly or wrongly, that they may have had an impact on philosophy. These events are the following: a *call* that would exercise an influence on philosophy, independently of any relation to the question of Being (first question); the *translation* of a fundamental text (second question); finally, a *world* that would not be the Greek world (third question). It is therefore not a matter here of Being or of God, or even of some confusion of the two, which could be referred to onto-theology. It is, rather, a matter of a possible contribution of the Bible to Western thought.

Does Heidegger respond to this question, three times repeated? The second part of his response, inasmuch as Beaufret renders it precisely, can only plunge the reader into great perplexity. There is no need, in effect, to "look closely at these things" in order to recognize that Aristotle's questioning takes its root in Greek thought and has no relation to the Bible! But that was obviously not the question. The question concerned knowing whether philosophy—and more broadly, as Ricoeur said, "our culture"— plunged *all* its roots into Greek thought, and none into the Bible. And the Bible is understood, let us repeat again, as a *text*, as a *world*, and as the shelter of a *call*. Now, to this question—which evokes the biblical contribution independently of the questions of God and of faith—Heidegger, to my knowledge, did not respond, at Cerisy or elsewhere.

Jean Beaufret, on the other hand, endeavors to do so. He ventures this in the article cited above, and comes back to it a few years later, in his discussions with Eryck de Rubercy and Dominique Le Buhan.[65] Confronting the question that Paul Ricoeur posed—that concerning a possible tie, within philosophy, between the Greek contribution and the biblical-Jewish one[66]—Beaufret first opposes the response he deems habitual to the "unusual" one given by Heidegger.[67] Now, whereas the first answer, the largely dominant one, would see in the biblical-Jewish contribution one of the sources of philosophy, the second response asserts that "the Greek contribution is precisely philosophy *itself*," or again, metaphysics itself, "the two terms [philosophy and metaphysics] being largely synonymous."[68] Thus, "Heidegger's audacity was to consider that which is today universally extolled in philosophy as an immanent source, as an external contribution."[69]

That the Jewish contribution should be "universally extolled" as a source of philosophy is certainly something that would merit discussion. It is incontestable, on the other hand, that for Heidegger philosophy is Greek in its origin and that, though it may have found itself dominated, during a certain phase of its history, "by Christian conceptions,"[70] it remains no less "Greek in its very being."[71] Why is it Greek in its very being? Because philosophy defines itself entirely "by the secret permanence of an initial question, that which became a question only with the Greeks only to persist beyond them and up to our time."[72]

What status, then, should we accord to that which could exist in the West, in its *history* and eventually even in its *thought*, without being oriented toward the question of Being and, therefore, without proceeding from the Greeks? That is a complex question, for it is firstly a matter of knowing *whether* something can exist in the West that would not arise out of (even in an inapparent fashion) this problematic, something, therefore, that would not come (even unconsciously) from that which the Greeks inaugurated. It is on this question that Beaufret's explanations seem to me to diverge from Heidegger's thought, without intending to do so—that is, on this point they become, properly speaking, unfaithful to Heidegger.

Beaufret's response is, in effect, the following: "Heidegger, to be sure, does not deny that there might be something other than metaphysics in the West, in other words, something other than philosophy. There are also sciences and technologies, data processing and psychoanalysis, religions and wars, governments and ministries, public services and private initiatives, trade unions and art shows."[73] Heidegger would grant that all that is not "without thought." But philosophy, which is also to say metaphysics, is neither a "specialist of generalities" nor a "general framework that one may fill indifferently": philosophy is "a differentiated problematic, that is, the problematic of the *Being of beings.*"[74] All that which the above list enumerated in its ironic inventory thus belongs neither to philosophy nor to metaphysics, in Beaufret's eyes.

The pages we are following here go further still. Even the questions one believed to be, by all rights, proper to the philosophical domain, up until now—such as the questions "concerning the *origin* or the *cause* of the world and of things, as well as the presumed *end* that should reveal their history"[75]—are little else than "some kind of magma or amalgamation of general ideas." And it would precisely be Heidegger's "most radical contribution" to have made it "impossible to use the word *philosophy*" to designate all of that.[76] For, only that "differentiated problematic," which we owe to the Greeks, can be called "philosophy."

Such a response, as I said, does not appear to me to accord with Heidegger's thought. It brings about a double exclusion, in effect: first, there occurs the exclusion from *metaphysics* of all that which is not directly *philosophical*; second, it effects the exclusion from philosophy itself of all the questions that would not be directly that of *Being.* Now, none of these exclusions is authorized by Heidegger's text. Let us consider the first among them. All that Beaufret names, psychoanalysis and data processing, war and ministries, and the rest, certainly does not belong to the determinate discipline that is philosophy. But, in Heidegger's vocabulary, philosophy and metaphysics are in no way synonyms. Philosophy is the domain that poses explicitly the question of the Being of beings (such as it was inaugurated by Plato). Metaphysics is the entirety of domains apparently foreign to philosophy, but secretly governed by the question that philosophy alone has posed as such.[77] In this sense, trade unions are metaphysical, like data processing, and so on; they are matters for the question of Being to the precise degree that they are carried, albeit unconsciously, by a certain comprehension (Greek in its principle) of the Being of beings.

Thus Heidegger draws no *separation* between a specific and privileged question (that of Being, initiated by the Greeks) and all the other questions (including that evoked by Ricoeur), which would presumably then be secondary and have no value as arguments because they would be foreign to the central question of philosophy-metaphysics. On the contrary, Heidegger's gesture is one of *integration*: all these questions, so apparently foreign to that of which the Greeks spoke, are in fact secretly governed by the question that intrigued the Greeks. And they may therefore be restored, in the last instance, to a framework that remains Greek. They may be restored, that means also illuminated, by that framework. It is for that reason that these questions may be held to be secondary: *not because they would be other than the question of Being, but because they come down to the same.* Ultimately, they say nothing other than that to which Heidegger, in his debate with the Greeks, has already responded. It is therefore impossible to assert, with Beaufret, that there is in the West "something other than metaphysics."[78] It is precisely because even wars and religions are thoroughly metaphysical that the objection concerning the other source, or the other component, is without relevance in Heidegger's eyes.

The second exclusion appears to me riskier still, that by which Beaufret sets apart from philosophy questions such as those of the origin, causality, and finality. For, not only do these concern—by the same right as the others—a certain comprehension of Being and thus enter into the framework of a metaphysical system [*d'un dispositif métaphysique*], but they moreover belong by all rights to philosophy *stricto sensu*. That philosophy here shares certain of its questions (though not always its answers) with "biblical dogmatics" is something that can indeed be accounted for within the framework (in this case, legitimately called upon) of onto-theology. In other circumstances, Beaufret himself recognizes that philosophy "over almost two millennia, has not ceased to be in debate with Judeo-Christianism."[79] But he is here so concerned to separate "biblical dogmatics" from this "Greek thought" that is philosophy, that he finds himself led to exclude from philosophy certain among its central questions—and this, for the sole reason that they might be shared by the "dogmatics" in question.

It thus appears that Heidegger did not directly answer the question posed initially by Ricoeur, that of the eventual place of the biblical contribution within philosophy, or, at the least, in Western thought. Jean Beau-

fret, who proposed to answer in his place, provided a clearly negative answer, while using arguments that move away, on several decisive points,
from Heidegger's intentions. We must therefore attempt to establish a possible response by Heidegger, and this, otherwise than Beaufret proposed to
do. This is his possible response, that is, it is one that could be given within
the framework of Heidegger's thought, although it was not formulated by
Heidegger himself.

The first side of the response concerns that which has been explored
up to now, of which we will limit ourselves to recalling only its conclusions. Philosophy is Greek. Philosophy is—perhaps in a more profound
and determinant way than Heidegger says—in frequent debate with the
biblical sources. Yet we will readily grant Beaufret that this debate does
not constitute philosophy's "center."[80] Metaphysics, meanwhile, is that in
which the entire history of the West is gathered. Whole swathes of that history may well recognize no tie at all with the Greeks, but they nonetheless
appertain to what was initially established by the Greeks: a certain question (that of Being), and at the same time a first comprehension of this
question, which remains a guide later on (Being as constant presence). For
this reason, philosophy, as well as the whole of Western history that the
word *metaphysics* encapsulates, may be said to be "Greek, in their very being." The Jewish contribution of which Ricoeur spoke may well "sustain
its questioning address" inside of philosophy, but one could not assert that
it constitutes philosophy. It remains, as Beaufret argued following Heidegger, an "external contribution."

Yet this is but a first side of the response. Though all the foregoing history of the West—and the thinking that unfolds therein—may be
gathered under the name of metaphysics, Heidegger's thought nevertheless is in no way reducible to metaphysics. Heidegger's thought surpasses metaphysics's frame, just as much by *that* which it thinks as by the
way in which it thinks it. What it thinks—in other words, the question
upon which Heidegger's thought takes its bearings—is no longer "what the
Greeks sought,"[81] as Beaufret also admits, but rather the truth of Being that
was never taken in charge by metaphysics, nor even by philosophy, which
nevertheless claimed to treat it. And it is precisely in order to think about
this question, which went uncontemplated by the Greeks, that Heidegger
must develop a *manner* of thinking that is no longer that of the Greeks.
The two aspects are evidently indissociable insofar as thinking takes its

being from *that* which it thinks: thought oriented toward beings (that is, toward the given, the available, the manipulable) is calculation, representation, mastery. Thinking oriented toward Being (that is, toward the unavailable, the mystery, the withdrawal) is memory, acquiescence, welcome, and serenity. In a word, we have on one side a question in its Greek development, which forms the axis of what Heidegger gathers under the name "metaphysics." On the other side, we have a renewal or reelaboration of this question, in a Heideggerian mode, which leads one to define a nonmetaphysical thinking.

For this reason there is indeed, *within the framework of what Heidegger called thinking* (in the rigorous sense of the term, and not as an amalgamation of general ideas), room for something other than the Greek understanding of Being, as well as for something other than the Greek way of thinking. That is, there is room also for something other than all the modalities of thinking (scientific, political, etc.) that remain governed by the Greek origin, even if they do not recognize their tie to the Greeks.

Heidegger assigns to this other thing, which is no longer Greek, the status of an *unthought condition of possibility* of what was opened up by the Greeks. Yet, while he defines it merely negatively (as unthought), that is, *relative*, still, to the Greeks (as their condition), he thinks this other thing in terms that recall a very old, non-Greek tradition. Better: he recalls it in terms that tie up too closely with this old tradition—too closely not to have been drawn, and to derive, at least partially, from it. What then should we conclude?

It seems to me that two conclusions may be drawn from this, determined according to whether one limits oneself to noting the *proximity* [*voisinage*] of this other thing and the tradition, or whether one accepts interpreting their close tie as a *filiation*.

In the first case, we are permitted to conclude that Heidegger accords, on the one hand, that which he refuses on the other. He accords a place, in the field of thinking, to nonmetaphysical possibilities, while elsewhere refusing to envision that these same possibilities might interest thinking if they at all rest on the Bible. Yet features such as the attention to language, the concern for a summons or a call, fidelity to a trace, the memory of a founding withdrawal, and so on, are recognized as essential when they are voiced by Heidegger. But they are simply overlooked as biblical features, which they nonetheless incontestably are. This is an oversight made possible by the fact that the biblical universe *in its entirety*, and in the multiplicity of its aspects, has been reduced from the outset to the two dimensions that, *stricto sensu*, prohibit our thinking (in the sense in which we speak of prohibiting someone from staying somewhere [*interdit de séjour*]): first, the dimension of faith (foreign to thought) and that of onto-theology (reducible to Greek thought).[82]

I admit that I have considerable difficulties understanding why this nonmetaphysical thinking, when it is encountered in the Bible, should be referred back to art shows or trade unions (that is, it would not merit the rigorous name of "thought"), whereas when we find it in Heidegger's own writing, it should be grasped not only as thought, but as the only authentic thought, as the very essence of contemplative thinking, and so forth. We can certainly grant that metaphysics be Greek: but why should all nonmetaphysical thought, notably that developed by Heidegger himself, be Greek in principle, or be dependent on the Greeks? What justifies such an assertion, if not precisely a pure *petitio principii*? Such is the first question, which is raised by the simple observation of a *proximity* between Heidegger's own thought and certain fundamental features of the Hebraic heritage.

On the other hand, if we agree to understand this proximity as a *filiation*—that is, if we admit that Heidegger's own thought drew from the Hebraic and the Old Testament reserves, via paths that are not completely clear—then we may conclude that there is indeed a difference between what Heidegger *says* about the Hebraico-biblical heritage and what he *does* with it.[83] For, on the one hand, he affirms that the Bible, when he consents to speak of it at all, offers nothing (in any case, nothing specific or original) that could interest thinking. On the other hand, he makes use of it to renew thinking and to orient it in a new direction. And even concerning the question of Being, he never ceases to argue, on the one side, that it is Greek and that the Bible is as foreign to it as possible, while on the other side he seeks in the Bible that which the Greeks did not seek—that to which he was himself awakened thanks to his theological "provenance."[84]

The Bible—at the same time as any possibility that an *identity* other than the Greek one might be significant for the West—has thus been excluded by Heidegger from the domain of thinking, all the while being constantly called upon by him. It is therefore the validity of this exclusion that we are placing in question here. We do this not because this exclusion would be, by all rights, indefensible, but because Heidegger *states* the principle of exclusion without *respecting* it.

If we bring these two partial conclusions together, it would appear, on the one hand, that the principle in question functions precisely as a principle, that is, as a postulate. On the other hand, it would appear that this postulate is indefensible, since Heidegger himself does not respect it. Now what would happen—I am returning here to my initial question—if Heidegger's statements and his acts agreed, rather than being discrepant? What would happen if Heidegger stated that which he is, in fact, carrying out? That is, what if the principle of exclusion ceased to play its role? We would then recognize—as Beaufret did at first in his response to Ricoeur— that philosophy is Greek, as is metaphysics in its entirety. But we would add that metaphysics is not all of thought. Heidegger recognized this. He did more than recognize it: it is he who taught us this. Heidegger wanted to root this other possibility of thinking, which metaphysics did not take in charge, in an unthought that was to be credited to our Greek heritage. I do not see what prohibits [*interdit*] us from recognizing therein the non-Greek part of our heritage—I see, rather, what would demand it of us. Heidegger had the merit to unfold this part, to sustain it with his authority alone, and to resituate it within the whole course of Western thought. In a word, he restored it to us as ours, to us thinkers, tearing us away from the domination, or the fascination, of metaphysics alone. Quite simply, he attributed paternity of it to one of our sources, whereas it ought perhaps to have been attributed to the other, at least in part. And if he did so, it is because he had from the first reduced the Judeo-Christian West—itself marked by an unsurpassable duality, *which Heidegger himself never ceased to attest*—to only one of its components, the Greek one.

This is why, in closing, I would like to "repeat" or "take back" ["*reprendre*"] from Beaufret some verses of Hölderlin. These are verses in which Beaufret hears resonating the critique of the "putative monotheism,"[85] but which it is possible, I believe, to read completely differently—as a resistance to any simplification and, above all, to the simplification of the origin. These verses are entitled "The Root of All Evil":

> To be in unity is divine and good; whence then the mania
> Among men, that there be one alone but no more,
> And one thing but no more?[86]

Conclusion: Deconstruction or Reconstruction?

Against mediators. Those who want to mediate between two resolute thinkers show that they are mediocre; they lack eyes for seeing *that which happens but once.* Seeing things as similar and making things the same is the sign of weak eyes.

—NIETZSCHE, *The Gay Science,* § 228

By dint of wanting too much to prove something . . . Every endeavor to establish parallels or line things up is risky. There is a risk of conferring credit to approximate, or distant, analogies; a risk of skirting round the differences or not perceiving what still differs even in the most confirmed proximities. There is a risk, in a word, of being the weak-eyed go-between that Nietzsche denounced.

If I have taken this risk, it is in the conviction that one cannot rigorously assert a difference without having first recognized resemblances. The latter are, I admit, without importance. They never constitute more than the shared base, from which is detached, in its singularity, "that which happens but once," and which alone sketches the "shape" [*la "figure"*] of a thought. But if these resemblances are without importance, then their denial [*dénégation*] only takes on a sharper relief. This denial inevitably leads to a question. In what respect was it necessary, then, within the system of a thought or a philosophy, to deny that which by right should have been recognized (i.e., that which could have been recognized without taking away the specificity of the thought in question)? What indeed can be the function of such a denial?

It is to this question that the entirety of this study must ultimately open. Before being able, legitimately, to pose it, this researcher had to take charge of a task one can only call unrewarding: that of reconstituting the fabric of resemblances that Heidegger denied. An unrewarding task, because it was called for entirely by the denial in question; an unavoidable task, however, because it determined the first chapters of this book: it was a matter of laying out thematically, and justifying, a proximity (between certain of Heidegger's themes and their Hebraico-biblical correspondents), which *only* required demonstration because Heidegger continually refused to recognize it. That is, it was a matter of recalling the evidence for this sole reason, that it was silenced, a matter of patiently tying up connections rendered indiscernible and of neglecting nothing in all the proximities that could be reestablished. And this, against Heidegger's explicit declarations, or against his silences.[1]

It was only in a second moment that we could abandon the merely factual terrain and work *on the basis* of that recognized proximity, confronting some of the problems it brought up.[2] After having endeavored to detect this proximity in the place where, moreover, it was not visible—showing that it had been able to creep all the way into the question where the greatest difference existed[3]—I sought to understand how this proximity might have been established. I inquired by which paths (or which detours) could a heritage, in large part ignored or quite largely unrecognized, have come to mark Heidegger's work.[4] It then became possible to extend this proximity toward that which it was liable to teach us, not so much about Heidegger as about the tradition he utilized in silence. What might such "utilization" show us, had the denial not played its part?[5]

Such was, cursorily redrawn, the path followed here. Where has it led us? Before examining its possible repercussions for the entirety of Heidegger's thought, it is appropriate to recall what can be taken for granted concerning the "occasional" question of Heidegger's relationship to the Hebraic heritage.

I. Assessment

We have seen that Heidegger consistently opposed a dominant essence (or rather nonessence), characteristic of metaphysics, to a wholly other and more originary essence, which he endeavored to unfold for itself, and which would have remained, up until then, as unthought as it was "unheard of." However, we have also seen that this other essence could be found [*se retrouvait*], just as consistently, in the non-Greek component of our tradition. And it could even serve properly to characterize that component. It is not that this other essence was thematically "thought out" ["*pensée*"] therein, nor that it might have taken the form of a "conception,"[6] but that it was indeed present from the origin. Such an essence has, therefore, in the entirety of Western history, a status wholly other than that which Heidegger bestowed on it. This essence is not just sheltered, *in a concealed mode*, within the Greek morning or in its first words. Instead, it has always been there—*in the open*, in other words. Far from being marked by an unavoidable and essential forgetting, this essence is a part of our memory, at least by right. That "philosophy" had not taken it in charge constitutes another problem, and it in no way allows one to assert that this essence would thus have deserted the "West" from the origin.[7]

Heidegger's "rule of interpretation" ["*règle de lecture*"], which we presented from the beginning of this work, may now appear, at the end, in its problematic character. This rule came down to asserting that the entirety of our history knew only the essence said to be dominant, while the other essence could only be discovered, in a properly posthistorial experience (Heidegger's own experience), on condition that it was discerned as a prehistorial possibility (i.e., sheltered in the first Greek words).[8] Yet as soon as we agree to consider, without effecting exclusions, the different components of our entire history, it appears that we can find the two essences, including their provenance, unfolded *in it*. To stay with the main themes developed over the course of this study, it is indeed *within history*—not on its margins, whether pre- or posthistorial—that we find, on one side, the conception of the word as sign and that of thinking as logic, both of which are undeniably of Greek origin, and on the other side, a conception of the word as presence of the thing itself, at the same time as we find an experience of thinking as memory—both of which are just as undeniably of biblical origin.

Heidegger, who recognized—even emphasized—this duality of essences, excludes from the outset the duality of sources. Affirming the one while refusing the other, he is necessarily led to credit the hypothetical unthought of the Greek text, with all the "experiences" he resolutely ignored in the biblical text. Let us state this once again: I am not doubting the fact that such experiences *might* be attributed to the Greeks' unthought, to that which they had not thought. I have simply sought to show that these experiences were present elsewhere. In clear terms, I in no way assert that these experiences could not be found, between the lines, among the Greeks. I am simply recalling that they were set down, in letters black on white, among the Jews.

This reminder is not without consequences. It signifies, in effect, that Heidegger reconsiders the entire metaphysical edifice in light of a horizon of meaning that already belongs to our tradition, and that forms a part of our heritage. But this he did not recognize as a heritage. And he thus referred it back, in circular fashion, in part to the Greek heritage, in part to a new thinking, which sets forth on unprecedented paths, opens onto experiences never ventured before, risks going into the complete unknown—and would be his own thought.⁹ That is, at the very least, what can be sketched out as a possible conclusion, if we accept as valid the preceding analyses.

II. Opening

I have endeavored in this way to circumscribe in Heidegger's work an occasional element that remained unacknowledged there, something like a blind spot. To close, it remains to measure its impact and possible repercussions, that is, to reconsider the entirety of his work in light of this blind spot. My very last inquiries shall therefore be the following: how is the question treated here inscribed in the general system of Heidegger's work, and what is its function?

Two interpretive directions can be envisaged. The first (which was my own when I took up this study) would consist in seeing therein only a purely punctual or incidental misprision [*méconnaissance*]—even a sort of lapse, as Derrida would have it. This would thus have been a misprision without major repercussions after all for the order of his thinking, since the essential part of the Hebraic contribution found itself, in the final analysis, taken in charge. Those who hold this perspective would say that, if Heidegger had truly dismissed, in its very content, one of the constitutive dimensions of our history, then one might consider this prejudicial. But what is it to forget an *identity?* Now this question belongs, it seems, exclusively to the "history of philosophy," and perhaps even to history *tout court.* That Heidegger's thought might have referents other than those it declares, that it might have failed to do sufficient justice to some of its sources—this is perhaps worth indicating in passing, but it is without major impact on his thought taken as a whole, and alters nothing of its meaning.

It seems to me, nevertheless, that the question considered here largely overflows its own terrain. This is what I discovered only gradually. At the beginning, I was troubled by an occasional silence: it seemed to me that there was a specific point there, poorly clarified up until then, which merited further examination. In the end, this point had enlarged in an unexpected way, becoming something like a center, a center that enlisted all of Heidegger's thought, and caused it to appear in a different light. Let us try to set down the moments, and motives, of this turnaround.

Already in the Introduction, we saw a considerable—and imperceptible—enlargement of Heidegger's project. At the beginning, it was still only a matter of questioning the history *of ontology*, that is, of illuminating our past as philosophers. Yet, because the question of Being is recognized as overflowing the mere terrain of ontology, it is, at the end of his oeuvre, the global figure of the West and the entirety of its history that Heidegger claims he is thinking. That is, he claims to refer this question back to its fundamental unity and, thereby, to its truth.

Now, it seems to me today that Heidegger has thought or written our history less than he has *rewritten* it, in the precise sense of the expression "to rewrite history"—that is, after having revised and corrected it. What I took to be a precious labor of deconstruction ultimately appears to me as a work of reconstruction.

In what sense are we justified in asserting that Heidegger rewrote history? It is in that he remains silent on one of its dimensions, *without managing however to really spare himself its use.* In order that there be "writing," that is, interpretation—an interpretation as innovative as one would like, but which would not pass beyond its own rights—the thinker, in the present case, had but two solutions. He would have had to show, either that our history owed effectively nothing to such a dimension—and therefore *effectively do without it*, reconstitute history in its coherence without having it intervene therein—or, if he drew things from it, he *would have had to recognize their provenance.* But Heidegger reintroduced it without ever recognizing it or permitting us to identify it. Better still, he reintroduced the dimension while he in other respects suppressed any possible marks by which to identify it. One may as well say he *smuggled* it back in.

What thus seems to me contestable in Heidegger's text is not that the Hebraic component is passed over in silence (one might accept, in effect, that this silence was legitimate). What seems contestable is that this component *should return* without ever being identified, that it could return in a text that does everything to make its identification impossible. And, again, that it returns, as I have tried to show, while being constantly attributed either to the unthought (which must evidently be understood as the Greek unthought), or to a wholly new and properly Heideggerian thinking (one that is postmetaphysical only because it perceives or prolongs the premetaphysical possibilities of the Greek text). At the outcome of this operation, we indeed find all the wealth of the foregoing history, which is still presented as a complex history, marked by a splitting or cleavage. But the advantage is that, henceforth, the two sides of this history are Greek, or of Greek inspiration. The duality is maintained, but it is expelled from the origin.

For this reason, Heidegger's own development of the question of the origin is much more complex than what one might grasp on first reading it. This development is not limited to *bringing to language* a certain heritage. It contains a second aspect, by which Heidegger, at the same time, works to *reduce* another heritage *to speechlessness.*

To speak of two aspects may nonetheless lead us into error. It is not that there are two distinct moments to the problematic here, but rather the two sides of one and the same act, which is firstly an act of speech [*acte de parole*]. Heidegger's word *speaks* on one side, and is *silent* on the other. That is to say that it covers up, in the active sense of that expression. That is why it seems indispensable to me to read his text—in the present case and perhaps in others as well—according to this double perspective: not to limit oneself to hearing what is said there, but to pay attention to *what is silenced by this saying.* It is only on condition of holding together these two aspects that we can finally grasp integrally that which is Heidegger's problematic of the origin, that is, the *work* that Heidegger does on the origin. It is not, as has so often been said, the simple "return to the Greeks," but indissociably the return to the Greek and the effacement of the Hebraic.

And it is there that we find that which makes up the specificity of Heidegger's procedure in regard to the general horizon to which it is often referred: the nostalgia for Greece (or the invention of another Greece), such as it was constituted at the dawn of German Romanticism and incarnated, in so pregnant a manner, in Hölderlin. In that constant parallel with Hölderlin's Greece, one invariably omits a point, nonetheless fundamental: that, in Hölderlin, the Judeo-Christian memory subsists beside the Greek dream. At Apollo's side stands the recurring figure of the Father. Heidegger is the only one, at least to my knowledge, who did not simply limit himself to dreaming of Greece, but who fulfilled this Greek dream at the cost of a radical erasure of all that could be recognized as the Other of the Greek [*comme l'Autre du grec*].

It is in this sense that Western history is not simply *interpreted* by Heidegger (which is what would have happened had he accentuated one or another dimension that he judged essential): it is, properly speaking, corrected. It is corrected, *because parts of it are crossed out.* What constitutes the distinctiveness of Heidegger's enterprise, and what makes him pass beyond the limits of mere interpretation, is precisely this crossing out that effaces and makes indiscernible.

At the outcome of this correction, we find ourselves with a new West. It is a West that indeed has at its disposal (and we should perhaps even say: that has at its disposal, finally and for the first time) all the dimensions that constituted it, from the origin. This is a West returned to its rich plenitude of content, and yet mysteriously, phantasmatically (unpardonably?) *purified.* It is purified because it is sent back to the putative simplicity of its origin—an origin without duality or alterity, and so, immaculate.

Notes

INTRODUCTION

1. Cf. Martin Heidegger, "Aus einem Gespräch von der Sprache," in *Unterwegs zur Sprache* (Tübingen: Neske, 1971), p. 138. In Heidegger, *Gesamtausgabe*, 102 vols. (Frankfurt am Main: Klostermann, 1975–), 12: 130. (Henceforth, wherever possible, the German single-volume page will appear first, followed by the *Gesamtausgabe*-edition page, and *Gesamtausgabe* will be abbreviated as *GA*.) In English, "A Dialogue on Language: Between a Japanese and an Inquirer," in *On the Way to Language*, trans. Peter D. Hertz (San Francisco: HarperSanFrancisco, 1982), pp. 42–43: "The metamorphosis [of thought] comes to pass like a migration, in which one site is abandoned for another. . . . The first site is metaphysics. And the other? We will leave it without a name." [Translation modified for fluency with the text.—Trans.]

2. Marlène Zarader, *Heidegger et les paroles de l'origine* (Paris: Vrin, 1986).

3. Otto Pöggeler, *Martin Heidegger's Path of Thinking*, trans. Daniel Magurshak and Sigmund Barber (Atlantic Highlands, N.J.: Humanities Press International, 1987), p. 6.

4. Ibid.

5. See Part II, Chapter 1, Section I, "Heidegger's Position: God or Being. 'The Two Paths.'"

6. At least it had, until 1987, an exceptional status. Since then, numerous texts have raised the problem. For a discussion of the principle ones among them, cf. Part II, Chapter 3, Section I, "Heidegger, or the 'Supplement of Originarity'? Jacques Derrida's Interpretation."

7. Ricoeur made this remark at the Cerisy Colloquium (Cerisy, France) in 1955. On this discussion, and the different positions represented there, see Part II, Chapter 3, notably Section II, "Western Thought and Metaphysics."

8. Paul Ricoeur, introductory note in Richard Kearney and Joseph Stephen O'Leary, eds., *Heidegger et la question de Dieu* (Paris: Grasset, 1980).

9. Heidegger distinguishes *Historie* and *Geschichte* in *Being and Time*, trans. John Macquarrie and Edward Robinson (New York: Harper and Row, 1962), division 2, § 73, p. 430 (Heidegger's p. 378), "The Ordinary Understanding of History

[*Geschichtlichkeit*] and Dasein's Historizing." Macquarrie and Robinson translate Heidegger's *Historie* as "historiology." This refers to objective treatments of history as the object of a science or learned discourse. On the other hand, Heidegger's *Geschichte* denotes the enlargement of Dasein's own temporalizing. "Authentic being-towards-death—that is to say, the finitude of temporality—is the hidden basis of Dasein's historicality [*Geschichtlichkeit*]." He adds, "Dasein does not first become historical [*geschichtlich*] in repetition; but because it is historical [*geschichtlich*] as temporal [*zeitliches*] it can take itself over in its history [*Geschichte*] by repeating. For this no historiology [*Historie*] is as yet needed" (§ 74, p. 438; Heidegger, *Sein und Zeit* [Tübingen: Niemeyer, 1977], p. 386; in Heidegger, *GA*, 2: 510).—Trans.

Thus Dasein is essentially historical (*geschichtlich*), given its way of deploying its own futural time, as it exists. This essential quality of Dasein precedes and makes possible any science of history per se.

10. James Barr, *The Semantics of Biblical Language* (London: Oxford University Press, 1961). The theses of this book are directed against the principal representatives of "biblical theology" (Boman, Knight, Torrance, Hebert, etc.). It does not so much contest the theological orientation they take in regard to linguistic data in theology. Barr's critique unfolds in two registers. In the first place, he contests the theoretical principles that direct their study of linguistic facts (i.e., their lexical method and the importance they accord to etymology, which entails an "illusion of roots," etc.). In the second place, he challenges the legitimacy of recourse to linguistics—whatever the orientation of the latter—to support or illustrate differences in thought (such recourse being founded on "a naive philosophy of language, for which structures of thought find a direct echo in linguistic structures"; see ibid., p. 279; also see p. 145 for the etymological illusion).

If his sometimes seductive argument does not completely convince us, this is because it is hardly better founded than those which it rejects. In the linguistic register, Barr opposed the double authority of the use and the intention of the interlocutor to the prevalence of etymology (pp. 290 ff.); in this respect it remains determined, despite its intentions, by an unavowed metaphysics, which gives the most significant role to the speaking subject. As to the "philosophy of language," which should form the ultimate presupposition of the proceedings used in biblical theology, Barr makes extensive use of it: asserting, with rare consistency, that there is no *relationship* between language and thought, he simply opposes one philosophy to another. That is, Barr criticizes certain linguistic principles only to substitute others, which are no less uncertain than his objects of criticism, and he grapples with a philosophy that he simply inverts without properly putting it down.

For a response on the part of one of the principal "defendants," see Thorleif Boman, *Hebrew Thought Compared with Greek*, trans. Jules L. Moreau (Philadelphia: Westminster Press, 1960); originally, *Das hebräische Denken im Vergleich mit dem griechischen* (Göttingen: Vandenhoeck and Ruprecht, 1952). This book, which I will be using extensively throughout this study, constitutes one of the main targets of Barr's criticism. It has been enlarged in the fifth German edition of 1968 by a final chapter entitled "Language and Thought." The final chapter is designed to respond to Barr's criticism. [The English translation of Boman's is from the second German edition, and does not feature the final chapter to which Zarader alludes.—Trans.]

11. See, in this work, Part I, Chapter 2, "The Question of Language."

12. Barr, *Semantics of Biblical Language*, p. 160, n. 1.

13. Ibid., p. 284. [Barr actually calls this "Midrashic romances."—Trans.]

14. See, in particular, Emmanuel Lévinas, *Difficult Freedom: Essays on Judaism*, trans. Seán Hand (Baltimore: Johns Hopkins University Press, 1990), pp. 6–7.

15. For more developed analyses of this point, please see the chapters devoted to these questions of time and language; see Zarader, *Heidegger et les paroles de l'origine*.

16. See below Part II, Chapters 1 and 2, "And How Is It with Being?" and "The Problem of Transmission."

17. I am borrowing the expression from Maria Villela-Petit, who applied it to the relation between Christianity and Hegelian philosophy. See "Le Narratif biblique et la philosophie de l'histoire," in *Cristianismo e história*, (São Paulo: Soyola, 1982), p. 119.

18. See Part II, Chapters 1 and 2.

PART I, CHAPTER 1: HEIDEGGER'S READING OF HISTORY

This chapter takes up and reworks large passages from an article entitled "Le Miroir aux trois reflets: Histoire d'une évolution," published in the *Revue de philosophie ancienne* 4, no. 1 (1986): 10–20. The first English translation of this essay is "The Mirror with a Triple Reflection," in Christopher MacAnn, ed., *Martin Heidegger: Critical Assessments*, 4 vols. (New York: Routledge, 1992), 2: 17–36. The essay was republished in MacAnne, ed., *Critical Heidegger* (New York: Routledge, 1996), pp. 7–27.

1. See Jean Greisch, *La Parole heureuse: Heidegger entre les choses et les mots* (Paris: Beauchesne, 1987), p. 214. Greisch writes, "Metaphysics would be a mere system of representations if it were not capable of manifesting itself elsewhere than in the discourse of the metaphysicians. . . . In domains apparently wholly free of any 'metaphysical prejudice,' *the economy of the metaphysical mechanism unfolds its effects.*" See also, ibid., p. 190.

2. Recall that ontology, understood as "that which properly brings beings to the word and the concept," Martin Heidegger, *Nietzsche*, vols. 1 and 2, trans. David Farrell Krell (San Francisco: HarperSanFrancisco, 1991), is constantly defined

by Heidegger as the "heart" or the "essence" of metaphysics. See *Nietzsche* (Pfullingen: Neske, 1998), 2: 208; in *Gesamtausgabe*, 102 vols. (Frankfurt am Main: Klostermann, 1975–), 6.2: 185. [English translation modified for fluency with the text. Henceforth *Gesamtausgabe* will be abbreviated as *GA*.—Trans.] See, notably, Heidegger's introduction to *What Is Metaphysics?* (*Was ist Metaphysik?*), in *Pathmarks* (*Wegmarken*), trans. and ed. William McNeill (Cambridge: Cambridge University Press, 1998). French edition in Henri Corbin, Roger Munier, Alphonse de Waelhens, Walter Biemel, et al., trans. and eds., *Questions I* (Paris: Gallimard, 1968), p. 39. Hereafter cited as *Questions I*.

3. See *Pathmarks*. In French, Kostas Axelos, Jean Beaufret, Dominique Janicaud, Lucien Braun, Michel Haar, André Préau, François Fédier, trans. and eds., *Questions II* (Paris: Gallimard, 1968). Hereafter cited as *Questions II*.

4. In Martin Heidegger, *On Time and Being*, trans. Joan Stambaugh (Harper and Row, 1972). See Heidegger, *Zur Sache des Denkens* (Tübingen: Niemeyer, 1976); in *GA*, vol. 14. French citation from Jean Beaufret, François Fédier, Jean Lauxerois, and Claude Roels, trans. and eds., *Questions IV* (Paris: Gallimard, 1976).

5. Martin Heidegger, *Was heisst Denken?* (Tübingen: Niemeyer, 1971), p. 2; in *GA*, 8: 6. [Zarader uses the French translation of Aloys Becker and Gérard Granel, *Qu'appelle-t-on penser?* (Paris: Presses Universitaires de France, 1959), p. 22.—Trans.] In English, see *What Is Called Thinking?* trans. J. Glenn Gray (New York: Harper and Row, 1972), p. 3.

6. Martin Heidegger, "Platons Lehre von der Wahrheit," in *Wegmarken*, 2nd expanded ed. (Frankfurt am Main: Klostermann, 1978), p. 143; in *GA*, 9: 237. In *Pathmarks*, p. 182.

7. Heidegger, *Zur Sache des Denkens*, p. 78. Zarader cites *Questions IV*, pp. 135–36. In English, see Joan Stambaugh, trans., *On Time and Being* (Harper and Row, 1972), p. 70.

8. Martin Heidegger, "Einleitung," in "Was ist Metaphysik?" in *Wegmarken*, p. 199; in *GA*, 9: 369. In English, see Heidegger's introduction to "What Is Metaphysics?" in *Pathmarks*. French citation from *Questions I*, p. 28.

9. Heidegger, *Zur Sache des Denkens*, p. 79. In English, Heidegger, *On Time and Being*, p. 71. See also Heidegger, "A Dialogue on Language: Between a Japanese and an Inquirer," in *On the Way to Language*, trans. Peter D. Hertz (San Francisco: HarperSanFrancisco, 1982), p. 39. For the German, see Heidegger, *Unterwegs zur Sprache* (Frankfurt am Main: Klostermann, 1985), p. 127; *GA*, 12: 127 (in the Neske edition, see p. 135). In French, Jean Beaufret, Wolfgang Brockmeier, and François Fédier, trans. and eds., *Acheminement vers la parole* (Paris: Gallimard, 1976), p. 125. "To pursue more originarily what the Greeks have thought, to see it the source of its reality. To see it so is in its own way Greek, and yet in respect of what it sees is no longer, is never again, Greek" (p. 39).

10. "Language in the Poem: A Discussion on Georg Trakl's Poetic Work," in Heidegger, *On the Way to Language*, p. 191. Heidegger says, "This language sings the song of the homecoming in apartness, the homecoming which, from the lateness of decomposition, comes to rest in the earliness of the stiller, and still impending, beginning [*des stilleren, noch ungewesenen Anbeginns einkehrt*]." For the German, see p. 74.

11. This is a movement whose mere outlines I have limited myself to tracing, in a way that remains necessarily formal. In the process, we will encounter a certain number of questions that constitute so many incarnations of this movement. It is only after having unfolded these, one by one, that we shall be able to "fill in" the formal structure presented here, thereby returning to its native "land" [*rapatriant*] as it were, the entire series of figures encountered in the meanwhile (truth, language, thought, etc.). See below, in this book, Part II, Chapter 3, Section I, "Heidegger, or the 'Supplement of Originarity': Jacques Derrida's Interpretation."

12. Heidegger, *Seminar über den Vortrag "Zeit und Sein,"* in *Zur Sache des Denkens*, p. 45. In English, see *On Time and Being*, p. 41: "Appropriation [*Ereignis*] is in itself *expropriation* [*Enteignis*]. This word contains in a manner commensurate with appropriation, the early Greek *léthé* in the sense of concealing."

13. Ibid., p. 58 (German), p. 54 (in Stambaugh's English translation).

14. Ibid., pp. 44–45 (German), p. 41 (English); also see p. 53 (German), p. 50 (English).

15. Martin Heidegger, *Gelassenheit* (Pfullingen: Günther Neske, 1959), p. 18; *GA*, 16: 528–29. In English, see Heidegger, *Discourse on Thinking*, trans. John M. Anderson and E. Hans Freund (New York: Harper and Row, 1966), pp. 55–56. Heidegger's *Gelassenheit* appeared in *GA*, broken up as follows: the "Memorial Address," called, in German "Gelassenheit (30 October 1955)," appeared in *GA*, vol. 16; the "Conversation on a Country Path About Thinking" appeared in *GA*, vol. 13, entitled "Zur Erörterung der Gelassenheit: Aus einem Feldweggespräch über das Denken (1944/45)." The English brings them all together in one volume.

16. See notably, Heidegger's letter to Ernst Jünger, "Zur Seinsfrage," in *Wegmarken*, p. 389; *GA*, 9: 95. In English, see *Pathmarks*, p. 294.

17. Heidegger, "Ueberwindung der Metaphysik (1936–1946)," in *Vorträge und Aufsätze* (Pfullingen: Neske, 1976), pp. 72–73; *GA*, vol. 7, *I. Abteilung: Veröffentlichte Schriften 1910–1976*, pp. 70–71. In English, *The End of Philosophy*, trans. Joan Stambaugh (New York: Harper and Row, 1973), pp. 86–87.

18. See "Das Wesen der Sprache," in *Unterwegs zur Sprache*, p. 165; *GA*, 12: 155. In English, see Heidegger, "The Nature of Language," in *On the Way to Language*, p. 62.

19. Heidegger, *Wegmarken*, p. 337; *GA*, 9: 267. For the English, see "Letter on Humanism," in *Pathmarks*, p. 259.

20. Martin Heidegger, *Einführung in die Metaphysik* (Tübingen: Niemeyer,

1976), p. 152; *GA*, 40: 208. In English, see "The Restriction of Being," in Heidegger, *Introduction to Metaphysics*, trans. Gregory Fried and Richard Polt (New Haven, Conn.: Yale University Press, 2000), p. 213.

21. Heidegger, *Gelassenheit*, p. 12; *GA*, 16: 524. In English, see *Discourse on Thinking*, p. 51.

22. Whence comes the entire theme of *Austrag* as "settlement of the difference or dispute." See Heidegger, *Identität und Differenz* (Pfullingen: Günther Neske, 1957), p. 63, and *Unterwegs zur Sprache*, p. 26; *GA*, 12: 23. In English, see *Identity and Difference*, trans. Joan Stambaugh (New York: Harper and Row, 1969), p. 65, and *On the Way to Language*, p. 181.

23. See below, Part I, Chapter 4, "The Question of Interpretation."

PART I, CHAPTER 2: THE QUESTION OF LANGUAGE

1. See the following principal texts: *The Origin of the Work of Art* (1936) and Heidegger's first lecture courses on Hölderlin, notably *Hölderlin and the Essence of Poetry* (1936) and "As When on a Holiday . . . " [delivered in 1939], in Heidegger, *Erläuterungen zu Hölderlins Dichtung*, *GA*, vol. 4. To these we must add the three courses on Hölderlin, in Martin Heidegger, *Gesamtausgabe*, 102 vols. (Frankfurt am Main: Klostermann, 1975–), vols. 39, 52, and 53 [the *Gesamtausgabe* is abbreviated as *GA*]. These lecture courses span the years 1934 (*Hölderlins Hymnen "Germanien" und "Der Rhein"*) through 1942 (*Hölderlins Hymne "Andenken"* and *Hölderlins Hymne "Der Ister"*) is translated into English in Heidegger, *Hölderlin's Hymn "The Ister,"* trans. William McNeill and Julia Davis (Bloomington: Indiana University Press, 1996). The "As When on a Holiday . . . ," "Remembrance," and "Hölderlin and the Essence of Poetry" appear in Heidegger, *Elucidations of Hölderlin's Poetry*, trans. Keith Hoeller (Amherst, N.Y.: Humanity Books, 2000), pp. 67–99, 101–73, and pp. 51–65, respectively.

2. See Heidegger's article, "Logos" (1944), in *Vorträge und Aufsätze* (Pfullingen: Neske, 1976), pp. 207–29; *GA*, 7: 211–34; the lecture course *Heraklits Lehre vom Logos*, in Heidegger, *GA*, vol. 55, and then later, the second part of *Was heisst Denken?* (Tübingen: Niemeyer, 1971); see *GA*, vol. 8. In English, *What Is Called Thinking?* trans. J. Glenn Gray (New York: Harper and Row, 1972). Also see Heidegger, "Logos (Heraclitus, Fragment B 50)," in *Early Greek Thinking: The Dawn of Western Philosophy*, trans. David Farrell Krell and Frank A. Capuzzi (San Francisco: HarperSanFrancisco, 1984).

3. See the following principal texts: the second part of Heidegger's *Vorträge und Aufsätze* ("Was heisst Denken?" [1952], "Bauen Wohnen Denken" [1951], "Das Ding" [1950], " . . . dichterisch wohnet der Mensch" [1952]). English, *What Is Called Thinking?*; "Building Dwelling Thinking," in *Martin Heidegger: Basic Writings*, ed. David Farrell Krell (New York: Harper and Row, 1993). "The Thing"

and "Poetically Man Dwells" are in Heidegger, *Poetry, Language, Thought*, trans. Albert Hofstadter (New York: Perennial Classics, 2001).

Finally, see the texts *Unterwegs zur Sprache* (Pfullingen: Neske, 1976); *GA*, vol. 12; in English, *On the Way to Language*, trans. Peter D. Hertz (San Francisco: HarperSanFrancisco, 1982) [the different articles in this work span the years 1950 to 1960], as well as the final texts on Hölderlin, notably "Hölderlin's Earth and Heaven" (1958), in Heidegger, *Elucidations of Hölderlin's Poetry*, pp. 175–207.

4. Heidegger, *Unterwegs zur Sprache*, p. 245; *GA*, 12: 233–34. In English, "The Way to Language," in *On the Way to Language*, p. 115.

5. Ibid.

6. Heidegger, *Vorträge und Aufsätze*, pp. 203–5; *GA*, 7: 217–18. In English, see "Logos," in *Early Greek Thinking*, pp. 63–64.

7. See *Vorträge und Aufsätze*, p. 139; *GA*, 7: 147 ff. In English, see "Building Dwelling Thinking," in Heidegger, *Basic Writings*, pp. 347 ff.

8. Heidegger, *Was heisst Denken?* (pt. 2, from 8 to 9), p. 171; *GA*, 8: 208. For English, see pt. 2, lecture 8, "Summary and Transition," in *What Is Called Thinking?* p. 205.

9. See notably the movement of thought followed in ibid., pt. 2, lecture 1, pp. 79–86; *GA*, 8: 117–25. English: pt. 2, lecture 1, pp. 113–25.

10. Ibid., p. 83; *GA*, 8: 122; English, p. 118.

11. Ibid.; *GA*, 8: 123.

12. Ibid., p. 84; English, p. 119. [Translation modified for fluency with Zarader's text. The English translation reads: "Is it playing with words when we attempt to give heed to this game of language and to hear what language really says when it speaks?"—Trans.]

13. Ibid., p. 83; *GA*, 8: 122; English, p. 118. Translation modified for fluency with Zarader's text. The English translation reads: "If we may talk here of playing games at all, it is not we who play with words but the nature of language plays with us, not only in this case, not only now, but long since and always."—Trans.]

14. Heidegger, "Heraklit: 1. Der Anfang des Abendländischen Denkens," *GA*, 55: 148. [Not yet published in English.—Trans.]

15. Jean Greisch, *La Parole heureuse: Martin Heidegger entre les choses et les mots* (Paris: Beauchesne, 1987), pp. 393–94.

16. A definition often taken up by Heidegger. See notably, *Unterwegs zur Sprache*, pp. 20–21; *GA*, 12: 18. For the English, see *Poetry, Language, Thought*, p. 198. Also see Heidegger, *Erläuterungen zu Hölderlins Dichtung*, pp. 34–35; *GA*, 4: 36–37. In English, *Elucidations of Hölderlin's Poetry*, p. 215.

17. Heidegger, *Unterwegs zur Sprache*, p. 164; *GA*, 12: 154: "Das Wort verschafft dem Ding erst das Sein." English see "The Nature of Language," in *On the Way to Language*, p. 62: "The word alone gives being to the thing."

18. Heidegger, *Erläuterungen zu Hölderlins Dichtung*, p. 38; *GA*, 4: 41; in Eng-

lish, *Elucidations of Hölderlin's Poetry*, p. 56. [Translation modified slightly for fluency with the text; the English reads, "as the founding of being, poetry is bound in a *twofold* sense."—Trans.]

19. Greisch, *La Parole heureuse*, p. 250.

20. Heidegger, *Erläuterungen zu Hölderlins Dichtung*, p. 36; *GA* 4: 39. "Reden-können und Hörenkönnen sind gleich ursprünglich. Wir sind ein Gespräch— und das will sagen: wir können voneinander hören . . . wir sind ein Gespräch." In English, see *Elucidations of Hölderlin's Poetry*, p. 57.

21. Heidegger, *Hölderlins Hymnen "Andenken,"* in *GA*, 52: 157. "Das Gespräch, so genommen, ist nicht ein Gebrauchsform der Sprache. Vielmehr hat die Sprache ihren Ursprung im Gespräch und d. h. im Fest und somit in dem, worin dieses selbst gründet."

22. Heidegger, "Germanien," § 7: "Der Sprachcharakter der Dichtung," in "Hölderlins Hymnen 'Germanien' und 'Der Rhein,'" *GA*, 39: 69–70.

23. The expression *fait être* is uncommon in French and belongs to a largely Heideggerian register; implicit in this expression is "language makes 'what-is' be," or "language makes all things 'be.'"—Trans.

24. This is indeed the reason why it can be called the "house of being."

25. Heidegger, *Unterwegs zur Sprache*, p. 16; *GA* 12: 13–14; "Language," in *Poetry, Language, Thought*, p. 194. *Erläuterungen zu Hölderlins Dichtung*, p. 40; *GA* 4: 43; *Elucidations of Hölderlin's Poetry*, p. 64.

26. See *Erläuterungen zu Hölderlins Dichtung*, p. 44; *GA* 4: 47. *Elucidations of Hölderlin's Poetry*, pp. 64–65.

27. Such as they appear notably throughout the meditation on Hölderlin, in whom this mission is incarnate in an exemplary fashion.

28. See Heidegger, *Parmenides*, in *GA*, 54: 188; In English, see *Parmenides*, trans. André Schuwer and Richard Rojcewicz (Bloomington: Indiana University Press, 1992), p. 126. Schuwer and Rojcewicz translate this as "the primordial free salvation and preservation of Being."

29. André Neher, *The Exile of the Word: From the Silence of the Bible to the Silence of Auschwitz*, trans. David Maisel (Philadelphia: Jewish Publication Society of America, 1981), p. 91. A translation of *L'Exil de la parole: Du silence biblique au silence d'Auschwitz* (Paris: Éditions du Seuil, 1970), p. 99.

30. Ibid.

31. Rabbi Shlomo Yitzchaki (1040–1105 C.E.), or "Rashi," is considered the greatest biblical and Talmudic commentator of the Middle Ages. Born in Troyes, France, he survived the First Crusade (1095–1201 C.E.). His exegesis was punctilious, concerned with each word in the text that required explanation (written down by his students). His biblical commentary first appeared in 1517 in the original, printed Bomberg text. It is for his explanations of Gemara that he is more famous still, as he explained the discussions of the sages who put the Gemara to-

gether, thereby rendering the Talmud more accessible to the nonscholar.—Trans.

32. André Neher, *The Prophetic Existence*, trans. William Wolf (South Bruns-wick, N.J.: A. S. Barnes, 1969), pp. 137–38. A translation of *L'Essence du prophé-tisme* (Paris: Calmann-Lévy, 1972), p. 125.

33. N. de Cacqueray, *Connaissance et langage symboliques dans la Bible* (Rennes: Université de Rennes, 1981), unpublished thesis.

34. See ibid., pp. 31 ff.

35. See, for example, in Numbers 15:38–40, the obligation upon the sons of Is-rael to wear fringes on their shawls: "It shall be to you a tassel to look upon and remember all the commandments of the Lord, to do them, not to follow after your own heart and your own eyes . . . " The connection thus established rests a pure proximity of consonants: in Hebrew, the fringe or tassel (*tsit-tsit*) recalls obe-dience due to Yahweh (*tsiyts*), and the requirement of practicing his command-ments (*mitzvot*). See de Cacqueray, *Connaissance et langage symboliques dans la Bible*, p. 73.

36. Ibid., pp. 67–86.

37. Hence the opposition sketched by Martin Buber and developed by Da-vid Bannon, between *logophany* and *hierophany*. See David Banon, *La Lecture in-finie: Les Voies de l'interprétation midrachique* (Paris: Éditions du Seuil, 1987), pp. 33, 139, and so on.

38. See Alexandre Safran, *La Cabale*, 3rd ed. corrected (Paris: Payot, 1983), p. 82. In English, *The Kabbalah: Law and Mysticism in the Jewish Tradition*, trans. Margaret A. Pater (New York: Feldheim, 1975, trans. of the 1st ed.), p. 55.

39. This is a verse often cited by André Neher in his *The Exile of the Word*, pp. 10, 17.

40. See ibid., pp. 94–100.

41. Ibid., pp. 112–13.

42. Ibid., pp. 113–20.

43. Emmanuel Lévinas, *Autrement qu'être ou au-delà de l'essence* (The Hague: Martinus Nijhoff, 1974; 1991, 5th ed., by Kluwer), pp. 185–94. For the English, see *Otherwise Than Being; or, Beyond Essence*, trans. Alphonso Lingis (Pittsburgh: Duquesne University Press, 1998), pp. 145–53.

44. Emmanuel Lévinas, *Noms propres* (Montpellier: Fata Morgana, 1976), pp. 59–66; *Proper Names*, trans. Michael B. Smith (Stanford, Calif.: Stanford Univer-sity Press, 1996), pp. 40–46.

45. Ibid., p. 65; in English, pp. 45–46.

46. See notably Henri Birault, *Heidegger et l'expérience de la pensée* (Paris: Gal-limard, 1978), p. 398: "The word about which Heidegger is speaking to us in the book *Die Sprache*—a secret, originary, and solitary word, concerned only with itself, speaking only with itself, and one which, even in its essential relationship with the essence of man, still refers only to itself—is without kinship with the

Word or the spoken word of God [*le Verb ou la Parole de Dieu*]."

We find the same position articulated by Jean Greisch who, in his "La Contrée de la sérénité" [The Land of Serenity] emphasizes "the dual incompatibility of Heidegger's serenity with the serenity of the mystic and the listening to a revealed god." See *Heidegger et la question de Dieu*, eds. Richard Kearney and Joseph Stephen O'Leary (Paris: Grasset, 1980), p. 177.

On the other hand, the opposition to this position, inaugurated by Lévinas, is thrown into doubt in another article in the same collection, see Joseph Stephen O'Leary, "Topologie de l'être et topographie de la révélation," in *Heidegger et la question*, p. 209.

47. Jürgen Habermas, "Penser avec Heidegger contre Heidegger?" in *Profils philosophiques et politiques*, trans. Françoise Dastur, Jean-René Ladmiral, and Marc B. Delaunay (Paris: Gallimard, 1974), p. 96. The original work was entitled, *Philosophisch-politische Profile* (Frankfurt am Main: Suhrkamp, 1987). [Frederick G. Lawrence, translator of the German volume, did not include "To Think with Heidegger Against Heidegger," in his *Philosophical-Political Profiles* (Cambridge, Mass.: MIT Press, 1983), which combines essays from the above German edition and from Habermas's *Kultur und Kritik: Versträute Aufsätze* (1973). The closest citation is from page 60. We therefore translate the French, here, for fluency with the text: "The call is modified, whereas the structures of philosophical meaning retain their stability over the decades of his evolution. . . . The tone of the call has changed at least two times . . . while neither the intellectual theme of exhortation to authenticity, nor that of the polemic against decadence has varied."—Trans.]

48. See below, Part II, Chapter 1, Section III, "From God to Being: The Abandonment of Ethics. The Debate with Emmanuel Lévinas."

49. Heidegger, *Erläuterungen zu Hölderlins Dichtung*, p. 108; *GA*, 4: 114. In English, *Elucidations of Hölderlin's Poetry*, p. 137.

50. Paul Beauchamp, *L'Un et l'autre testament* (Paris: Éditions du Seuil, 1990), p. 79. [All translations are by the translator of this volume, unless otherwise stated.—Trans.]

51. De Cacqueray, *Connaissance et Langage symboliques dans la Bible*, p. 228.

52. Neher, *The Exile of the Word*, pp. 156–57, 164.

53. *Erläuterungen zu Hölderlins Dichtung*, p. 64; *GA*, 4: 66. In English, *Elucidations of Hölderlin's Poetry*, p. 88: "such an excess of meaning as can scarcely be uttered."

54. Ibid., p. 98; *GA*, 4: 103; in English, p. 126.

55. Ibid., p. 101; *GA*, 4: 106; in English, pp. 129–30.

56. Ibid., p. 44; *GA*, 4: 47; in English, p. 64.

57. Ibid., p. 139–40; *GA*, 4: 148; in English, pp. 169–70.

58. Ibid.

59. Ibid., p. 64; *GA*, 4: 66; in English, p. 88: "even a poet is never capable of

attaining the holy through his own meditation, or indeed exhausting its essence [*Wesen*] and forcing it to come to him through his questioning [*durch das Fragen*]."

60. Ibid., p. 37; *GA*, 4: 40; in English, p. 58.

61. See, on this subject, the last chapter, "Prophetic Existence," of Neher, *The Prophetic Existence*, pp. 282 ff.

62. *Erläuterungen zu Hölderlins Dichtung*, p. 69; *GA*, 4: 71. In English, see *Elucidations of Hölderlin's Poetry*, p. 93 [" . . . so gilt es doch, den vermittelnden Strahl 'mit eigner Hand zu fassen' und selbst in den 'Wettern' des aufgehenden Anfänglichen auszuharren (. . . it is still necessary 'to grasp with our own hands' the mediating ray, and to endure the rising 'storms' of the primordial one)"].

63. Neher, *The Prophetic Existence*, p. 331.

64. *Erläuterungen zu Hölderlins Dichtung*, p. 104; *GA*, 4: 110. In English, see *Elucidations of Hölderlin's Poetry*, p. 133.

65. See, notably, Isaiah 8:18; Ezekiel 24:24–27.

66. *Erläuterungen zu Hölderlins Dichtung*, p. 42; *GA*, 4: 46. In English, see *Elucidations of Hölderlin's Poetry*, p. 63: "The poet's saying is the intercepting of these hints, in order to pass them on to his people."

67. Ibid. The Hölderlin poem is "Mnemosyne," cited by Heidegger in *Was heisst Denken?*, and in *GA*, vol. 8; in English, *What Is Called Thinking?*

68. Ibid., p. 119; *GA*, 4: 126; in English, p. 148.

69. Ibid., p. 56; *GA*, 4: 58; in English, p. 80. [I follow Zarader's translation for fluency with her text.—Trans.]

70. Ibid., p. 104; *GA*, 4: 110; in English, p. 133: "Because the night, in such sheltering-concealing darkness, is not nothing, it also has its own vast *clarity* and the *peacefulness* of the silent preparation for something which is coming. To the latter belongs its own vigil, not that sleeplessness that needs sleep, but rather that which keeps watch over and protects the night."

71. Talmud, "Makhoth," 24a. The discussion is resumed in Gershom Scholem, *Zur Kabbala und ihrer Symbolik*. In English, *On the Kabbalah and Its Symbolism*, trans. Ralph Manheim, foreword by Bernard McGinn (New York: Schocken Books, 1996), pp. 29–30.

72. *Erläuterungen zu Hölderlins Dichtung*, p. 43; *GA*, 4: 47. In English, see *Elucidations of Hölderlin's Poetry*, p. 64.

73. Ibid., pp. 68–69; *GA*, 4: 70–71; in English, p. 92.

74. On this theme, see Neher, *The Prophetic Existence*, pp. 337–38.

PART I, CHAPTER 3: THE QUESTION OF THOUGHT

1. On the basis of context, the French distinguishes, for the nominalized participle *la pensée*, between the ongoing activity of "thinking" and the "thought" that,

as a kind of totality, belongs to intellectual or spiritual traditions. I therefore translate *la pensée* generally as "thought," but also, according to variations in context, as the noun formed from the present participle, "thinking."—Trans.

2. Heidegger, *Was heisst Denken?* (Tübingen: Niemeyer, 1971), p. 2; *Gesamtausgabe*, 102 vols. (Frankfurt am Main: Klostermann, 1975–), 8: 6 [henceforth, citations from the *Gesamtausgabe* will be abbreviated as *GA*]. In English, *What Is Called Thinking?* trans. J. Glenn Gray (New York: Harper and Row, 1972), p. 4.

3. Ibid., p. 7; *GA*, 8: 13; in English, p. 11.

4. Etymology frequently recalled by Heidegger. See notably, Heidegger, "Vortrag," in *Der Satz vom Grund* (Pfullingen: Neske, 1957), pp. 210–11; *GA*, 10: 189. In English, *The Principle of Reason*, trans. Reginal Lilly (Bloomington: Indiana University Press, 1996), p. 129.

5. *Was heisst Denken?* p. 5; *GA*, 8: 10; *What Is Called Thinking?* p. 8. Also see Heidegger, *Identität und Differenz* (Pfullingen: Neske, 1957), 42. In English, *Identity and Difference*, trans. Joan Stambaugh (New York: Harper and Row, 1969), p. 53.

6. Marlène Zarader, *Heidegger et les Paroles de l'origine* (Paris: Vrin, 1986), pp. 263 ff.

7. See Heidegger, "Die Sprache," in *Unterwegs zur Sprache* (Pfullingen: Neske, 1976), pp. 16, 242; *GA*, 12: 13, 230. In English, see "Language," in *Poetry, Language, Thought*, trans. Albert Hofstadter (New York: Perennial Classics, 2001), p. 189; then see *On The Way to Language*, trans. Peter D. Hertz (San Francisco: HarperSanFrancisco, 1982), p. 112.

8. "Das Wesen der Sprache," in *Unterwegs zur Sprache*, p. 186; *GA*, 12: 175. In English, see "The Nature of Language" in *On the Way to Language*, p. 81.

9. *Was heisst Denken?* p. 79; *GA*, 8: 117. *What Is Called Thinking?* p. 113.

10. Ibid. [Translation modified for fluency with text.—Trans.]

11. The old word *Gedanc* [said to correspond with the Old English *thanc* or *thonc*] will come to be *Gedanke*, or "thought," "notion," "memory." But *Gedanc* does not mean these; it means "the gathered . . . gathering thinking that recalls." It contains both *denken* and *danken*, "to think" and "to thank, to acknowledge," as Heidegger notes in the seminar. Thinking in its originary form contains a thankfulness to Being. See *What Is Called Thinking?* p. 139.

12. *Was heisst Denken?* pp. 81–83; *GA*, 8: 114–22. In English, *What Is Called Thinking?* pp. 116–18.

13. See Marlène Zarader, "Le Miroir aux trois reflets: Histoire d'une évolution," [The Mirror with Three Reflections: The History of an Evolution], in *Revue de philosophie ancienne* 4, no. 1 (1986): 10–20. This chapter takes up and reworks large passages from the original article just cited. The first English translation of this essay is "The Mirror with a Triple Reflection," in Christopher Macann, ed., *Martin Heidegger: Critical Assessments*, 4 vols. (New York: Routledge, 1992), 2: 17–

36. The essay was subsequently republished in Macanne, ed., *Critical Heidegger* (New York: Routledge, 1996), pp. 7–26.

14. This is what the theme of "lightning abruptly lay[ing] before us everything present in the light of its presencing" [Zarader's "inaugural flash"] is about. See Heidegger's article "Logos (Heraklit, Fragment B 50)," in *Vorträge und Aufsätze* (Pfullingen: Neske, 1976), pp. 222, 228–29; *GA*, 7: 227, 233; in English, "Logos (Heraclitus, Fragment B 50)," in *Early Greek Thinking: The Dawn of Western Philosophy*, trans. David Farrell Krell and Frank A. Capuzzi (San Francisco: HarperSanFrancisco, 1984), pp. 72, 78.

15. See Heidegger, *Vorträge und Aufsätze*, pp. 207–29; *GA*, 7: 211–34.

16. *Was heisst Denken?* p. 91; *GA*, 8: 142; *What Is Called Thinking?* p. 138.

17. Ibid., pp. 2–3, 85; *GA*, 8: 6–7, 125; in English, pp. 3–4, 125.

18. Ibid., pp. 4–6; *GA*, 8: 9–12; in English, pp. 7–11.

19. Ibid., pp. 6–8, 92; *GA*, 8: 11–14, 143; in English, pp. 9–12, 139. [J. Glenn Grey drops the sentence "'Der Gedanc' sagt soviel wie das Gemüt, der muot, das Herz" in his translation. The *Thanc* says as much as feeling or *muot*, "the heart," on p. 92 of the German 3rd ed.—Trans.]

20. Ibid., pp. 93–95; *GA*, 8: 143–47; in English, pp. 140–43.

21. Heidegger, § 9, "Das Thema der Analytik des Daseins," in *Sein und Zeit* (Tübingen: Niemeyer, 1977), and *GA*, vol. 2. For English, see *Being and Time*, trans. John Macquarrie and Edward Robinson (New York: Harper and Row, 1962), § 9. (A subsequent translation, sanctioned by Heidegger himself, was published by Joan Stambaugh: see *Being and Time* [Albany: State University of New York Press, 1997], § 9.)

22. See Heidegger, "Zur Erörterung der Gelassenheit: Aus einem Feldweggespräch über das Denken," in *Gelassenheit* (Pfullingen: Neske, 1959), pp. 29–73. Heidegger's *Gelassenheit* appeared in *GA*, broken up as follows: the "Memorial Address," called, in German "Gelassenheit (30 October 1955)," appeared in *GA*, vol. 16; the "Conversation on a Country Path About Thinking" appeared in *GA*, vol. 13, entitled "Zur Erörterung der Gelassenheit: Aus einem Feldweggessspräch über das Denken (1944/45)." The English brings them all together in one volume.

Therein lies an assertion that we find in certain texts explicitly treating the *Discourse on Thinking* (notably the accompanying *Zur Erörterung der Gelassenheit* or "Conversation on a Country Path About Thinking"), which the French entitles "Pour Servir de Commentaire à *Sérénité* (see Heidegger, *Questions III*, trans. André Préau, Julien Hervier, and Roger Munier [Paris: Gallimard, 1966]). For the English, see Heidegger, *Discourse on Thinking: A Translation of "Gelassenheit,"* trans. John M. Anderson and E. Hans Freund (New York: Harper and Row, 1966), pp. 58–90.

However, this assertion is contradicted by other texts, where the themes of waiting and of desire remain prevalent (this is the case in the essay that we have followed in this book, i.e., *What Is Called Thinking?*).

23. A problematic assertion, as Jean Greisch has clearly shown us when he reminds that, in speculative mysticism (notably that of Meister Eckhart), it is God himself who divests himself of his creative will. On this question, see Greisch, "La contrée de la sérénité et l'horizon de l'espérance," in *Heidegger et la question de Dieu*, pp. 178–84.

24. Heidegger, *Gelassenheit*, p. 41; *GA*, 13: 47. In English, see *Discourse on Thinking*, pp. 65–66.

25. Ibid., p. 47; *GA*, 13: 53–54; in English, pp. 70–71. The English is awkward in rendering *Gelassenheit* as "releasement."

26. See notably Henri Birault, *Heidegger et l'expérience de la pensée* (Paris: Gallimard, 1978), pp. 387–88.

27. Jean Greisch, "La Contrée de la sérénité et l'horizon de l'espérance," in *Heidegger et la question de Dieu*, p. 176.

28. This is the sense of one of its criticisms by Habermas. See Habermas, "Penser avec Heidegger contre Heidegger?" p. 97. [This essay does *not* appear in the shorter English translation by Frederick G. Lawrence, *Philosophical-Political Profiles* (Cambridge, Mass.: MIT Press, 1983).—Trans.]

[The French translation reads, "If one does not recognize that, after Descartes— alongside a method of thinking founded on calculation and reducing things to objects available for variable use, there exists the other attitude of intuitive apprehension and comprehension of meaning—then one will not be able to account for the dialectical fluidity of movement of the ideas in the modern age."—Trans.]

29. See above, Part I, Chapter 1, Section III, Subsection 1, "From the Derivative to the Originary."

30. Or, more modestly, if the elements that will serve, in Heidegger's work, to characterize the essence of thought were not already set down in another text.

31. Cf. for example, *Was heisst Denken?* p. 91; *GA*, 8: 142. Heidegger is evidently speaking of *der Wink* (German for "clue," "sign," "hint"). J. Glenn Gray translates *der Wink* as "the clue." See English, *What Is Called Thinking?* p. 138.

32. A remark by Paul Ricoeur at the Colloque de Cerisy (September 4, 1955), following Heidegger's lecture "What Is Philosophy?" [Qu'est-ce que la philosophie?]. It was cited by Jean Beaufret (using the notes taken by him in the meeting); see "Heidegger et la théologie," in *Heidegger et la question de Dieu*, p. 22, and reprinted in Beaufret, *Dialogue avec Heidegger*, vol. 4 (Paris: Éditions de Minuit, 1985).

33. Jacques Derrida, *De l'esprit: Heidegger et la question* (Paris: Éditions Galilée, 1987). In English, *Of Spirit: Heidegger and the Question*, trans. Geoffrey Bennington and Rachel Bowlby (Chicago: University of Chicago Press, 1989).

34. Ibid., p. 148n1. In English, p. 129n5: " . . . before any contract, a sort of promise of originary alliance to which we must have in some sense already acquiesced, already said *yes*, given a pledge . . . "

35. *Was heisst Denken?* p. 83; *GA*, 8: 122; *What Is Called Thinking?* p. 118. "Das Wesen der Sprache," in *Unterwegs zur Sprache*, p. 174; *GA*, 12: 163–64. In English, "The Nature of Language," in *On the Way to Language*, pp. 70 ff.

36. Jacques Derrida, *De l'esprit*, p. 148; In English, *Of Spirit: Heidegger and the Question*, p. 129n5. The English note reminds us that Derrida will not translate Heidegger's *Zusage*, preferring four related terms for it: "promise, agreement, consent, originary abandonment to what is given in the promise itself."

37. Otto Pöggeler, *Martin Heidegger's Path of Thinking*, trans. Daniel Magurshak and Sigmund Barber (Atlantic Highlands, N.J.: Humanities Press International, 1987), p. 233. [The French reads somewhat differently, therefore it is worth noting. "Cependant le questionnement . . . est au contraire determiné par ce qui se consent à lui. . . . Il se révèle ainsi que ce n'est pas l'interrogation, mais l'audition de ce qui est accordé, qui est l'attitude véritable de la pensée" (in the French translation, p. 392).—Trans.]

Pöggeler refers, moreover, to a passage in *Unterwegs zur Sprache*, on which Derrida also relies. See *Unterwegs zur Sprache*, p. 174; *GA*, 12: 163–64. In English, *On the Way to Language*, pp. 70–71.

38. Ibid.; Zarader's emphasis.

39. Gershom Scholem, *On the Kabbalah and Its Symbolism*, trans. Ralph Manheim, foreword by Bernard McGinn (New York: Schocken Books, 1996), p. 20; David Banon, *La Lecture infinie: Les Voies de l'interprétation midrachique* (Paris: Éditions du Seuil, 1987), p. 151; Thorleif Boman, *Hebrew Thought Compared with Greek* (a translation of *Das hebräische Denken im Vergleich mit dem griechischen*), Jules L. Moreau (New York: Norton, 1970), pp. 113–15, 176; Rudolf Bultmann, "La Notion de parole de Dieu dans le Nouveau Testament," in *Foi et compréhension*, vol. 1, *L'Historicité de l'homme et de la révélation*, trans. André Malet, trans. (Paris: Éditions du Seuil, 1969–70), pp. 304–5, 308. See also "La Signification de l'Ancien Testament pour la foi chrétienne," in Bultmann, p. 361. For the English, *The Concept of the Word of God in the New Testament* (London: S.C.M. Press, 1969), pp. 286 ff. and 290. [The English selection does not contain the chapter "The Signification of the Old Testament for Christian Faith."—Trans.]

40. Alexandre Safran, *La Cabale*, 3rd ed. corrected (Paris: Payot, 1983), p. 231. In English, *The Kabbalah: Law and Mysticism in the Jewish Tradition*, trans. Margaret A. Pater, (New York: Feldheim, 1975, trans. of 1st ed.), p. 188. [Translation modified slightly for fluency with the French text.—Trans.]

41. See notably Florent Gaboriau, *Le Thème biblique de la connaissance* (Paris: Desclée de Brouwer, 1970).

42. Banon, *La Lecture infinie*, p. 151.

43. Cited by Richard Kearney, "Heidegger, le possible et Dieu," in *Heidegger et la question de Dieu*, p. 146.

44. On this subject, cf. notably, Yosef Hayim Yerushalmi, *Zakhor: Jewish His-*

tory and Jewish Memory (Seattle: University of Washington Press, 1996), p. 9. [The English original does not use "Yahweh." Bible quotations for this translation are taken from *Tanakh: A New Translation of the Holy Scriptures According to the Traditional Hebrew Text* (Philadelphia: The Jewish Publication Society, 1985).—Trans.]

45. Scholem, *On the Kabbalah and Its Symbolism*, pp. 120–21.

46. Yerushalmi, *Zakhor*, p. 5.

47. When, in *What Is Called Thinking?* Heidegger evokes Mnémosyne in passing, it is as the title of the hymn by Hölderlin. But above all, this evocation takes place in the very first lesson (introduction) of the winter semester course of 1951–52. On the other hand, when he undertakes, the following semester, to thematically unfold the up till then hidden thematic essence of thought (which corresponds to the third of four questions brought out in the course), he does so starting from a constellation of meaning, sketched from the German words, a choice that he does not fail to emphasize himself on several occasions (see, for example, *Was heisst Denken?* p. 102; *GA*, 8: 166–67. In English, *What Is Called Thinking?* pp. 163–64). And it is only when he has arrived at the end of this unfolding that he can *return* to the Greek, to find there a confirmation of what was set down elsewhere (ibid., p. 149; *GA*, 8: 246–47; in English, pp. 243–44).

48. *Was heisst Denken?* p. 7; *GA*, 8: 13; in English, p. 11. "Gedächtnis ist die Versammlung des Andenkens" ["Memory is the gathering of recollection, thinking back"].

49. Yerushalmi dates from the sixteenth century (after the Expulsion from Spain) "the birth of the cultural phenomenon that one can call historiography" (Yerushalmi, *Zakhor*, p. 52).

50. Ibid., p. 6.

51. This is why the biblical figure who explicitly takes charge of history is less that of the historian than that of the prophet.

52. Paul Beauchamp, *L'Un et l'autre testament* (Paris: Éditions du Seuil, 1990), p. 120.

53. Ibid., 121.

54. See the Pirke Avot ["Sayings of the Fathers"] 2: 21, cited by David Banon in *La Lecture infinie*, pp. 33, 139, and elsewhere. [Also see Bernard Scharfstein, ed., *Pirke Avot: Sayings of the Fathers* (New York: Ktav, 1968).—Trans.]

55. See below, Part II, Chapter 1, Section II, Subsection 3, "Withdrawal."

56. See above, Part I, Chapter 2, Section II, Subsection 4, "Poetry and Prophetism."

57. Freud, *Die Verneinung, Gesammelte Werke*, 18 vols. (Frankfurt am Main: Fischer, 1968), 14: 11–15. In English, *Standard Edition of the Complete Psychological Works of Sigmund Freud*, trans. James Strachey and Anna Freud, 24 vols. (London: Hogarth, 1957–74), vol. 14 (1914–16).

Jean Hyppolite's presentation on Freud's "Negation," ("Commentary on the

Verneinung of Freud") was held in 1954, in the framework of Jacques Lacan's seminar on the technical writings of Freud [we can grasp the context, and some of Lacan's responses, in *Freud's Papers on Technique, 1953–1954,* pp. 52–61; see also *The Seminar of Jacques Lacan,* ed. Jacques-Alain Miller, trans. John Forrester (New York: Norton, 1991), pp. 289–97]. The Hyppolite text was first reproduced as "Appendix I: Commentaire parlé sur le *Verneinung* de Freud," in Lacan, *Écrits* (Paris: Éditions du Seuil, 1966), pp. 879–87; and in English in *Freud's Papers on Technique,* pp. 289–97. See also *Écrits: The First Complete Translation in English,* trans. Bruce Fink (New York: Norton, 2005). The presentation was thereafter reprinted in Jean Hyppolite, *Figures de la pensée philosophique,* (Paris: Presses Universitaires de France, 1971), 1: 385–96.

58. See Rudolf Bultmann, "Le Christianisme comme religion orientale et comme religion occidentale," in *Foi et compréhension,* 2 vols. (Paris: Éditions du Seuil, 1969–70), 1: 578. The English abridged volume, *Faith and Understanding,* cited above, does not contain this essay. "We do not find there, save in outline, the abstract formulation of a theme, the exposition of a problem . . . That does not mean that all the meaning of the problems, all the depth of thought are excluded from it. But the ideas are commandments there, imperatives summarily inscribed."

59. In the sense of the second question distinguished by Heidegger in *Was heisst Denken?* (p. 79; *GA,* 8: 117; in English, *What Is Called Thinking?* p. 113): "how does traditional doctrine conceive and define [*aufgefasst und ungrenzt*] what we have named thinking? What is it that for two and a half thousand years has been regarded as the basic characteristic of thinking?"

60. See notably, Gianni Vattimo, *The Adventure of Difference: Philosophy After Nietzsche and Heidegger,* trans. Cyprian Blamires and Thomas Harrison (Baltimore: Johns Hopkins University Press, 1993), pp. 149, 174 ff. Also see Derrida, *De l'esprit,* pp. 183–84; in English, *Of Spirit,* pp. 112–13.

61. See Zarader, "Le Miroir aux trois reflets," p. 17.

62. For example, the distinction between essence and existence, which can be taken for the birth of metaphysics (see Heidegger, *Nietzsche,* vol. 2, § 8, "Die Metaphysik als Geschichte des Seins. Leibniz: Die Zusammengehörigkeit von Wirklichkeit und Vorstellen" ["Metaphysics as the History of Being. Leibniz: The Co-belonging of Reality and Representation"] (Pfullingen: Neske, 1961), p. 401; in *GA,* vol. 6.2, chap. 8, p. 365), is a "trace" of Difference, that is, of the principal 'unthought' of metaphysics. [The Krell English translation does not feature this or subsequent sections.—Trans.]

63. Heidegger, "Die Sprache," in *Unterwegs zur Sprache,* p. 12; *GA,* 12: 10. In English, *Poetry, Language, Thought,* p. 190. [The Hofstadter translation reads, "But we do not want to get anywhere. We would like only, for once, to get to just where we are already."—Trans.]

64. See above in this work, our Introduction.

65. See below in this work, Part II, Chapter 1, Section I, "Heidegger's Position: God or Being. 'The Two Paths.'"

66. This is why I agree fully with David Banon's judgment in his *La Lecture infinie*, p. 19: "Heidegger poses . . . the questions of the possibility of thought, of the becoming of the world, of our language, and of poetry—but also and above all he poses the questions of the origin of philosophy and of the West, which he has going back to the Greeks. . . . [It is] as though the mode of intelligibility suggested by the Scriptures, contrary to [writings] which would go back to the Presocratics, could not preserve, separated from the faith, the slightest vigor or any intellectual fecundity of their own." To this Banon replies, a few lines below [ibid., p. 20]: "Now, biblical discourse and the questioning to which it gives rise are as justifiably constitutive of the West as are the *Iliad*, the *Odyssey*, or the Presocratics." Note that the sentence beginning "as though the mode of intelligibility . . . " is, in reality, without Banon mentioning it, a citation. It is taken from a text of Emmanuel Lévinas, "De la significance du sens," in *Heidegger et la question de Dieu*, p. 238.

67. See below in this work, Part I, Chapter 4, "The Question of Interpretation."

PART I, CHAPTER 4: THE QUESTION OF INTERPRETATION

1. The word *Pardes* (*paradise*) is composed of the initials of the four meanings of the Torah: *pshat* (the literal meaning), *rémèze* (the allegorical meaning), *drash* (the haggadic or moral meaning), and *sod* (the mystical meaning).

2. See for example, Henry Corbin, *Alone with the Alone: Creative Imagination in the Sufism of ʿArabī*, trans. Ralph Manheim (Princeton, N.J.: Princeton University Press, 1991), particularly pp. 77–78.

3. On this question, see Henri de Lubac, *Medieval Exegesis*, trans. Mark Sebanc (Grand Rapids, Mich.: Eerdmans, 1998).

4. Who takes up the thesis presented by Wilhelm Bacher in his article "L'Exégèse biblique dans le Zohar," in *Revue des études juives* 22 (1891): 33–46.

5. See Gershom Scholem, *On the Kabbalah and Its Symbolism*, trans. Ralph Manheim, foreword by Bernard McGinn (New York: Schocken Books, 1996). "Two different branches, coming from the same ancient root, are found in the final formation of the doctrine of the *Zohar*. . . . Philo of Alexandria certainly stands at the origin of this root, and it is to him that all the differentiations between the literal and the spiritual meanings ultimately go back; these differentiations reached Patristic Christianity and that of the Middle Ages, as well as Islam (by way of Christian-oriental sources)."

6. George Steiner, *After Babel: Aspects of Language and Translation* (New York: Oxford University Press, 1998), pp. 299 ff.

7. See particularly Betty Rojtman, *Black Fire on White Fire: An Essay on Jewish*

Hermeneutics, from Midrash to Kabbalah, trans. Steven Rendall (Berkeley: University of California Press, 1998).

8. See above, Chapter 2, Section II, Subsection 1, "Language and Presence: The Biblical Teaching."

9. This question becomes particularly crucial when the interpretive word reaches its highest degree of freedom, namely, in mystical literature. How can the mystics, who have an eminently personal and innovative experience of God, find this experience reflected, this is anticipated, in the sacred texts of their tradition? Scholem, who presents this problem very clearly at the beginning of his study on the Kabbalah, responds in the following way: "What happens when a mystic encounters the holy scriptures of his tradition is briefly this: the sacred text is smelted down and a new dimension is discovered in it" (Scholem, *On the Kabbalah and Its Symbolism*, pp. 11–12). The entirety of our exposition will attempt to determine what the expression "the smelting down of the sacred text" could well mean, beyond the single question of the relationship between mysticism and a tradition. What conception of interpretation—and, more fundamentally, of the text itself—is required for such a reshaping to be possible?

10. For discussion of this question, see Marlène Zarader, *Heidegger et les paroles de l'origine* (Paris: Vrin, 1986), pp. 28–30.

11. See Hans-Georg Gadamer, *Truth and Method*, trans. Joel Weinsheimer and Donald G. Marshall (New York: Continuum, 1993), pp. 250–67.

12. Rojtman, *Black Fire on White Fire*, pp. 2–3. See also David Banon, *La Lecture infinie: Les Voies de l'interprétation midrachique* (Paris: Éditions du Seuil, 1987), p. 42.

13. The kabbalists even go as far as to see in these two Torahs the two faces of the Divinity: the written Torah would be the symbol of the dispensing part of the Divinity, the oral Torah would be that of its receptive part. See Scholem, *On the Kabbalah and Its Symbolism*, pp. 47–48.

14. We find, in the *Zohar* 2, 99a–b, a superb parable (taken up in Alexandre Safran, *La Cabale*, 3rd ed. corrected [Paris: Payot, 1983], p. 82; in English, *The Kabbalah: Law and Mysticism in the Jewish Tradition*, trans. Margaret A. Pater [New York: Feldheim, 1975, trans. of the 1st ed.], pp. 241–42; as well as by Gershom Scholem, *On the Kabbalah and Its Symbolism*, p. 55), well illustrating this idea, according to which the text only speaks to the one who has already proceeded to encounter it and who, for this reason, knows how to understand it. This is the parable of the Torah as a fiancée: "Verily, the Torah lets out a word and emerges a little from her sheath and then hides herself again. But she does this only for those who know and obey her. For the Torah resembles a beautiful and stately damsel, who is hidden in a secluded chamber of her palace and who has a secret lover, unknown to all others. For love of her, he keeps passing the gate of her house, looking this way and that in search of her. She knows that her lover haunts the gate of

her house. What does she do? She opens the door of her hidden chamber ever so little, and for a moment reveals her face to her lover, but hides it again forthwith. Were anyone with her lover, he would see nothing and perceive nothing. He alone sees it and he is drawn to her with his heart and soul and his whole being, and he knows that for love of him she disclosed herself to him for one moment, a flame with love for him. So is it with the word of the Torah, which reveals herself only to those who love her. . . . And this is why the Torah is visible and hidden."

15. André Neher, *The Exile of the Word: From the Silence of the Bible to the Silence of Auschwitz*, trans. David Maisel (Philadelphia: Jewish Publication Society of America, 1981), p. 18.

16. Cited by Scholem, *On the Kabbalah and Its Symbolism*, p. 65. See also, Scholem, *Major Trends in Jewish Mysticism* (New York: Schocken Books, 1995).

17. Cited by Scholem, *On the Kabbalah and Its Symbolism*, p. 80.

18. Rojtman, *Black Fire on White Fire*, p. 1.

19. Ibid., p. 2. [Translation modified slightly for fluency with the text.—Trans.]

20. Banon, *La Lecture infinie*, p. 90.

21. Scholem, *On the Kabbalah and Its Symbolism*, pp. 35, 50–66.

22. Recall that the number seventy is, for biblical men, the number of all the nations existing on the earth, and of all existing languages.

23. Scholem, *On the Kabbalah and Its Symbolism*, p. 63; Zarader's emphasis.

24. Banon, *La Lecture infinie*, p. 220.

25. Ibid., 75.

26. Ibid.

27. N. de Cacqueray, *Connaissance et Langage symboliques dans la Bible* (Rennes: Université de Rennes, 1981), unpublished thesis, p. 114.

28. James Barr, *The Semantics of Biblical Language* (London: Oxford University Press, 1961).

29. See particularly the letters to F. Willmans from September 20, 1803, and April 2, 1804. One can also consult, on this subject, the excellent analysis of George Steiner in his *Antigones* (New York: Oxford University Press, 1984), pp. 72–73.

30. Ibid., 72.

31. Ibid., p. 73.

32. Ibid., p. 75.

33. I will not go into depth here on this question. Recall nonetheless that German Idealism has drawn from the dual source of German mysticism and Jewish mysticism (essentially, the Kabbalah). This connection is notably emphasized by Habermas, who remarks that "Bloch recurs to Schelling, and Schelling had brought from the spirit of Romanticism the heritage of the Kabbalah into the Protestant philosophy of German Idealism" ("The German Idealism of the Jewish Philosophers," in Jürgen Habermas, *Philosophical-Political Profiles*, trans. Freder-

ick G. Lawrence [Cambridge, Mass.: MIT Press, 1983], p. 40).

34. The image is used by Scholem, *On the Kabbalah and Its Symbolism*, p. 12.

35. David Banon, *La Lecture infinie*, p. 220. This link between the infinity of reading and the incompleteness of history is often emphasized in the Jewish tradition. Different parables on the complete elucidation of the text, which would ultimately be realized in the messianic age, bear witness to this link. The best known of these parables (as is taken up, notably, by Jacques Derrida in *Dissemination*, trans. Barbara Johnson [Chicago: University of Chicago Press, 1981]), is the one attributed to Rabbi Levi Isaac of Berdichev: "The white, the spaces in the Torah scroll likewise come from letters, but we do not know how to read them the way we do the black of the letters. In the messianic age, God will reveal the white [the blank] spaces of the Torah, whose letters are presently invisible for us."

36. See letters to Böhlendorf, December 4, 1801, and of November 1802. Compare Friedrich Hölderlin, *Essays and Letters on Theory*, ed. and trans. Thomas Pfau (Albany: State University of New York Press, 1982).

37. Letter to F. Willmans, September 20, 1803.

38. That is, the translation leads it back to its "natal element," neglected initially in the "cultural tendency" of the Greeks. On this opposition, see Beda Allemann, *Hölderlin und Heidegger* (Zurich: Atlantis, 1954); in French, *Hölderlin et Heidegger*, trans. François Fédier, 2nd ed. corrected (Paris: Presses Universitaires de France, 1987), pp. 42–54.

39. Steiner, *Antigones*, p. 75.

40. Friedrich Hölderlin, "Patmos," in *Sämtliche Werke* (Stuttgart: Kohlhammer, 1943–72), 2: 165. In English, see *Friedrich Hölderlin: Poems and Fragments*, trans. Michael Hamburger (Ann Arbor: University of Michigan Press, 1968), p. 463.

41. In his letter to Hegel of July 14, 1804, Schelling wrote, on the subject of Hölderlin whose visit he had just received: "His translation of Sophocles betrayed his mental deterioration." See G. W. F. Hegel, *Briefe von und an Hegel*, ed. Johannes Hoffmeister (Hamburg: Felix Meiner, 1952–60), vol. 1. Zarader cites the French translation by Jean Carrère, *Correspondance* (Paris: Gallimard, 1962–67), p. 82. In English, see Clark Butler and Christiane Seiler, trans., *Hegel: The Letters* (Bloomington: Indiana University Press, 1884), p. 66. [This letter, from Hegel *to* Schelling, points to the deterioration of Hölderlin; the citation from Schelling's letter is not reproduced in the English.—Trans.]

42. An element frequently noted by commentators. See, for example, Michel Haar, *The Song of the Earth: Heidegger and the Grounds of the History of Being*, trans. Reginald Lilly, foreword by John Sallis (Bloomington: Indiana University Press, 1993), p. 56. "He [Heidegger] has without a doubt minimized the non-Greek elements of Hölderlin: the Asiatic, the Christian."

43. The last two terms are clearly defined by Heidegger, as much for them-

selves as in their differences. Confronting them is thus automatic. On the other hand, the setting into perspective relative to *Erklärung*—the explanation proper to the metaphysical field—is not as clearly accomplished by Heidegger. We owe it to Otto Pöggeler, who, in his book *Martin Heidegger's Path of Thinking* (trans. Daniel Magurshak and Sigmund Barber [Atlantic Highlands, N.J.: Humanities Press, 1987], pp. 217–42), devoted an analysis, which has become classic, to the relationship between these three terms. This analysis has been taken up again, in its main themes, by Gianni Vattimo, *Introduction à Heidegger*, trans. Jacques Rolland (Paris: Éditions du Cerf, 1985), pp. 145–49. [No English translation is available.—Trans.] For my part, if I take my inspiration from Pöggler in considering *Erklärung*, as he has done, I thereafter demur to his analysis of the other two terms. We will see, further on, where the difference gets situated.

44. Pöggeler, *Martin Heidegger's Path of Thinking*, p. 228.

45. As well as Vattimo, *Introduction à Heidegger*, pp. 145–46.

46. See above, Part I, Chapter 3, Section I, Subsection 3, "Characteristics of the Originary Essence."

47. See notably "Platons Lehre von der Wahrheit," in *Wegmarken*, 2nd expanded ed. (Frankfurt: Klostermann, 1978), p. 109; *Gesamtausgabe*, 102 vols. (Frankfurt am Main: Klostermann, 1975–), 9: 203 [henceforth *Gesamtausgabe* will be abbreviated as *GA*]. In English, see "Plato's Doctrine of Truth," trans. Thomas Sheehan, in Martin Heidegger, *Pathmarks*, trans. and ed. William McNeill (Cambridge: Cambridge University Press, 1998), p. 155.

48. Here is the first point on which I differ from Pöggeler; the latter defines *Erörterung* clearly as a leap toward the unthought and the unformulated (see Pöggeler, *Martin Heidegger's Path of Thinking*, pp. 230, 232, etc.). On the other hand, he only grants a minor place to the *Erläuterung* (cf. ibid., p. 387). He does not see, it appears, that this is the precise counterpoint of the preceding movement: it is an elucidation of *what is thought and formulated*. Pöggeler certainly mentions, in passing, that Heidegger establishes a tie between the two terms (p. 230), but he does not show in what this tie consists.

49. That was the initial title of the text, at the time of its first publication in the journal *Merkur* in 1953.

50. Here, I am translating by "Poem" (with a capital) the German word *Gedicht*, which Jean Beaufret and Wolfgang Brokmeier translate as *Dict* or *Dit* (see the French translators' note in Heidegger, *Acheminement vers la parole* [On the Way to Language], p. 39).

51. *Unterwegs zur Sprache* (Pfullingen: Neske, 1976), p. 38; *GA*, 12: 34. In English, see "Language in the Poem: A Discussion of Georg Trakl's Poetic Work," in *On the Way to Language*, trans. Peter D. Hertz (San Francisco: HarperSanFrancisco, 1982), pp. 159–60.

52. Ibid.

53. See Heidegger, *Der Satz vom Grund* (Pfullingen: Neske, 1957), pp. 105–6; *GA*, 10: 87–88; in English, *The Principle of Reason*, trans. Reginald Lilly (Bloomington: Indiana University Press, 1991), pp. 59–60.

54. Ibid. [Translation modified for fluency with the French text.—Trans.] Also see on this question, Heidegger, "Bauen Wohnen Denken," in *Vorträge und Aufsätze* (Pfullingen: Neske, 1976), 153–54; *GA*, 7: 156. In English, see "Building Dwelling Thinking," trans. Albert Hofstadter, in *Martin Heidegger: Basic Writings*, ed. David Farrell Krell (New York: Harper and Row, 1993), p. 356. Also see Heidegger, "Zur Seinsfrage," in *Wegmarken*, p. 240; *GA*, 9: 412; in English, "On the Question of Being," in *Pathmarks*, pp. 311–12.

55. Pöggeler insists strongly on this aspect. He presents what is thought as a sign or an index of the unthought, a "reference" to the unthought (cf. Pöggeler, *Martin Heidegger's Path of Thinking*, p. 230). There is, therefore, indeed a "leap" from the one to the other, but "this leap escapes arbitrariness only *then* when what is to be thought of, towards which thinking springs, is in truth the unthought of what has been thought, what is *intended* [Zarader uses the term *accorded* and *proposed* from the French translation, p. 405.—Trans.] (ibid., p. 241). The *Erörterung* [emplacement] that aims to explicate the unnoticed presuppositions (ibid., pp. 234–35) will thus have as its exclusive task "to attend to the decisive claim and bring to word" (ibid., p. 236).

56. Neither Pöggeler nor Vattimo note this. Pöggeler, on the contrary, never fails to juxtapose the two types of Heideggerian formulas (those relating to the unthought, and those relative to the unsaid), as though the two formulas were strictly equivalent to each other. See, for example, ibid., p. 388: "To explicate what is already thought in the direction of what is not thought, to give the word to that which remained unformulated in what was formulated." Or, see ibid., p. 397: "To bring to the word what has escaped listening and what is silent . . . "

57. On this definition of the unthought see Zarader, *Heidegger et les paroles de l'origine*, p. 22.

58. I have shown elsewhere that if the warranty of language were preserved (or even expanded) to the end of the work, the warranty of history would diminish to the point, perhaps, of disappearing in the later works. See Zarader, "Le Miroir aux trois reflets: Histoire d'une évolution," published in the *Revue de philosophie ancienne* 4, no. 1 (1986): 19n14, 25.

59. Vattimo, *Introduction à Heidegger*, p. 146.

60. See above, Part I, Chapter 1, Section III, Subsection 1, "The Premetaphysical Margin."

61. See Jacques Derrida, *De l'esprit: Heidegger et la question* (Paris: Éditions Galilée, 1987), pp. 183–84. In English, see Derrida, *Of Spirit: Heidegger and the Question*, trans. Geoffrey Bennington and Rachel Bowlby (Chicago: University of Chicago Press, 1989). "But access to thought, the thinking access to the *possibil-*

ity of metaphysics or pneumato-spiritualist religions opens onto something quite other than what the possibility makes possible" (p. 113). And " . . . the thinking of this *Frühe* to come, while advancing towards the possibility of what you think you recognize, is going towards what is quite other than what you think you recognize" (pp. 112–13). Also see below, Part II, Chapter 3, Section I, Subsection 3, "A Critical Perspective."

62. Heidegger translates the fragment thus: "It is useful to let-lie-before-us and so the taking-to-heart also = beings in being." See *What Is Called Thinking?* trans. J. Glenn Gray (New York: Harper and Row, 1968), p. 176.—Trans.

63. Translation modified for fluency with Zarader's text.—Trans.

64. Heidegger, *Was heisst Denken?* (Tübingen: Niemeyer, 1971), p. 109; *GA*, 8: 180. In English, see *What Is Called Thinking?* p. 176. [Translation modified for fluency with Zarader's text.—Trans.]

65. Heidegger, "Hermeneutische Situation und methodischer Charakter," *Sein und Zeit* (Tübingen: Niemeyer, 1977), § 63 ; *GA*, 2: 413. In English, see *Being and Time*, trans. John Macquarrie and Edward Robinson (New York: Harper and Row, 1962), § 63, "The Hermeneutical Situation, . . . " pp. 359–60.

66. Ibid., p. 311; *GA*, 2: 411–12; in English, pp. 358–59.

67. Ibid., pp. 312–13; *GA*, 2: 414–15; in English, pp. 360–61.

68. Ibid., pp. 312–13; *GA*, 2: 413–14; in English, pp. 359–60. [Translation modified for fluency with the French.—Trans.]

69. Ibid.

70. Ibid., 417; in English, p. 362. Heidegger's emphasis.

71. See above, Chapter 3, Section III, Subsection 1, "Heidegger's Taking in Charge."

72. Jacques Derrida, *De l'esprit*. For a discussion of Derrida's text, see below in this work, Part II, Chapter 3, Section I, "Heidegger, or the 'Supplement of Originarity'? Jacques Derrida's Interpretation."

PART II, CHAPTER I: AND HOW IS IT WITH BEING?

1. Richard Kearney and Joseph Stephen O'Leary, eds., *Heidegger et la question de Dieu* (Paris: Grasset, 1980).

2. Henri Birault, "Philosophie et théologie: Heidegger et Pascal," in Michel Haar, ed., *Cahier de l'herne: Heidegger* 45 (1983): 398–99.

3. See Heidegger, "Einleitung in die Phänomenologie der Religion (Winter Semester 1920–21)," and "Augustinus und der Neuplatonismus (Summer Semester 1921)," in *Martin Heidegger: Phänomenologie des religiösen Lebens*, pts. 1 and 2 (Frankfurt am Main: Klostermann, 1995); also in *Gesamtausgabe*, 102 vols. (Frankfurt am Main: Klostermann, 1975–), vol. 60 [henceforth *Gesamtausgabe* will be abbreviated as *GA*]. In English, *Martin Heidegger: Phenomenology of Religious Life*,

trans. Matthias Fritsch and Jennifer Anna Gosetti (Bloomington: Indiana University Press, 2004). These courses were the object of two summaries, which, judging from their points of similarity, are quite complete: one of Otto Pöggeler, "The Factical Experience of Life in the Christian Faith," in *Martin Heidegger's Path of Thinking*, trans. Daniel Magurshak and Sigmund Barber (Atlantic Highlands, N.J.: Humanities Press International, 1987), pp. 24–31, and certainly Karl Lehmann, "Christliche Geschichtserfahrung und ontologische Frage beim jungen Heidegger," in Otto Pöggeler, ed., *Martin Heidegger: Perspektiven zur Deutung seines Werkes* (Königstein: Athenäum, 1984), pp. 140–68. It is also necessary to mention the *Becker Nachschrift*, unpublished notes made by Oskar Becker on Heidegger's courses at Fribourg in 1920–21, which I have, unfortunately, not been able to consult.

4. Heidegger, *Being and Time*, trans. John Macquarrie and Edward Robinson (New York: Harper and Row, 1962) [first published in 1927], pp. 74–75, 271, 293n6, 479n13, and so on (in the 14th edition of the German, published by Niemeyer (Tübingen, 1977), see pp. 49, 229, 249n2, 427n1, etc.). In *GA*, 2: 65–66, 303, 331n2, 564n7.

5. "Phänomenologie und Theologie," in *Wegmarken*, 2nd expanded ed. (Frankfurt: Klostermann, 1978), pp. 45–77; *GA*, 9: 45–77. For the English see "Phenomenology and Theology," trans. James G. Hart and John C. Maraldo, in *Pathmarks*, trans. and ed. William McNeill (Cambridge: Cambridge University Press, 1998), pp. 39–62. The French translation, introduced by Pierre Aubenque, appears as an appendix to *Débat sur le kantisme (Entretiens de Davos)* (Paris: Beauchesne, 1972), pp. 101 ff.

6. The problematic of the sacred and the gods is sketched out from the years 1935, in "The Origin of the Work of Art," collected in Heidegger, *Poetry, Language, Thought*, trans. Albert Hofstadter (New York: Perennial Classics, 2001). And, above all, "Hölderlin and the Essence of Poetry," in Heidegger, *Elucidations of Hölderlin's Poetry*, trans. Keith Hoeller (Amherst, N.Y.: Humanity Books, 2000), pp. 51–65. First published in German as "Hölderlin und das Wesen der Dichtung," in *Erläuterungen zu Hölderlins Dichtung* (Frankfurt: Klostermann, 1971), pp. 31–45; *GA*, 4: 33–48.

7. *Sein und Zeit* (Tübingen: Niemeyer, 1977), p. 49; *GA*, 2: 65–66. In English, *Being and Time*, pp. 74–75.

8. "Réponse de Heidegger à un étudiant," transcribed by Raymond Savioz in the *Revue de théologie et de philosophie* (1951): 300. This text is cited by Bernard Dupuy, "Heidegger et le Dieu inconnu," in *Heidegger et la question de Dieu*, p. 104.

9. Heidegger, *Einführung in die Metaphysik* (Tübingen: Niemeyer, 1976), p. 6; *GA*, 40: 9–10. In English, *Introduction to Metaphysics*, trans. Gregory Fried and Richard Polt (New Haven, Conn.: Yale University Press, 2000), p. 8.

10. "Einleitung zu 'Was ist Metaphysik?'" in *Wegmarken*, p. 203; *GA*, 9: 374. In English, introduction to *What Is Metaphysics?* trans. Walter Kaufmann, in *Pathmarks*, pp. 283–84. [Translation modified for fluency with the French text.—Trans.]

11. Heidegger, *Identität und Differenz* (Pfullingen: Neske, 1957), p. 58; in English, *Identity and Difference*, trans. Joan Stambaugh (New York: Harper and Row, 1969), p. 70. [Translation modified for fluency with the French text.—Trans.]

12. See "Die onto-theo-logische Verfassung der Metaphysik," in *Identität und Differenz*, and "The Onto-theo-logical Constitution of Metaphysics," in *Identity and Difference*, pp. 142–74. But also, *Die Frage nach dem Ding: Zu Kants Lehre von den transzendentalen Grundsätzen* (Tübingen: Niemeyer, 1987), p. 92; in English, see *What Is a Thing?* trans. W. B. Barton, Jr., and Vera Deutsch (Chicago: Regnery, 1970), p. 119. Heidegger, *Nietzsche* (Pfullingen: Neske, 1998), vol. 2, pp. 348–49; *GA*, 6.2: 314–15. In English, "Nihilism as Determined by the History of Being," in *Nietzsche*, vol. 4, trans. David Farrell Krell (San Francisco: HarperSanFrancisco, 1991), pp. 240–41.

13. Birault, "Philosophie et théologie," p. 398 and p. 402n45.

14. *Identität und Differenz*, p. 70; in English, *Identity and Difference*, pp. 70 ff.

15. Ibid.

16. Birault, "Philosophie et théologie," p. 398.

17. Heidegger, *Wegmarken*, p. 52; *GA*, 9: 52. "Phänomenologie und Theologie," *GA*, 9: 45–78; in English, "Phenomenology and Theology (1927)," in *Pathmarks*, pp. 39–62.

18. Ibid., p. 52; *GA*, 9: 52; in English, *Pathmarks*, pp. 43–44.

19. Heidegger, *Sein und Zeit*, § 6, "Aufgabe einer Destruktion der Geschichte der Ontologie," pp. 21–23; *GA*, 2: 28–31. in English, *Being and Time*, § 6, "The Task of Destroying the History of Ontology," pp. 42–45.

20. Lehmann, "Christliche Geschichtserfahrung und ontologische Frage beim jungen Heidegger," p. 157.

21. Hans-Georg Gadamer, "Martin Heidegger und die Marburger Theologie," in *Martin Heidegger: Perspektiven zur Deutung seines Werkes*, p. 170.

22. "Phänomenologie und Theologie," in *Wegmarken*, p. 52; *GA*, 9: 52; in English, see *Pathmarks*, p. 44.

23. Birault, "Philosophie et théologie," p. 398.

24. Ibid., p. 392.

25. Ibid., p. 398.

26. These two points are clearly set forth and examined in an interesting article by Maria Villela-Petit, "Parler à Dieu, parler de Dieu," in *Institut Catholique de Paris: Dieu* (Paris: Beauchesne, 1985), pp. 19–22, above all.

27. Cf. the often-commented remarks from "Phänomenologie und Theolo-

gie," in *Wegmarken*, p. 58; *GA*, 9: 57. In English, *Pathmarks*, p. 47 ff. "If indeed faithfulness is attested in the Scriptures, systematic theology is, in its essence, a New Testament theology."

28. Ibid., p. 66; *GA*, 9: 66; in English, p. 53.

29. *Dialogue with Martin Heidegger*, from November 6, 1951 (seminar held at the University of Zurich), translated in the appendix of *Heidegger et la question de Dieu*, p. 334.

30. *Berichte aus der Arbeit der Evangelischen Akademie Hofgeismar* [Report from the Work of the Evangelical Academy at Hofgeismar], vol. 1 (1954), p. 33, translated in the appendix of *Heidegger et la question de Dieu*, p. 335.

31. Following in this, a remark by Villela-Petit, "Parler à Dieu, parler de Dieu," p. 24n.

32. Heidegger, "Brief über den Humanismus," in *Wegmarken*, pp. 347–48; *GA*, 9: 347–48. In English "Letter on Humanism," in *Martin Heidegger: Basic Writings*, trans. David Farrell Krell (New York: HarperCollins, 1993), p. 242, and in William McNeill, ed., *Pathmarks*, p. 258. [Translation modified for fluency with the text.—Trans.]

33. See Heidegger, "Esquisses tirées de l'atelier" (1959) [Outlines from the Workshop], trans. Michel Haar, in *Cahier de l'herne: Heidegger* 45 (1983): 83. "God is not dead. For his divinity lives on. It [divinity] is even closer to thinking than is faith, if it is true that divinity draws its origin from the truth of Being, and if Being, as the appropriating inception (*ereignender Anfang*), 'is' something other than the foundation and the cause of beings."

34. Heidegger, *Identität und Differenz*, p. 71; in English, *Identity and Difference*, p. 72.

35. See Heidegger, "Beilage zu den Hinweisen," in *Wegmarken*, p. 78; *GA*, 9: 78; in English, "Addition to the Pointers" [following "Phenomenology and Theology"], in *Pathmarks*, p. 61. "Poetic thinking is being in the presence of . . . and for the god. Presence means: purely letting the god's presence be said."

36. See above, note 32.

37. *Berichte aus der Arbeit der Evangelischen Akademie Hofgeismar* 1 (1954): 33. French translation in the appendix of *Heidegger et la question de Dieu*, p. 336.

38. Heidegger, "Esquisses tirées de l'atelier," trans. Michel Haar, in *Cahier de l'herne: Heidegger* 45 (1983): 83.

39. See *Die Technik und die Kehre* in Heidegger, *Opuscula I* (Pfullingen: Neske, 1962), p. 46. In English, "The Turn," in *The Question Concerning Technology and Other Essays* (New York: Harper and Row, 1977): "If God is God, he comes to be starting from the constellation of being and within the latter."

40. Interview with Heidegger in *Der Spiegel*, May 31, 1976. Translated into French by Jean Launay, *Réponses et Questions sur l'histoire et la politique* (Paris: Mercure de France, 1977), p. 49. This has appeared in numerous places in Eng-

lish, see for example, "Only a God Can Save Us: *Der Spiegel*'s Interview with Martin Heidegger (1966), in Richard Wolin, ed., *The Heidegger Controversy: A Critical Reader* (Cambridge, Mass.: MIT Press, 1993), p. 107.

41. Ibid.

42. *Berichte aus der Arbeit der Evangelischen Akademie Hofgeismar*, p. 34, in the appendixes of *Heidegger et la question de Dieu*, p. 336.

43. *Aussprache mit M. Heidegger* (seminar at the University of Zurich), in the appendixes of *Heidegger et la question de Dieu*, p. 334.

44. *Berichte aus der Arbeit der Evangelischen Akademie Hofgeismar* 1 (1954): 33, in *Heidegger et la question de Dieu*, p. 336.

45. Heidegger, *Einführung in die Metaphysik* (Tübingen: Niemeyer, 1976), p. 5. In the *GA*, 40: 9. In English see, *Introduction to Metaphysics*, trans. Gregory Fried and Richard Polt (New Haven, Conn.: Yale University Press, 2000), pp. 7–8.

46. *Prolegomena zur Geschichte des Zeitbegriffs*, in Heidegger, *GA*, 20: 109–10; in English, *History of the Concept of Time: Prolegomena*, trans. Theodore Kisiel (Bloomington: Indiana University Press, 1985), p. 80: "Philosophical research is and remains atheism, which is why philosophy can allow 'the arrogance of thinking.'"

47. *Einführung in die Metaphysik*, p. 6; *GA*, 40: 9–10; *Introduction to Metaphysics*, pp. 8–9.

48. Jean Greisch, *La Parole heureuse: Heidegger entre les choses et les mots* (Paris: Beauchesne, 1987), p. 34.

49. *Aussprache mit M. Heidegger* (from November 6, 1951, seminar at Zurich), in *Heidegger et la question de Dieu*, p. 134.

50. Heidegger, *Unterwegs zur Sprache* (Pfullingen: Neske, 1976), p. 96; *GA*, 12: 91. In English, see *On the Way to Language*, trans. Peter D. Hertz (San Francisco: HarperSanFrancisco, 1982), pp. 9–10.

51. Ibid., pp. 96–97; *GA*, 12: 92; in English, p. 12.

52. Greisch, *La Parole heureuse*, p. 321.

53. Ibid., p. 32.

54. Ibid., p. 34.

55. See above, Heidegger, "Einleitung in die Phänomenologie der Religion" and "Augustinus und der Neuplatonismus"; in English, *Martin Heidegger: Phenomenology of Religious Life*, trans. Matthias Fritsch and Jennifer Anna Gosetti (Bloomington: Indiana University Press, 2004).

56. Heidegger, "Metaphysik und Anthropomorphie," in *Nietzsche*, vol. 2 (Pfullingen: Neske, 1998), p. 132; *GA*, 6.2: 116; in English, in *Nietzsche*, vol. 4, *Nihilism*, trans. Frank A. Capuzzi, ed. David Farrell Krell (New York: Harper and Row, 1982), p. 103.

57. Lehmann, "Christliche Geschichtserfahrung und ontologische Frage beim jungen Heidegger," p. 160.

58. Ibid., p. 154.

59. Pöggeler, *Martin Heidegger's Path of Thinking*, pp. 28–29.

60. Ibid., p. 18.

61. Lehmann, "Christliche Geschichtserfahrung und ontologische Frage beim jungen Heidegger," p. 154.

62. Ibid., p. 155.

63. Pöggeler, *Martin Heidegger's Path of Thinking*, p. 33.

64. Ibid., pp. 25–26; Lehmann, "Christliche Geschichtserfahrung und ontologische Frage," p. 155.

65. Pöggeler, *Martin Heidegger's Path of Thinking*, pp. 27–28; Lehmann, "Christliche Geschichtserfahrung und ontologische Frage," p. 157.

66. Ibid., p. 26.

67. See above, Part II, Chapter 1, Section I, "Heidegger's Position: God or Being. 'The Two Paths.'" There, we saw how, later on, it would be precisely every *relationship* between faith and the question of Being that appeared as a misunderstanding.

68. Lehmann, "Christliche Geschichtserfahrung und ontologische Frage," p. 155.

69. See above, Part II, Chapter 1, Section I.

70. This is the whole problematic of Heidegger's lecture "What Is Metaphysics?" delivered in 1929.

71. "Was ist Metaphysik?" in *Wegmarken*, p. 114; *GA*, 9: 114; in English, "What Is Metaphysics?" in *Pathmarks*, pp. 91–92.

72. "Nachwort zu: 'Was ist Metaphysik?'" in *Wegmarken*, p. 303; *GA*, 9: 303. "Postscript to What is Metaphysics," in *Pathmarks*, pp. 232–33.

73. Heidegger, *Erläuterungen zu Hölderlins Dichtung*, p. 61; *GA*, 4: 62; in English, *Elucidations of Hölderlin's Poetry*, p. 83.

74. The translation of this term is controversial. Literally, it could mean "desert and desolation," but André Chouraqui mentions the possibility that this might be the name of the primordial divinities; see Chouraqui's translation *La Bible* (Paris: Desclée de Brouwer, 1985), p. 18n2.

75. André Neher, *The Exile of the Word: From the Silence of the Bible to the Silence of Auschwitz*, trans. David Maisel (Philadelphia: Jewish Publication Society of America, 1981), pp. 61–62.

76. Ibid.

77. Neher, *Exile of the Word*, p. 63.

78. Gershom Scholem, *Major Trends in Jewish Mysticism* (New York: Schocken Books, 1995), p. 25.

79. Alexandre Safran, *The Kabbalah: Law and Mysticism in the Jewish Tradition*, trans. Margaret A. Pater (New York: Feldheim, 1975), p. 233.

80. Ibid., p. 255. [Translation modified for correspondence with the French text.—Trans.]

81. Scholem, *Major Trends in Jewish Mysticism*, p. 13.

82. Ibid., p. 25.

83. *Zohar II*, 63b, and *III*, 696. Cited by Scholem in *Major Trends in Jewish Mysticism*, p. 33.

84. Gershom Scholem, *On the Kabbalah and Its Symbolism*, trans. Ralph Manheim, foreword by Bernard McGinn (New York: Schocken Books, 1996), p. 103.

85. Safran, *The Kabbalah*, p. 257.

86. This is a kinship that ought to have been "foreseen" [*pressentie*] by the Greeks. If chaos "appears to be the undifferentiated and thus, simple confusion," Heidegger asserts that this is "but the deviation (*Unwesen*) of what Chaos should mean." Thought more originally (that is, on the basis of *phusis* and of *alètheia*), chaos "signifies firstly the gaping, the open abyss, the Opening that opens first" (*Erläuterungen zu Hölderlins Dichtung*, p. 62; *GA*, 4: 63–64; in English, *Elucidations of Hölderlin's Poetry*, p. 84).

See Michel Haar, *The Song of the Earth: Heidegger and the Grounds of the History of Being*, trans. Reginald Lilly, foreword by John Sallis (Bloomington: Indiana University Press, 1993), p. 56. Haar is of the opinion that, in such an interpretation, "Heidegger greatly diminishes the connotation of 'panic,' which the term [chaos] has in Hölderlin, by interpreting it as 'gaping,' which means '*opening*,'" and thus "he minimizes the non-Greek elements in Hölderlin." However, it is in no way certain that to interpret "chaos" as "gaping" is to place the accent only on the dimension of opening and thus, actually to go in the "Greek" direction. It seems to me that the alternative here is shaped less by the couple [Greek] open and [Asian or Christian] panic, than it is by that of the creative abyss, on the one side, and an ineffective confusion, on the other. Hölderlin, singing of "the engendering from sacred Chaos," would have noticed, in effect, the dizzying power of the creative abyss, which would in no way have diminished the "non-Greek" elements of his poetry (except for Heidegger).

87. Heidegger, "Zeit und Sein," in *Zur Sache des Denkens* (Tübingen: Niemeyer, 1976), p. 31; in English, *On Time and Being*, trans. Joan Stambaugh (New York: Harper and Row, 1972), p. 29.

88. This is an evolution already sketched in "The Origin of the Work of Art" (1935), and which will find its full deployment in *Nietzsche*, vol. 2 (1940–46), notably in "Nihilism as Determined by the History of Being," pp. 197–250.

89. Heidegger, *Der Satz vom Grund* (Pfullingen: Neske, 1957), p. 110; in *GA*, 10: 91; in English, *The Principle of Reason*, trans. Reginald Lilly (Bloomington: Indiana University Press, 1996), p. 62.

90. Ibid., p. 109; *GA*, 10: 91; in English, p. 65. [Translation modified for fluency with the French text.—Trans.]

91. Heidegger, "Zeit und Sein," in *Zur Sache des Denkens*, p. 32; in English, *On Time and Being*, p. 30.

92. Stanislas Breton, "La Querelle des dénominations," in *Heidegger et la Question de Dieu*, p. 257.

93. Translation modified for fluency with the French text ("A Toi, seul le silence convient en guise de louange").—Trans.

94. The French text reads, "and I will place hope in him."—Trans.

95. On this doctrine, the principle source of information remains Gershom Scholem. See his *Major Trends in Jewish Mysticism*, pp. 244–86. However, one may also see Safran, *The Kabbalah*, pp. 62, 88, 251, 271–74, and so on. Finally, one can also see Betty Rojtman, *Black Fire on White Fire: An Essay on Jewish Hermeneutics, from Midrash to Kabbalah*, trans. Steven Rendall (Berkeley: University of California Press, 1998), pp. 150, 160–61.

96. Scholem, *Major Trends in Jewish Mysticism*, pp. 260–61.

97. Ibid.

98. *Abîmer* generally means "to damage," "to spoil," "to submerge," by analogy with *abîme* or abyss, so that the verb implies that which has been somehow cast into an abyss, into the depths. In this understanding of contraction, God is submerged in himself, engulfed in his own depths.—Trans.

99. Scholem, *On the Kabbalah and Its Symbolism*, p. 110.

100. Safran, *The Kabbalah*, p. 270. [Translation modified for fluency with the French.—Trans.]

101. Rojtman, *Black Fire on White Fire*, p. 150.

102. Scholem, *Major Trends in Jewish Mysticism*, p. 261.

103. Rojtman, *Black Fire on White Fire*, p. 161.

104. Lehmann, "Christliche Geschichtserfahrung und ontologische Frage beim jungen Heidegger," p. 154.

105. Emmanuel Lévinas, "Exégèse et culture: Notes sur un verset," in *Le Nouveau Commerce* 50 (1983): 91.

106. Pierre-Jean Labarrière, "Avant Propos" [Introduction], in *Autrement que savoir: E. Lévinas. Entretiens du Centre Sèvres* (Paris: Osiris, 1988), p. 8.

107. Lévinas, *L'Au-delà du verset: Lectures et discours talmudiques* (Paris: Éditions de Minuit, 1982), pp. 233–34. In English, Lévinas, *Beyond the Verse: Talmudic Readings and Lectures*, trans. Gary D. Mole (Bloomington: Indiana University Press, 1994), p. 200.

108. The two major exceptions to this are the Platonic idea of the Good beyond Being, and the Cartesian idea of the Infinite. As Derrida puts it, these are "the only two philosophical gestures that, excluding their authors, could be totally acquitted, found innocent by Lévinas." (See Derrida, *L'Écriture et la différence* [Paris: Éditions de Minuit, 1967], p. 146). [Translation modified for fluency with the French text.—Trans.] A later work, Lévinas's *Otherwise Than Being; or, Beyond Essence*, trans. Alphonso Lingis (Pittsburgh: Duquesne University Press, 1998), p. 133, adds the Kantian gesture to these exceptions.

109. Emmanuel Lévinas, "La Trace de l'autre," in *En découvrant l'existence avec Husserl et Heidegger* (Paris: Vrin, 1967), p. 188. This essay is not reproduced in the partial English translation. It may be found in Mark C. Taylor, ed., *Deconstruction in Context* (Chicago: University of Chicago Press, 1986), pp. 345–46.

110. Ibid., p. 169; in English, pp. 50–51.

111. Emmanuel Lévinas, *Totalité et infini: Essai sur l'extériorité* (The Hague: Martinus Nijhoff, 1984), p. 9; in English, *Totality and Infinity: An Essay on Exteriority*, trans. Alphonso Lingis (Pittsburgh: Duquesne University Press, 1998), p. 39.

112. Ibid., p. 47; in English, p. 75.

113. Ibid., p. 188; in English, p. 213.

114. Lévinas, "La Trace de l'autre," p. 198. See Taylor, ed., *Deconstruction in Context*, pp. 355–56.

115. Maurice Blanchot, *L'Entretien infini* (Paris: Gallimard, 1969), p. 77; in English, see *The Infinite Conversation*, trans. Susan Hanson (Minneapolis: University of Minnesota Press, 1993), p. 54. [Translation modified slightly for fluency with the French text.—Trans.]

116. Silvano Petrosino, "D'un livre à l'autre: *Totalité et infini—autrement qu'être*," trans. G. Iannella, in *Les Cahiers de "La nuit surveillée"* 3 (1984): 204.

117. Lévinas, *Otherwise Than Being*. "Otherwise than being" is an expression privileging the adverbial "otherwise" as a strategy to work against the verbal quality of Heidegger's Being as "essence" or pure verbality. The "otherwise than being" is not another being, as we know from Lévinas's work, it is the enigma of another modality that suggests itself (within and without being) even as it loses all meaningfulness in ontology proper and must be resaid, restated in the form sincerity, witnessing, and a giving-to the other person. A good discussion of the otherwise is provided by Jacques Rolland, *Parcours de l'autrement . . .* (Paris: Presses Universitaires de France, 2000)—Trans.

118. Lévinas, *Totalité et infini*, p. 18; in English, see *Totality and Infinity*, p. 47. [Lévinas's first major work, and his Doctorat d'État, defended at the Sorbonne in 1961, was *Totality and Infinity: Essay on Exteriority*. Of the two *magna opera*, Richard Cohen maintains that they are two sides to the same question of the Other: the first opus works through the alterity of *exteriority*, the second work, *Otherwise Than Being*, is a phenomenology of immanence. See Richard A. Cohen, *Ethics, Exegesis, and Philosophy: Interpretation After Lévinas* (New York: Cambridge University Press, 2001). For his part, Jacques Rolland counters that *Otherwise Than Being* is the more significant work, because it explores the adverbial "modalities" of self, other, and illeity.—Trans.]

119. Lévinas, preface to the second edition of *De l'existence à l'existant* (Paris: Vrin, 1977). English translation, *Existence and Existents*, trans. Alphonso Lingis, foreword by Robert Bernasconi (Pittsburgh: Duquesne University Press, 2001). This edition contains only Lévinas's *Avant-propos*, and not the preface to the 2nd

edition. This evolution has been extensively discussed. The preeminence of the being or entity in *Totality and Infinity* has been put in question by Jean-Luc Marion in his *The Idol and the Distance: Five Studies*, trans. Thomas Carlson (New York: Fordham University Press, 2001), p. 219. "Obviously, in being displaced from being to a being or entity, the privilege consecrates the preeminence of the latter, as Other [person], only by inverting the ontological difference, and hence in consecrating it" [translation modified—Trans.]. Lévinas responds to this objection in the preface just cited; there he attempts to circumscribe "the philosophical procedure going from *Totality and Infinity* to *Otherwise than Being*." The entirety of the debate has been summed up by Jacques Rolland and Silvano Petrosino, in *La Vérité nomade: Introduction à E. Lévinas* (Paris: La Découverte, 1984), pp. 100–102.

120. Lévinas, *Totalité et infini*, p. 281; in English, see *Totality and Infinity*, p. 304. Also see the aforementioned preface to the 2nd edition of *De l'existence à l'existant*, where Lévinas presents *Totality and Infinity* as "the first step of a movement that opens upon an ethics more ancient than ontology."

121. *De l'existence à l'existant*, p. 171; in English, p. 104.

122. See above, note 107, Lévinas, *L'Au-delà du verset*, pp. 233–34.

123. Lévinas, *En Découvrant l'existence avec Husserl et Heidegger*, p. 169; Zarader's emphasis. The essay in question is not in the English translation; see Alphonso Lingis, trans., *Lévinas: Collected Philosophical Papers* (Pittsburgh: Duquesne University Press, 1998), pp. 50–51.

124. Ibid.; French, p. 171; in English, see Lingis, trans., *Lévinas: Collected Philosophical Papers*, p. 53; Zarader's emphasis.

125. This is a term that appears for the first time in Lévinas's 1963 text on Kierkegaard ("Existence et éthique," reprinted in Emmanuel Lévinas, *Noms propres* (Montpellier: Fata Morgana, 1996), p. 104; in English, *Proper Names*, trans. Michael B. Smith (Stanford, Calif.: Stanford University Press, 1996), p. 71. We again find the term in 1980, in "De la signifiance du sens," in *Heidegger et la question de Dieu*, p. 239.

126. For example, see Lévinas, *De Dieu qui vient à l'idée* (Paris: Vrin, 1982), p. 174; in English, *Of God Who Comes to Mind*, trans. Bettina Bergo (Stanford, Calif.: Stanford University Press, 1998), p. 113.

127. Lévinas, *Autrement qu'être*, p. 167; in English, *Otherwise Than Being*, p. 131.

128. I add "with one another" to preserve the sense of the reflexive in French, which Lingis translates as a passive, "où l'être et l'étant peuvent *s'*entendre et *s'*identifier"; see *Autrement qu'être ou au-delà de l'essence*, p. 55. In English, *Otherwise than Being*, p. 42.—Trans.

129. A possibility merely evoked in *Otherwise Than Being* ("to write essence with an 'a,' as the history of language would demand . . . "), then adopted in certain texts from the 1975–76 (reprinted in *Of God Who Comes to Mind*, p. 113), only to be abandoned, finally, in the later writings.

130. Lévinas, *Autrement qu'être*, p. ix; in English, *Otherwise than Being*, p. xli.

131. Ibid., p. 9; in English, p. 8.

132. See ibid., p. 211; in English, p. 166. "A difference—a non-coinciding, an arrhythmia in time, a diachrony refractory to thematization, refractory to the reminiscence that synchronizes the phases of a past."

133. Ibid., p. 200; in English, p. 158.

134. Ibid., p. 67; in English, p. 52.

135. Ibid., p. 9; in English, p. 8.

136. Ibid., p. 112; in English, p. 89.

137. For the meaning of this word, see "Énigme et phénomène," in *En découvrant l'existence*, p. 203; in English, *Lévinas: Collected Philosophical Papers*, p. 61.

138. Jacques Rolland, "Une Logique de l'ambiguïté," in *Autrement que savoir*, p. 51.

139. Ibid., p. 52.

140. The term is used by Lévinas himself, in the interrogative mode to be sure: "These lines, and those that follow, owe much to Heidegger. Deformed and ill-understood? Perhaps. At least this deformation will not have been a way to deny the debt. Nor this debt a reason to forget"; in *Autrement qu'être*, p. 49n28: in English, p. 189.

141. Lévinas, *Autrement qu'être*, p. 223; in English, *Otherwise Than Being*, p. 177.

142. See "Dieu et la philosophie," in *De Dieu qui vient à l'idée*, p. 107; in English, "God and Philosophy," in *Of God Who Comes to Mind*, p. 64. Note that passivity appears in Heidegger's interpretation of will; this makes up part of his argument against Nietzsche's active will to power. [See Heidegger, *Nietzsche*.—Trans.]

143. Lévinas, *En découvrant l'existence*, p. 170. In English, "Philosophy and the Idea of the Infinite," in *Lévinas: Collected Philosophical Papers*, p. 52.

144. Ibid.

145. Lévinas, *Noms propres*, p. 115; in English, p. 78.

146. Lévinas, "La Trace de l'autre," p. 189; in English, see "The Trace of the Other," in Taylor, ed., *Deconstruction in Context*, p. 347.

147. See above, Part II, Chapter 1, Section II, Subsection 4, "Provisional Conclusion."

148. Notably in "Philosophy and the Idea of the Infinite" (1957, reprinted in the last part of *En Découvrant l'existence*. In English, see *Lévinas: Collected Philosophical Papers*, pp. 56–60.

149. Martin Heidegger, "Zur Erörterung der Gelassenheit: Aus einem Feldweggespräch über das Denken," in *Gelassenheit* (Pfullingen: Neske, 1959), p. 42; *GA*, 13: 48. In English, "Conversation on a Country Path About Thinking," in *Discourse on Thinking* (New York: Harper and Row, 1966), p. 66. Heidegger's *Gelassenheit* appeared in *GA*, broken up as follows: the "Memorial Address," called, in

German "Gelassenheit (30 October 1955)," appeared in *GA*, vol. 16; the "Conversation on a Country Path About Thinking" appeared in *GA*, vol. 13, entitled "Zur Erörterung der Gelassenheit: Aus einem Feldweggespräch über das Denken (1944/45)." The English brings them all together in one volume.

150. See above, Part I, Chapter 2, note 47. Jürgen Habermas, "Penser avec Heidegger contre Heidegger?" in *Profils philosophiques et politiques*, trans. Françoise Dastur, Jean-René Ladmiral, and Marc B. de launay (Paris: Gallimard, 1974), p. 96. The original work was entitled, *Philosophisch-politische Profile* (Frankfurt am Main: Suhrkamp, 1987). Frederick G. Lawrence, translator of the German volume, did not include "To Think with Heidegger Against Heidegger" in his *Philosophical-Political Profiles* (Cambridge, Mass.: MIT Press, 1983), which combines essays from the above German edition and from Habermas's *Kultur und Kritik: Versträute Aufsätze* (1973) (Cambridge, Mass.: MIT Press, 1983).

151. Marion, *L'Idole et la distance* (Paris: Grasset, 1977), p. 274; in English, *The Idol and the Distance*, pp. 216 ff.

152. Maria Villela-Petit, "Heidegger est-il idolâtre?" in *Heidegger et la question de Dieu*, p. 96.

153. Lévinas, *Autrement qu'être*, p. 207; in English, *Otherwise Than Being*, pp. 162–63.

154. Rolland and Petrosino, *La Vérité nomade*, p. 12.

PART II, CHAPTER 2: THE PROBLEM OF TRANSMISSION

1. Bernard Dupuy, "Heidegger et le Dieu inconnu," in Richard Kearney and Joseph Stephen O'Leary, eds., *Heidegger et la question de Dieu* (Paris: Grasset, 1980), p. 104.

2. See above Part II, Chapter 1, Section II, Subsection 1, "The Point of Departure in the Questioning of the Greek Understanding of Being: The Experience of Christian Faith."

3. The Greek term *kairos* denotes the time or instant appropriate for action, the right moment, a temporal window of opportunity.—Trans.

4. See Otto Pöggeler, *Martin Heidegger's Path of Thinking*, trans. Daniel Magurshak and Sigmund Barber (Atlantic Highlands, N.J.: Humanities Press International, 1987), pp. 24–25. Also see Karl Lehmann, "Christliche Geschichtserfahrung und ontologische Frage beim jungen Heidegger," in Otto Pöggeler, ed., *Heidegger: Perspektiven zur Deutung seines Werkes* (Königstein: Athenäum, 1984), p. 143. For both of these references, see above Part II, Chapter 1, note 3.

5. Text modified for fluency with the French translation.—Trans.

6. See Pöggeler, *Martin Heidegger's Path of Thinking*, p. 25. Also see Lehmann, p. 143. "Any attempt to objectify, even provisionally, the coming of the *Kairos*, transforms the enigma of the coming into a determination of content."

7. Pöggeler, *Martin Heidegger's Path of Thinking*, p. 24. [Translation modified for fluency with the French.—Trans.]

8. Lehmann, "Christliche Geschichtserfahrung und ontologische Frage beim jungen Heidegger," p. 143.

9. Ibid., p. 149.

10. Pöggeler, *Martin Heidegger's Path of Thinking*, p. 24.

11. Ibid., p. 25.

12. Lehmann, "Christliche Geschichtserfahrung und ontologische Frage beim jungen Heidegger," p. 144.

13. See Pöggeler, *Martin Heidegger's Path of Thinking*, p. 25: "It lives not only in time, but lives time itself." Also see Lehmann, "Christliche Geschichtserfahrung und ontologische Frage beim jungen Heidegger," p. 144.

14. See Pöggeler, *Martin Heidegger's Path of Thinking*, pp. 25–26.

15. Ibid., pp. 18–19. Also see Lehmann, "Christliche Geschichtserfahrung und ontologische Frage beim jungen Heidegger," p. 160.

16. See Lehmann, "Christliche Geschichtserfahrung und ontologische Frage beim jungen Heidegger," p. 160.

17. Jean Greisch, *La Parole heureuse: Heidegger entre les choses et les mots* (Paris: Beauchesne, 1987), p. 264.

18. See above Part II, Chapter 1, Section II, Subsection 1.

19. Martin Heidegger, "Phänomenologie und Theologie," in *Wegmarken*, 2nd expanded ed. (Frankfurt: Klostermann, 1978), p. 64; *Gesamtausgabe*, 102 vols. (Frankfurt am Main: Klostermann, 1975–), 9: 64 [henceforth *Gesamtausgabe* will be abbreviated as *GA*]. In English, "Phenomenology and Theology," trans. James G. Hart and John C. Maraldo in *Pathmarks*, trans. and ed. William McNeill (Cambridge: Cambridge University Press, 1998), pp. 51–52.

20. Ibid. (for all sources).

21. Ibid., p. 65; *GA*, 9: 65; in English, p. 53.

22. Martin Heidegger, *Sein und Zeit* (Tübingen: Niemeyer, 1977), § 7, pp. 27–39; in the *Gesamtausgabe* (Frankfurt am Main: Klostermann, 1977), § 7, pp. 36–52; in English, *Being and Time*, trans. John Macquarrie and Edward Robinson (New York: Harper and Row, 1962), § 7, pp. 49–63.

23. "Existentiell experiences" of *Dasein* comprise the everyday experiences, sometimes denoted as "ontic" rather than "ontological." However, the existentiell experiences *can* lead us back to their formal conditions of possibility in the "ontological," which takes as its point of departure the "most basic and the most concrete question": that of Being. See *Being and Time*, § 3.—Trans.

24. Lehmann, "Christliche Geschichtserfahrung und ontologische Frage beim jungen Heidegger," p. 145.

25. These occasional problems, for example the risk of making of the future a pure horizon of consciousness (ibid., p. 46)—as well as a much more general

problem, which Lehmann expresses in these terms: "Can an experience be formalized? Can it let itself be extracted from its religious context, for example?" Ibid., p. 159.

26. Heidegger, "Phänomenologie und Theologie," p. 65; in English, "Phenomenology and Theology," in *Pathmarks*, p. 52. "The concept of sin is not simply built up upon the ontological concept of guilt. Nevertheless, the latter is determinative in one respect, in that it formally indicates the ontological character of *that* region of being in which the concept of sin *as a concept of existence* must necessarily maintain itself."

27. Lehmann, "Christliche Geschichtserfahrung und ontologische Frage beim jungen Heidegger," p. 150.

28. Ibid., p. 147.

29. Ibid.

30. Ibid.

31. See above, Part II, Chapter 1, Section II, Subsection 4, "Provisional Conclusion."

32. Lehmann, "Christliche Geschichtserfahrung und ontologische Frage beim jungen Heidegger," p. 149.

33. Ibid.

34. Ibid., p. 150.

35. See in this chapter, Section II, "From the New Testament to the Old: The Forgotten Connection"—notably the latter half of the section.

36. See above, Part II, Chapter 1, Section I, "Heidegger's Position: God or Being. 'The Two Paths.'"

37. Maria Villela-Petit, "Parler à Dieu, parler de Dieu," in *Institut Catholique de Paris: Dieu*, (Paris: Beauchesne, 1985), p. 22. Also see Henri Birault, "Philosophie et théologie: Heidegger et Pascal," in Michel Haar, ed., *Cahier de l'herne: Heidegger* 45 (1983): 395.

38. Heidegger, *Wegmarken*, p. 57; *GA*, 9: 57; in English, *Pathmarks*, pp. 47–48.

39. Pascal, *Pensées*, ed. Brunschwicg, Fragment 619 (Paris: Hachette, n.d.). In English, *Pensées*, trans. A. J. Krailsheimer, revised ed. (New York: Penguin, 1995).

40. Paul Beauchamp, *L'Un et l'autre Testament* (Paris: Éditions du Seuil, 1977), *passim.*

41. Henri de Lubac, *Histoire et esprit: L'intelligence de l'écriture d'après Origène* (Paris: Aubier, 1950), p. 170 (cited by Beauchamp in *L'un et l'autre Testament*, p. 24).

42. Villela-Petit, "Parler à Dieu, parler de Dieu," p. 22n12.

43. Ibid., p. 23.

44. Ibid.

45. Gerhard Kittel and Gerhard Friedrich, eds., *Theologisches Wörterbuch zum*

Neuen Testament, 12 vols. (Stuttgart: Kohlhammer, 1933–78). An abridged, one-volume English edition appeared under the title *Theological Dictionary of the New Testament,* trans. and ed. Geoffrey W. Bromiley (Grand Rapids, Mich.: Eerdmans, 1985).

46. That is Gerhard Friedrich, who continued the edition of the *Theologisches Wörterbuch.*

47. James Barr, *The Semantics of Biblical Language* (London: Oxford University Press, 1961), p. 242.

48. Thorleif Boman, *Hebrew Thought Compared with Greek,* trans. Jules L. Moreau (New York: Norton, 1960).

49. Rudolf Karl Bultmann, *Faith and Understanding,* trans. Louise Pettibone Smith, ed. Robert W. Funk (Philadelphia: Fortress Press, 1987). [This is a *selective* translation of *Glauben und Verstehen,* vol. 1. The organization of the English does not correspond to the French translation.—Trans.]

50. Pöggeler, *Martin Heidegger's Path of Thinking,* p. 27.

51. Ibid., p. 28.

52. See above, Part I, Chapter 1, Section I, Subsection 3, Part (a), "The Premetaphysical Margin."

53. On this question of the Greek-German connection, see ibid. Also see Part II, Chapter 3, Section I, Subsection 1, "Heidegger's 'Trajectory.'"

54. Heidegger recognizes naturally (especially in the later works) that the Greek of the Gospels is derived relative to classical Greek. But how can we seriously limit ourselves to confronting, here, Greek with Greek, without bringing in the Hebrew, which is the very motor of the transformation?

55. See Pöggeler, *Martin Heidegger's Path of Thinking,* p. 20. [Translation modified for fluency with the French. The English reads, "Does traditional conceptualization suffice for the determination of what history is, or must this conceptualization be revised when thinking demonstrates that reflection upon history belongs to the founding of philosophy itself?"—Trans.]

56. See Karl Jaspers, *Nietzsche und das Christentum* (Munich: Piper, 1946), pp. 43 ff.; in English, *Nietzsche and Christianity,* trans. E. B. Ashton (New York: Regnery, 1961), p. 49 ff.

57. Bultmann, "Adam, où es-tu?" in *Foi et compréhension* (Paris: Éditions du Seuil, 1969–70), p. 492. [This essay was not reproduced in the English translation.—Trans.]

58. Bultmann, "Le Christianisme comme religion orientale et comme religion occidentale," in ibid., p. 587. [This essay also was not reproduced in the English translation.—Trans.]

59. Bultmann, "Signification de la tradition vétéro-testamentaire juive pour l'Occident Chrétien," in ibid., p. 632. [This essay was not reproduced in the English translation.—Trans.]

60. One finds an impressive compendium of these observations on Hebrew time in Boman, *Hebrew Thought Compared with Greek*, pp. 135 ff.

61. Proverbs 7:22–24 reads: "Thoughtlessly he follows her, / Like an ox going to the slaughter, / Like a fool to the stocks for punishment— / Until the arrow pierces his liver. / He is like a bird rushing into a trap, / Not knowing his life is at stake. / Now, sons, listen to me; / Pay attention to my words . . . "—Trans.

62. Boman, *Hebrew Thought Compared with Greek*, pp. 145–46.

63. Ibid., p. 137.

64. Bultmann, *Foi et compréhension*, p. 586. [This is part of the essay on Christianity as 'Oriental' religion; it is not reproduced in the English translation. The translation above is mine.—Trans.]

65. See the article "Kairos" in Gerhard Kittel, *Theological Dictionary of the New Testament*.

66. On the question of eschatology and the transformation it undergoes in the Pauline letters, see Boman, *Hebrew Thought Compared with Greek*, pp. 168–74.

67. This is a tendency that marked Catholic theology above all, but which one also notes in certain currents of Protestantism. On this point see Karl Barth, *Protestant Theology in the Nineteenth Century: Its Background and History* (Grand Rapids, Mich.: Eerdmans, 2002), no translator listed.

68. George Steiner, *Antigones* (New York: Oxford University Press, 1984), p. 133. Also see George Steiner, *After Babel: Aspects of Language and Translation* (New York: Oxford University Press, 1975), pp. 22 ff.

69. Jürgen Habermas, "The German Idealism of the Jewish Philosophers," in *Philosophical-Political Profiles*, trans. Frederick G. Lawrence (Cambridge, Mass.: MIT Press, 1985), pp. 39–41. Also see Part I, Chapter 4, in this work, note 33.

70. Ibid., p. 21. Translation modified for fluency with the French. The English translation reads, " . . . it remains astonishing how productively central motifs of the philosophy of German Idealism, shaped so essentially by Protestantism, can be developed in terms of the experience of the Jewish tradition."

71. This is a misunderstanding, or misprision, that has been brought to light with increasing frequency. Contemporary thought, notably in France, never ceases recalling its Hebraic forebears, not so much to explore them per se, but rather *to underscore the forgetfulness of them.* Contemporary thought speaks—more so than had been done previously—of the Jews and of the Hebraic dimension, but precisely to recall that too little discussion of these has occurred. A good indication of this are the two principal terms, evoked today to account for the relationship that the "West" has with its Hebraic component: "repression" and "foreclosure." These terms punctuate, like so many leitmotifs, contemporary works nonetheless treating different areas, but all of them appeared at approximately the same time (in the space of one or two years), and they were all concerned with "the Hebraic." Thus, David Banon, in the area of Jewish studies (see *La Lecture infinie* [Paris:

Éditions du Seuil, 1987], p. 19) and Marie Balmary in psychoanalysis (*Le Sacrifice interdit: Freud et la Bible* [Paris: Grasset, 1986], p. 35). See, in philosophy, Jean-François Lyotard, *Heidegger and "The Jews"* (Minneapolis: University of Minnesota Press, 1990), pp. 22, 28–29, etc.). Whatever the divergences in their remarks, all agree on one point at least, that is, that the Hebraic heritage concerns Western thought intimately, but as that which is forgotten by it and in it (one says, according to the case in point, "censored," "falsified," "obscured," and so forth. Nevertheless, the word *foreclosed* predominates, like a sort of generic term). This unique convergence seems to me apt to take on the value of an indicator: if it is in no way certain that Western thought, over the entire course of its history, has forgotten the Hebraic, it is patent, on the other hand, that Western thought inclines today to interpret itself in this mode.

72. This is Jean-François Lyotard's entire thesis; see *Heidegger and "The Jews,"* trans. Andreas Michel and Mark S. Roberts (Minneapolis: University of Minnesota Press, 1990), pp. 56–57. "Heidegger's Nazism and his silence repeat, in their essence and their effect upon our thinking, a foreclosure that is constitutive of Western thought as philosophy and as politics."

73. See above, in this chapter, Section II, "From the New Testament to the Old: The Forgotten Connection."

PART II, CHAPTER 3: THE HEBRAIC HERITAGE AND WESTERN THOUGHT

1. Jacques Derrida, *De l'esprit: Heidegger et la question* (Paris: Éditions Galilée, 1987); in English, *Of Spirit: Heidegger and the Question,* trans. Geoffrey Bennington and Rachel Bowlby (Chicago: University of Chicago Press, 1989).

2. See this work, above, Introduction, Section II, "The Question."

3. See George Steiner, *Antigones* (New York: Oxford University Press, 1984), pp. 132–33. Jean-François Lyotard, *Heidegger and "The Jews,"* trans. Andreas Michel and Mark S. Roberts (Minneapolis: University of Minnesota Press, 1990).

4. It is indeed a matter of a movement, and of a movement that has just emerged. By way of a symptom thereof, let us recall that when I began the writing of this study (1986), I had found, to encourage me in my investigations, but one paragraph on this by Paul Ricoeur. Since then, we can scarcely count the texts that bring up (if only in passing) the problem treated here. That is to say that certain silences of Heidegger are beginning to evoke discussion: this is an entirely recent phenomenon, then, which no doubt has not finished showing its ultimate developments.

5. Derrida, *De l'esprit,* pp. 182; in English, *Of Spirit,* pp. 111–12.

6. Ibid., p. 164; in English, pp. 99–100.

7. Martin Heidegger, *Schelling: Vom Wesen der menschlichen Freiheit (1809)* (Tübingen: Niemeyer, 1971), p. 154; *Gesamtausgabe,* 102 vols. (Frankfurt am Main:

Klostermann, 1975–), 42: 221–22 [henceforth *Gesamtausgabe* will be abbreviated as *GA*]; in English, *Schelling's Treatise on the Essence of Human Freedom*, trans. Joan Stambaugh (Athens: Ohio University Press, 1985), p. 128. Compare Derrida, *De l'esprit*, p. 123; in English, *Of Spirit*, p. 77.

    8. Martin Heidegger, "Die Sprache im Gedicht: Eine Erörterung von Georg Trakls Gedicht," in *Unterwegs zur Sprache* (Pfullingen: Neske, 1976), pp. 59–60; *GA*, 12: 55–56. In English, "Language in the Poem: A Discussion on Georg Trakl's Poetic Work," in *On the Way to Language*, trans. Peter D. Hertz (San Francisco: HarperSanFrancisco, 1982), p. 179.

    9. See above Part I, Chapter 1, "Heidegger's Reading of History: The Split."

    10. See above, Part I, Chapter 1, Section I, Subsection 3, "Second Configuration: Metaphysics as History."

    11. See above, same section.

    12. For Heidegger's evolution on the question of truth, see Marlène Zarader, *Heidegger et les paroles de l'origine* (Paris: Vrin, 1986), pp. 79–82, as well as Zarader, "Le Miroir aux trois reflets," in *Revue de philosophie ancienne* 4, no. 1 (1986): 23–24. In English, "The Mirror with a Triple Reflection," in Christopher Macann, ed., *Martin Heidegger: Critical Assessments* (4 vols.) (New York: Routledge, 1992), 2: 27–28. The essay was republished in Macann, ed., *Critical Heidegger* (New York: Routledge, 1996).

    13. The term is introduced in Heidegger, "Der Spruch des Anaximander," *Holzwege* (Frankfurt: Klostermann, 1972), p. 321; *GA*, 5: 348. In English, Martin Heidegger, "Anaximander's Saying," in *Off The Beaten Track*, trans. Julian Young and Kenneth Haynes (New York: Cambridge University Press, 2002), p. 262. [For a discussion of "Wahrnis," as "Safeguarding," also see William Lovitt, "The Turning," in *The Question Concerning Technology, and Other Essays* (New York: Harper and Row, 1977), p. 42.—Trans.]

    14. Heidegger, *Was heisst Denken?* Zweiter Teil "Die Vorlesung im Sommersemester 1952," § 11 (Tübingen: Niemeyer, 1971), p. 149; *GA*, 8: 247. In English, part 2 in *What Is Called Thinking?* trans. J. Glenn Gray (New York: Harper and Row, 1972), pp. 243–44.

    15. A conclusion that is likewise that of Derrida; see *De l'esprit*, p. 114; in English, *Of Spirit*, pp. 71–72.

    16. Heidegger, "Logos, (Heraklit Fragment 50)" in *Vorträge und Aufsätze*, in *GA*, 7: 221. In English, "Logos (Heraclitus, Fragment B 50)," in *Early Greek Thinking: The Dawn of Western Philosophy*, trans. David Farrell Krell and Frank A. Capuzzi (San Francisco: HarperSanFrancisco, 1984), p. 78. Heidegger writes, "Once, however, in the beginning of Western thinking, the essence of language flashed *in the light* of Being [*im Lichte des Seins auf*]. . . . But the lightning abruptly vanished. No one held onto its streak of light and the *nearness* [*Nähe*] of what it illuminated" (Zarader's emphasis).

17. For this double movement, see Zarader, *Heidegger et les paroles de l'origine*, pp. 177–78.

18. Heidegger "Das Wesen der Sprache," in *Unterwegs zur Sprache*, p. 163; *GA*, 12: 153. In English "The Nature of Language," in *On the Way to Language*, pp. 60–61. Also see "Das Wort," in *Unterwegs zur Sprache*, pp. 219–20. In English, "Words," trans. Joan Stambaugh, in *On the Way to Language*, p. 150.

19. "Das Wesen der Sprache," in *Unterwegs zur Sprache*, p. 193; *GA*, 12: 182; in English "The Nature of Language," in *On the Way to Language*, p. 88. Where Heidegger, after having asserted: "If our thinking does justice to the matter, then we may never say of the word that it is, but rather that it gives [*dann nie sagen: Es ist, sondern: Es gibt*]—not in the sense that the words are given by an 'it,' but that the word itself gives." Heidegger acknowledges, further on, " . . . the word gives Being. Our thinking, then, would have to seek the word, the giver which itself is never given, in this 'there is that which gives.'" [The French translation is somewhat different, it reads: "Even Being still needs this '*Es gibt,*' as presence, in order to come to its ownmost [*à son propre*]."—Trans.]

20. Heidegger, *Heraklit*, in *GA*, vol. 55, § 8, p. 384. [Not yet translated into English.—Trans.] Also see *Unterwegs zur Sprache*, pp. 215–16, 226–27; *GA*, 12: 203–4, 214–15; in English, *On the Way to Language*, pp. 107, 143–44.

21. Derrida, *De l'esprit*, p. 141; *Of Spirit*, p. 90.

22. Ibid., p. 129; in English, pp. 81–82. "Derrida's formulas contain, nonetheless, an element of ambiguity. Does Heidegger manage to distance himself from the 'onto-theological' determination of *pneuma* or of its 'Greek' meaning? The question is not innocent. What is at stake here, is all the difference between a (derived) *conception* and a signification (sheltered in language). By frequently juxtaposing these two orders of qualification, Derrida *seems* not to decide the question of knowing whether Heidegger is setting himself apart from a thinking or from an unthinking, or an unthought. In reality, he does decide, since he recognizes in Heidegger's approach to spirit a passage beyond the Greek itself (" . . . the Greek language has no word to say—nor therefore, to translate—*Geist* . . . ," p. 112; in English, p. 70); it is that he opts for the second solution. But he sometimes formulates it in terms that might evoke the first solution. It is true that this ambiguity is also—and firstly—Heidegger's own ambiguity.

23. Ibid., p. 112; English, p. 70.

24. Ibid., p. 113; English, p. 71.

25. Ibid. Further on, when Derrida attempts to assemble, in a recapitulative mode, the different traits characteristic of the essence of spirit, such as it is ultimately thought by Heidegger, he declares, about the "second trait": "In this movement, the recourse to the German language appears irreducible. It appears to make the semantics of *Geist* depend on an 'originary meaning' [*ursprüngliche Bedeutung*] entrusted to the German idiom *gheis*." See Derrida, *De l'esprit*, p. 157; *Of Spirit*, p. 97.

26. Ibid., p. 157, also see p. 163; in English, p. 97, and pp. 99–100.

27. Ibid., p. 131; in English, p. 83.

28. Ibid.

29. Ibid., p. 144; in English, p. 92.

30. Ibid., p. 164; in English, p. 100.

31. Ibid., p. 165; in English, p. 101.

32. Ibid., p. 165; in English, p. 100.

33. Ibid. [Translation modified for fluency with the French text.—Trans.]

34. Ibid., p. 164; in English, p. 100.

35. Ibid.

36. Ibid., p. 167; in English, p. 102.

37. Ibid., pp. 179–81; in English, pp. 109–11.

38. Ibid., p. 180; in English, p. 110.

39. Ibid.

40. Ibid., p. 181; in English, p. 111.

41. See above, notably, Part I, Chapter 3, Section III, "Heidegger, Memory, and Denial."

42. Derrida, *De l'esprit*, p. 166; *Of Spirit*, p. 101.

43. Ibid., p. 183; in English, p. 112.

44. Ibid., p. 184; in English, p. 113; the French is *hétérogène à l'origine*. Also see ibid., pp. 176 ff.; in English, p. 108.

45. Ibid., p. 183; in English, p. 112: " . . . Heidegger, I imagine, would reply . . . "

46. Ibid., p. 177; in English, p. 107.

47. Ibid.; in English, p. 108.

48. Ibid., p. 182; in English, p. 111.

49. Ibid.; in English, p. 112.

50. Ibid., pp. 183–84; in English, p. 113. "But access to thought, the thinking access to the *possibility* of metaphysics or pneumato-spiritualist religions opens onto something quite other than what the possibility makes possible."

51. Ibid., p. 184; in English, p. 113.

52. Ibid., p. 182; in English, p. 112. [The words "nor even (I had forgotten that one)" are underlined by Zarader.—Trans.]

53. Ibid. [The words "or, since you insist" are underlined by Zarader.—Trans.]

54. See ibid., pp. 165–66; in English, pp. 100–101.

55. Ibid., p. 163; in English, p. 99.

56. Ibid., p. 164; in English, p. 100.

57. Ibid., p. 165; in English, p. 100.

58. See above, the first page of this chapter.

59. Derrida, *De l'esprit*, p. 184; *Of Spirit*, p. 113.

60. The reverse path (i.e., emphasizing the avoidance, without taking into

account, except in completely marginal way, the repetition) is followed by Jean-François Lyotard in his 1988 work, *Heidegger and "The Jews."*

61. See below, Conclusion.

62. See above, Part I, Chapter 3, note 32 (Paul Ricoeur's remark at Cerisy). I am citing this text in its first edition, in *Heidegger et la question de Dieu.*

63. Jean Beaufret, "Heidegger et la théologie," in *Heidegger et la question de Dieu,* p. 22.

64. Ibid.

65. See Eryck de Rubercy, Jean Beaufret, Dominique Le Buhan, *Douze Questions posées à Jean Beaufret à propos de Martin Heidegger* (Paris: Aubier-Montaigne, 1983), pp. 31–33.

66. Beaufret, "Heidegger et la théologie," p. 23: "The question is: can one really, on the basis of philosophy, tie to the Greek contribution the biblical one, in which the Old Testament is [or remains] an authentically Jewish contribution?"

67. See *Douze questions posées à Jean Beaufret,* p. 31.

68. Beaufret, "Heidegger et la théologie," p. 23.

69. See *Douze questions posées à Jean Beaufret,* pp. 31–32.

70. Heidegger, *Was ist das—die Philosophie?* (Pfullingen: Neske, 1976), p. 7. *What Is Philosophy?* trans. Jean T. Wilde and William Kluback (New Haven, Conn.: College and University Press, 1968), p. 31.

71. Ibid.

72. Beaufret, "Heidegger et la théologie," p. 24.

73. Ibid., p. 23.

74. Ibid.

75. Ibid., p. 24; Zarader's emphasis.

76. Ibid.

77. See above, Part I, Chapter 1, Section I, Subsection 1, "The Semantic Expansion."

78. See Beaufret, "Heidegger et la théologie," p. 23.

79. *Douze questions posées à Jean Beaufret,* p. 32.

80. Ibid.

81. Beaufret, "Heidegger et la théologie," p. 25. "Western history . . . is the history of Being in its clearing or lighting, such as it mutatively unfolds from a center which is not the god of biblical revelation. [But it is] neither 'that which the Greeks sought' if they sought merely the Being of beings [*l'être de l'étant*]."

82. See above, Introduction, Section II, "The Question."

83. A distinction between the real gesture and the saying, which Paul Ricoeur had already utilized relative to a completely different question, that of metaphor. See Paul Ricoeur, *La Métaphore vive* (Paris: Éditions du Seuil, 1975), p. 357; in English, Ricoeur, *The Rule of Metaphor: The Creation of Meaning in Language,* trans. Robert Czerny, Kathleen McLaughlin, et al. (London: Routledge, 2003), p.

280: " . . . the constant use Heidegger makes of metaphor is finally more important than what he says in passing against metaphor."

84. See Part II, Chapter 1, Section II, "Heidegger's Renewal of the Question of Being."

85. Beaufret, "Heidegger et la théologie," p. 34: " . . . this putative monotheism, a term formed quite late on the basis of the Greek, which the *Dictionnaire Littré* holds to be a disturbing neologism and which was never a part of any language.

86. Hölderlin, cited in Beaufret, "Heidegger et la théologie," p. 33. Michael Hamburger translates this epigraph: "Being at one is god-like and good / but human, too human, the mania / which insists there is only the One / one country, one truth and one way." See Friedrich Hölderlin, *Poems and Fragments*, trans. Michael Hamburger (Ann Arbor: University of Michigan Press, 1966), p. 71.

CONCLUSION: DECONSTRUCTION OR RECONSTRUCTION?

1. See above, Part I, "Readings."
2. See above, Part II, "Problems."
3. See above, Part II, Chapter 1, "And How Is It with Being?"
4. See above, Part II, Chapter 2, "The Problem of Transmission."
5. See above, Part II, Chapter 3, "The Hebraic Heritage and Western Thought."
6. In certain cases, it would be in no way excessive to assert that there is indeed, in the Jewish tradition for example, a determinate "conception" of language. But this question can remain open here.
7. On this question, see above, Part II, Chapter 3, Section I, Subsection 3, "A Critical Perspective."
8. For Heidegger's evolution on this point, see above Part I, Chapter 1, Section I, Subsection 2, "The Historical Expansion: Presentation."
9. I would in no way contest the fact that Heidegger's thought is new, risqué, and to a great degree "unprecedented." However, if it is all this, then this is no doubt for the reasons opposite to those which one is inclined, at times, to emphasize: its novelty comes, rather, from that which it has recalled, more amply than any other thought, that which philosophers had failed, in part, to recognize. What makes for its specificity, and the radicality of its difference from "philosophy," is precisely its resemblances, its close proximity, with other sources neglected up till then—or insufficiently called upon.

Bibliography

I. HEIDEGGER

1. Books

These works are listed in order of original publication date, which is in brackets following each citation. The most current translations or editions are listed; in those cases where an older version may be considered canonical, both will be included. Those translated into English are listed by the English translation publication information; those untranslated are listed in their original language and/or French translations—Trans.

Gesamtausgabe. 102 vols. Frankfurt am Main: Klostermann, 1975– . Abbreviated elsewhere in this Bibliography as *GA*.

———. *Being and Time.* Translation of *Sein and Zeit.* Trans. John Macquarrie and Edward Robinson. New York: Harper and Row, 1962 [1927].

———. Trans. Joan Stambaugh. Albany: State University of New York Press, 1997.

Elucidations of Hölderlin's Poetry. Translation of *Erläuterungen zu Hölderlins Dichtung.* Trans. Keith Hoeller. Amherst, N.Y.: Humanity Books, 2000 [1944].

Off the Beaten Track. A Translation of *Holzwege.* Trans. Julian Young and Kenneth Haynes. Cambridge: Cambridge University Press, 2002 [1950].

Introduction to Metaphysics. Translation of *Einführung in die Metaphysik.* Trans. Gregory Fried and Richard Polt. New Haven, Conn.: Yale University Press, 2000 [1954].

What Is Called Thinking? Translation of *Was heisst Denken?* Trans. J. Glenn Gray. New York: Harper and Row, 1972 [1954].

Vorträge und Aufsätze. Pfullingen: Neske, 1978 [1956]. [While this German work is not translated, all of the essays contained therein are translated in the following works as noted: *Basic Writings: Revised and Expanded Edition.* Ed. David Farrell Krell. New York: HarperCollins, 1993 [1977]. (Containing *Was heisst Denken?* [*What Calls for Thinking?*], pp. 365–91; *Bauen, Wohnen, Denken* [*Build-*

ing, Dwelling, Thinking], pp. 343–63; *Die Frage nach der Technik* [*The Question Concerning Technology*], pp. 307–41).—Trans.]

Early Greek Thinking: The Dawn of Western Philosophy. Trans. David Farrell Krell and Frank A. Capuzzi. San Francisco: HarperSanFrancisco, 1984 [1975]. [Containing "Logos (Heraklit, Fragment B 50)," pp. 59–78; "Moira (Parmenides, Fragment VIII, 34–41)," pp. 79–101; "Alèthéia (Heraklit, Fragment 16)," pp. 102–23.—Trans.]

Poetry, Language, Thought. Trans. Albert Hofstader. New York: Perennial Classics, 2001. [Containing "Bauen, Wohnen, Denken" (Building, Dwelling, Thinking), pp. 143–61; "Das Ding" (The Thing), pp. 165–86; "Dichterisch wohnet der Mensch" (". . . Poetically Man Dwells"), pp. 211–29.—Trans.]

The End of Philosophy. Trans. Joan Stambaugh. New York: Harper and Row, 1973. [Containing "Ueberwindung der Metaphysik" (Overcoming Metaphysics), pp. 84–110.—Trans.]

The Question Concerning Technology and Other Essays. Trans. William Lovitt. New York: Harper and Row, 1977. [Containing "Die Frage nach der Technik" (The Question Concerning Technology), pp. 3–64; "Wissenschaft und Besinnung" (Science and Reflection), pp. 155–82.—Trans.]

What Is Called Thinking? Translation of *Was heisst Denken?* Trans. J. Glenn Gray. New York: Harper and Row, 1972.

What Is Philosophy? Translation of *Was ist das—die Philosophie?* Trans. Jean T. Wilde and William Kluback. New Haven, Conn.: College and University Press, 1968 [1956].

The Principle of Reason. Translation of *Der Satz vom Grund.* Trans. Reginald Lilly. Studies in Continental Thought. General editor, John Sallis. Bloomington: Indiana University Press, 1996 [1957]. [*GA*, vol. 10.]

Identity and Difference. Translation of *Identität und Differenz.* Trans. Joan Stambaugh. New York: Harper and Row, 1969 [1957].

Discourse on Thinking. A Translation of *Gelassenheit.* Trans. John M. Anderson and E. Hans Freund. New York: Harper and Row, 1966 [1959].

On the Way to Language. Translation of *Unterwegs zur Sprache.* Trans. Peter D. Hertz. San Francisco: HarperSanFrancisco, 1982 [1959].

Nietzsche. 4 vols. Translation of *Nietzsche.* Trans. David Farrell Krell. San Francisco: HarperSanFrancisco, 1991 [1961]. [Containing "Wer ist Nietzsches Zarathustra?" (Who Is Nietzsche's Zarathustra?), 2: 209–33.—Trans.]

Martin Heidegger: Phänomenologie des religiösen Lebens. Frankfurt am Main: Klostermann, 1995. [*GA*, vol. 60.]

Pathmarks. Translation of *Wegmarken.* Trans. and ed. William McNeill. Cambridge: Cambridge University Press, 1998 [1967].

On Time and Being. Translation of *Zur Sache des Denkens.* Trans. Joan Stambaugh. New York: Harper and Row, 1972 [1969].

Schelling's Treatise on the Essence of Human Freedom. Translation of *Schellings Abhandlung: Über das Wesen der menschlichen Freiheit.* Trans. Joan Stambaugh. Studies in Continental Thought. General editor, John Sallis. Athens: Ohio University Press, 1985 [1971].

The Essence of Truth: On Plato's Cave Allegory and Theaetetus. Trans. Ted Sadler. Contemporary European Thinkers Series. New York: Continuum Press, 2002. [*GA*, vol. 34.]

The Essence of Human Freedom: An Introduction to Philosophy. Trans. Ted Sadler. New York: Continuum Press, 2002. [*GA*, vol. 31.]

Martin Heidegger: Phenomenology of Religious Life. Trans. of *Martin Heidegger: Phänomenologie des religiösen Lebens.* Trans. Matthias Fritsch and Jennifer Anna Gosetti. Bloomington: Indiana University Press, 2004.

2. Heidegger's Courses

The following appear in the complete works, the *Gesamtausgabe.* In her bibliography, Zarader cites vols. 20, 39, and 52–55. Those that have been translated are listed with the individually published German editions, followed by the *Gesamtausgabe* volume (abbreviated as *GA*) and then the English translation.—Trans.

History of the Concept of Time: Prolegomena. A Translation of *Prolegomena zur Geschichte des Zeitbegriffs* (Summer Semester 1925). Trans. Theodore Kisiel. Bloomington: Indiana University Press, 1985. [*GA*, vol. 20.]

Hölderlins Hymnen "Germanien" und "Der Rhine" (Winter Semester, 1934–35). [*GA*, vol. 39.]

Hölderlins Hymne "Andenken" (Winter Semester, 1941–42). [*GA*, vol. 52.]

Hölderlin's Hymn "The Ister." Translation of *Hölderlins Hymne "Der Ister"* (Summer Semester, 1942). Trans. William McNeill and Julia Davis. Studies in Continental Thought. Bloomington: Indiana University Press, 1996. [*GA*, vol. 53.]

Parmenides. Translation of *Parmenides* (Winter Semester, 1942–43). Trans. André Schuwer and Richard Rojcewicz. Bloomington: Indiana University Press, 1992. [*GA*, vol. 54.]

Heraclitus Seminar. Translation of *Heraklit* (Summer Semester, 1943–44). Trans. Charles H. Seibert. Evanston, Ill.: Northwestern University Press, 1993. [*GA*, vol. 55.]

3. Collections of Heidegger's Works

Questions I. Trans. Henri Corbin, Roger Munier, Alphonse de Waelhens, Walter

Biemel, Gérard Granel, and André Préau. Paris: Gallimard, 1968.

Questions II. Trans. Kostas Axelos, Jean Beaufret, Dominique Janicaud, Lucien Braun, Michel Haar, André Préau, and François Fédier. Paris: Gallimard, 1968.

II. RELATED WORKS IN ENGLISH

Barr, James. *The Semantics of Biblical Language.* London: Oxford University Press, 1961.

Barth, Karl. *Protestant Theology in the Nineteenth Century: Its Background and History,* 1972–73. New ed. Translation of *Protestantische Theologie im 19ten Jahrhundert.* Grand Rapids, Mich.: Eerdmans, 2002.

Boman, Thorleif. *Hebrew Thought Compared with Greek.* Translation of *Das hebräische Denken im Vergleich mit dem griechischen.* Trans. Jules L. Moreau. Philadelphia: Westminster Press, 1960.

Bultmann, Rudolf Karl. *Faith and Understanding.* Translation of *Glauben und Verstehen.* Trans. Louise Pettibone Smith. Ed. Robert W. Funk. Philadelphia: Fortress Press, 1987.

Corbin, Henry. *Alone with the Alone: Creative Imagination in the Sūfism of Ibn ʿArabī,* 1991. Translation of *Imagination créatrice dans le soufisme d'Ibn ʿArabi.* Trans. Ralph Manheim. Preface by Harold Bloom. Princeton, N.J.: Princeton University Press.

Derrida, Jacques. *Dissemination.* Translation of *La Dissémination.* Trans. Barbara Johnson. Chicago: University of Chicago Press, 1981.

———. *Of Spirit: Heidegger and the Question.* Translation of *De l'esprit: Heidegger et la question.* Trans. Geoffrey Bennington and Rachel Bowlby. Chicago: University of Chicago Press, 1989.

———. *Writing and Difference.* Translation of *L'Écriture et la différence.* Trans. Alan Bass. Chicago: University of Chicago Press, 1978.

Gadamer, Hans-Georg. *Truth and Method.* Translation of *Wahrheit und Methode.* Trans. Joel Weinsheimer and Donald G. Marshall. New York: Continuum, 1993.

Haar, Michel. *The Song of the Earth: Heidegger and the Grounds of the History of Being.* Translation of *La Chant de la terre.* Trans. Reginald Lilly. Foreword by John Sallis. Bloomington: Indiana University Press, 1993.

Habermas, Jürgen. *Philosophical-Political Profiles.* Translation of *Philosophisch-politische Profile.* Trans. Frederick G. Lawrence. Cambridge, Mass.: MIT Press, 1983.

Jaspers, Karl. *Nietzsche and Christianity.* Translation of *Nietzsche und das Christentum.* Trans. E. B. Ashton. New York: Regnery, 1961.

Kittel, Gerhard; Friedrich, Gerhard. *Theological Dictionary of the New Testament.* Abridged. Translation of *Theologisches Wörterbuch zum Neuen Testament.* Trans. and ed. Geoffrey W. Bromiley. Grand Rapids, Mich.: Eerdmans, 1985.

Lacan, Jacques. *Écrits: The First Complete Translation in English.* Trans. Bruce Fink. New York: Norton, 2005.

———. *The Seminar of Jacques Lacan.* Translation of *Séminaire de Jacques Lacan.* Trans. Jacques-Alain Miller. New York: Norton, 1998.

Lévinas, Emmanuel. *Difficult Freedom: Essays on Judaism.* Trans. Seán Hand. Translation of *Difficile liberté.* Baltimore: Johns Hopkins University Press, 1990.

———. *Discovering Existence with Husserl.* Trans. Richard A. Cohen and Michael B. Smith. Evanston, Ill.: Northwestern University Press, 1998.

———. *Existence and Existents.* Translation of *De l'existence à l'existant.* Trans. Alphonso Lingis. Foreword by Robert Bernasconi. Pittsburgh: Duquesne University Press, 2001.

———. *Otherwise Than Being; or, Beyond Essence.* Translation of *Autrement qu'être.* Trans. Alphonso Lingis. Pittsburgh: Duquesne University Press, 1998.

———. *Proper Names.* Translation of *Noms propres.* Trans. Michael B. Smith. Stanford, Calif.: Stanford University Press, 1996.

———. *Totality and Infinity: An Essay on Exteriority.* Translation of *Totalité et infini.* Trans. Alphonso Lingis. Pittsburgh: Duquesne University Press, 1998.

Lubac, Henri de. *Medieval Exegesis.* Translation of *Exegese médiévale.* Trans. Mark Sebanc. Grand Rapids, Mich.: Eerdmans, 1998.

Lyotard, Jean-François. *Heidegger and "The Jews."* Translation of *Heidegger et "les juifs."* Trans. Andreas Michel and Mark S. Roberts. Minneapolis: University of Minnesota Press, 1990.

Marion, Jean-Luc. *The Idol and Distance: Five Studies.* Translation of *L'Idole et la distance.* Trans. Thomas A. Carlson. New York: Fordham University Press, 2001.

Neher, André. *The Exile of the Word: From the Silence of the Bible to the Silence of Auschwitz.* Translation of *L'Exil de la Parole: Du silence biblique au silence d'Auschwitz.* Trans. David Maisel. Philadelphia: Jewish Publication Society of America, 1981.

———. *The Prophetic Existence.* Translation of *L'Essence du prophétisme.* Trans. William Wolf. South Brunswick, N.J.: A. S. Barnes, 1969.

Nietzsche, Friedrich Wilhelm. *The Gay Science: With a Prelude in German Rhymes and an Appendix of Songs.* Translation of *Fröhliche Wissenschaft.* Trans. Josefine Nauckhoff and Adrian Del Caro. Ed. Bernard Williams. Cambridge: Cambridge University Press, 2001. See also the Walter Kaufmann translation, published by Vintage Books and others.

Pascal, Blaise. *Pensées*. Trans. A. J. Krailsheimer. London: Penguin, 1995.

Pöggeler, Otto. *Martin Heidegger's Path of Thinking*. Translation of *Der Denkweg Martin Heideggers*. Trans. Daniel Magurshak and Sigmund Barber. Atlantic Highlands, N.J.: Humanities Press International, 1987.

Rojtman, Betty. *Black Fire on White Fire: An Essay on Jewish Hermeneutics, from Midrash to Kabbalah*. Translation of *Feu noir sur feu blanc*. Trans. Steven Rendall. Berkeley: University of California Press, 1998.

Safran, Alexandre. *The Kabbalah: Law and Mysticism in the Jewish Tradition*. Translation of *La Cabale*. Trans. Margaret A. Pater. New York: Feldheim, 1975.

Scholem, Gershom Gerhard. *Major Trends in Jewish Mysticism*. Original from which *Les Grands Courants de la mystique juive* was translated. Foreword by Robert Alter. New York: Schocken Books, 1995.

———. *On the Kabbalah and Its Symbolism*. Translation of *Zur Kabbala und ihrer Symbolik*. Trans. Ralph Manheim. Foreword by Bernard McGinn. New York: Schocken Books, 1996.

Vattimo, Gianni. *The Adventure of Difference: Philosophy After Nietzsche and Heidegger*. Translation of *La avventura della differenza*. Trans. Cyprian Blamires and Thomas Harrison, Baltimore: Johns Hopkins University Press, 1993.

Yerushalmi, Yosef Hayim. *Zakhor: Jewish History and Jewish Memory*. Original from which *Zakhor: Histoire juive et mémoire juive* was translated. Foreword by Harold Bloom. Seattle: University of Washington Press, 1996.

Zarader, Marlène. "The Mirror with the Triple Reflection." In Christopher MacAnn, ed., *Martin Heidegger: Critical Assessments*, vol. 2, *History of Philosophy*. New York: Routledge, 1992.

III. OTHER AUTHORS NOT TRANSLATED INTO ENGLISH

Allemann, Beda. *Hölderlin und Heidegger*. Zurich: Atlantis, 1959 [1954].

———. French trans. by François Fédier. *Hölderlin et Heidegger*. Paris: Presses Universitaires de France, 2nd ed. corrected, 1987.

Autrement que savoir: E. Lévinas: Les Entretiens du Centre Sèvres. Paris: Osiris, 1988.

Bacher, Wilhelm. "L'Exégèse biblique dans le Zohar," *Revue des études juives* 22 (1891): 33–46.

Banon, David. *La Lecture infinie: Les Voies de l'interprétation midrachique*. Paris: Éditions du Seuil, 1987.

Beauchamp, Paul. *L'Un et l'autre testament*. Paris: Éditions du Seuil, 1977.

Birault, Henri. *Heidegger et l'expérience de la pensée*. Paris: Gallimard, 1978.

———. "Philosophie et théologie: Heidegger et Pascal." In Michel Haar, ed., *Cahier de l'herne: Heidegger* 45 (1983): 398–99.

Blanchot, Maurice. *L'Entretien infini.* Paris: Gallimard, 1969.

Cacqueray, N. de. *Connaissance et langage symboliques dans la Bible.* Rennes: Université de Rennes. Unpublished thesis, 1981.

Cahier de l'herne: Heidegger 45 (1983). Under the direction of Michel Harr.

Gadamer, Hans-Georg. "Martin Heidegger und die marburger Theologie." In Otto Pöggeler, ed., *Martin Heidegger: Perspektiven zur Deutung seines Werkes.* Königstein: Athenäum, 1984.

Greisch, Jean. *La Parole heureuse: Heidegger entre les choses et les mots.* Paris: Beauchesne, 1987.

Hegel, G. W. F. *Briefe von und an Hegel.* Ed. Johannes Hoffmeister. 4 vols. Hamburg: Felix Meiner, 1952–60.

———. French trans. by Jean Carrère. *Correspondance.* Paris: Gallimard, 1962–67.

Heidegger et la question de Dieu. Ed. Richard Kearney and Joseph Stephen O'Leary. Paris: Grasset, 1980.

Hölderlin, Friedrich. *Sämtliche Werke.* Stuttgart: Kohlhammer, 1943–72.

———. French trans. by Philippe Jaccottet. *Oeuvres.* Paris: Gallimard, "Bibliothèque de la Pléiade," 1967.

Hyppolite, Jean. *Figures de la pensée philosophique.* Vol. 1. Paris: Presses Universitaires de France, 1971.

Lehmann, Karl. "Christliche Geschichtserfahrung und ontologische Frage beim jungen Heidegger." In Otto Pöggeler, ed., *Heidegger: Perspektiven zur Deutung seines Werkes.* Königstein: Athenäum, 1984.

Lévinas, Emmanuel. *L'Au-delà du verset: Lectures et discours talmudiques.* Paris: Éditions de Minuit, 1982.

———. "Exégèse et culture: Notes sur un verset," in *Le nouveau commerce,* 1983, no. 50.

———. *Sur Maurice Blanchot.* Montpellier: Fata Morgana, 1976.

Lubac, Henri de. *Histoire et esprit: L'Intelligence de l'écriture d'après Origène.* Paris: Aubier, 1950.

Payot, C. "Les Infortunes de la théologie biblique et de l'herméneutique." *Revue de théologie et de philosophie* 4 (1968): 218–35.

Petrosino, Silvano. "D'un livre à l'autre: *Totalité et infini—Autrement qu'être.*" French trans. by G. Iannella. In *Les Cahiers de "La nuit surveillée"* 3 (1984).

Otto Pöggeler, ed. *Heidegger: Perspektiven zur Deutung seines Werkes.* Königstein: Athenäum, 1984.

Ricoeur, Paul. *La Métaphore vive.* Paris: Éditions du Seuil, 1975.

Rolland, Jacques, and Silvano Petrosino. *La Vérité nomade: Introduction à E. Lévinas.* Paris: Découverte, 1984.

Rubercy, Eryck de, Jean Beaufret, and Dominique Le Buhan. *Douze questions posées à Jean Beaufret à propos de Martin Heidegger*. Paris: Aubier-Montaigne, 1983.

Vattimo, Gianni. *Introduction à Heidegger*. French trans. by Jacques Rolland. Paris: Éditions du Cerf, 1985.

Villela-Petit, Maria. "Parler à Dieu, parler de Dieu." In *Institut catholique de Paris: Dieu*. Paris: Beauchesne, 1985.

Zarader, Marlène. *Heidegger et les paroles de l'origine*. Paris: Vrin, 1986.

Cultural Memory | *in the Present*

Jacques Derrida and Elisabeth Roudinesco, *For What Tomorrow . . . : A Dialogue*

Elisabeth Weber, *Questioning Judaism: Interviews by Elisabeth Weber*

Jacques Derrida and Catherine Malabou, *Counterpath: Traveling with Jacques Derrida*

Martin Seel, *Aesthetics of Appearing*

Nanette Salomon, *Shifting Priorities: Gender and Genre in Seventeenth-Century Dutch Painting*

Jacob Taubes, *The Political Theology of Paul*

Jean-Luc Marion, *The Crossing of the Visible*

Eric Michaud, *The Cult of Art in Nazi Germany*

Anne Freadman, *The Machinery of Talk: Charles Peirce and the Sign Hypothesis*

Stanley Cavell, *Emerson's Transcendental Etudes*

Stuart McLean, *The Event and its Terrors: Ireland, Famine, Modernity*

Beate Rössler, ed., *Privacies: Philosophical Evaluations*

Bernard Faure, *Double Exposure: Cutting Across Buddhist and Western Discourses*

Alessia Ricciardi, *The Ends Of Mourning: Psychoanalysis, Literature, Film*

Alain Badiou, *Saint Paul: The Foundation of Universalism*

Gil Anidjar, *The Jew, the Arab: A History of the Enemy*

Jonathan Culler and Kevin Lamb, eds., *Just Being Difficult? Academic Writing in the Public Arena*

Jean-Luc Nancy, *A Finite Thinking*, edited by Simon Sparks

Theodor W. Adorno, *Can One Live after Auschwitz? A Philosophical Reader*, edited by Rolf Tiedemann

Patricia Pisters, *The Matrix of Visual Culture: Working with Deleuze in Film Theory*

Andreas Huyssen, *Present Pasts: Urban Palimpsests and the Politics of Memory*

Talal Asad, *Formations of the Secular: Christianity, Islam, Modernity*

Dorothea von Mücke, *The Rise of the Fantastic Tale*

Marc Redfield, *The Politics of Aesthetics: Nationalism, Gender, Romanticism*

Emmanuel Levinas, *On Escape*

Dan Zahavi, *Husserl's Phenomenology*

Rodolphe Gasché, *The Idea of Form: Rethinking Kant's Aesthetics*

Michael Naas, *Taking on the Tradition: Jacques Derrida and the Legacies of Deconstruction*

Herlinde Pauer-Studer, ed., *Constructions of Practical Reason: Interviews on Moral and Political Philosophy*

Jean-Luc Marion, *Being Given That: Toward a Phenomenology of Givenness*

Theodor W. Adorno and Max Horkheimer, *Dialectic of Enlightenment*

Ian Balfour, *The Rhetoric of Romantic Prophecy*

Martin Stokhof, *World and Life as One: Ethics and Ontology in Wittgenstein's Early Thought*

Gianni Vattimo, *Nietzsche: An Introduction*

Jacques Derrida, *Negotiations: Interventions and Interviews, 1971-1998*, edited by Elizabeth Rottenberg

Brett Levinson, *The Ends of Literature: The Latin American "Boom" in the Neoliberal Marketplace*

Timothy J. Reiss, *Against Autonomy: Cultural Instruments, Mutualities, and the Fictive Imagination*

Hent de Vries and Samuel Weber, editors, *Religion and Media*

Niklas Luhmann, *Theories of Distinction: Re-Describing the Descriptions of Modernity*, edited and Introduction by William Rasch

Johannes Fabian, *Anthropology with an Attitude: Critical Essays*

Michel Henry, *I am the Truth: Toward a Philosophy of Christianity*

Gil Anidjar, *"Our Place in Al-Andalus": Kabbalah, Philosophy, Literature in Arab-Jewish Letters*

Hélène Cixous and Jacques Derrida, *Veils*

F. R. Ankersmit, *Historical Representation*

F. R. Ankersmit, *Political Representation*

Elissa Marder, *Dead Time: Temporal Disorders in the Wake of Modernity (Baudelaire and Flaubert)*

Reinhart Koselleck, *The Practice of Conceptual History: Timing History, Spacing Concepts*

Niklas Luhmann, *The Reality of the Mass Media*

Hubert Damisch, *A Childhood Memory by Piero della Francesca*

Hubert Damisch, *A Theory of /Cloud/: Toward a History of Painting*

Jean-Luc Nancy, *The Speculative Remark: (One of Hegel's bon mots)*

Jean-François Lyotard, *Soundproof Room: Malraux's Anti-Aesthetics*

Jan Patočka, *Plato and Europe*

Hubert Damisch, *Skyline: The Narcissistic City*

Isabel Hoving, *In Praise of New Travelers: Reading Caribbean Migrant Women Writers*

Richard Rand, ed., *Futures: Of Jacques Derrida*